Contemporary Nigerian Politics

In 2015, Nigeria's voters cast out the ruling People's Democratic Party. Here, A. Carl LeVan traces the political vulnerability of Africa's largest party to elite bargains that facilitated a democratic transition in 1999. These "pacts" enabled electoral competition but ultimately undermined the party's coherence. While the PDP unsuccessfully stoked fears about the opposition's ability to stop Boko Haram's terrorism, the opposition built a winning electoral coalition on economic growth, anti-corruption, and electoral integrity. LeVan also crucially examines three institutional "stress points" that challenge future democratic development: Boko Haram's insurgency in the northeast, threats of Igbo secession in the southeast, and geographically dispersed farmer–pastoralist conflicts. Drawing on extensive interviews with politicians, generals, activists and voters, he argues that electoral accountability is essential but insufficient for resolving the representational, distributional, and cultural components of these challenges.

A. CARL LEVAN is Associate Professor in the School of International Service at American University. He is the author of *Dictators and Democracy in African Development: The Political Economy of Good Governance in Nigeria* (Cambridge University Press, 2015) and the co-author of *Constituents before Assembly: Participation, Deliberation, and Representation in the Crafting of New Constitutions* (Cambridge University Press, 2017). He tweets @Dev4Security.

Contemporary Nigerian Politics

Competition in a Time of Transition and Terror

A. CARL LEVAN

American University, Washington, DC

CAMBRIDGE
UNIVERSITY PRESS

University Printing House, Cambridge CB2 8BS, United Kingdom

One Liberty Plaza, 20th Floor, New York, NY 10006, USA

477 Williamstown Road, Port Melbourne, VIC 3207, Australia

314–321, 3rd Floor, Plot 3, Splendor Forum, Jasola District Centre,
New Delhi – 110025, India

79 Anson Road, #06-04/06, Singapore 079906

Cambridge University Press is part of the University of Cambridge.

It furthers the University's mission by disseminating knowledge in the pursuit of
education, learning, and research at the highest international levels of excellence.

www.cambridge.org
Information on this title: www.cambridge.org/9781108472494
DOI: 10.1017/9781108560467

First published 2019

Printed and bound in Great Britain by Clays Ltd, Elcograf S.p.A.

A catalogue record for this publication is available from the British Library.

Library of Congress Cataloging-in-Publication Data
Names: LeVan, A. Carl, author.
Title: Contemporary Nigerian politics : competition in a
time of transition and terror / A. Carl LeVan.
Description: New York: Cambridge University Press, 2019. |
Includes bibliographical references and index.
Identifiers: LCCN 2018039008 | ISBN 9781108472494 (hardback) |
ISBN 9781108459747 (pbk.)
Subjects: LCSH: People's Democratic Party (Nigeria) – History. |
Elections – Nigeria – 21st century. | Democracy – Nigeria. |
Nigeria – Politics and government – 2007–
Classification: LCC JQ3096.L485 2018 | DDC 324.9669056–dc23
LC record available at https://lccn.loc.gov/2018039008

ISBN 978-1-108-47249-4 Hardback
ISBN 978-1-108-45974-7 Paperback

For Emerson –

For the joys you bring,
and the dreams you multiply.

Contents

Figures

Tables

Acknowledgments

At various stages of this project, the American Political Science Association (APSA) provided critical support and encouragement. I am especially grateful for my time at the Centennial Center in Washington, DC, where I wrote much of the manuscript during a sabbatical leave I received from American University. I particularly want to thank Betsy Super. A grant from the APSA's William A. Steiger Fund for Legislative Studies for my proposal, "Terrorism and Party Turnover in Post-Transition Nigeria," enabled me to conduct field research in Rivers, Imo, Anambra, Enugu, and Abia states in 2017.

I also gratefully acknowledge a variety of support from American University, which provides a fertile ground for doing research and engaging policy-makers. A School of International Service (SIS) Dean's Summer Research Grant in 2015 for my proposal, "Counting on Contestation: Explaining Opposition Risk and Performance in Nigeria's 2015 Elections," funded preliminary research by Yoonbin Ha, who gathered some of the electoral data used in Chapters 3 and 4. An International Faculty Travel Award to study "Violent Insurgency and Partisan Realignment in Nigeria" later helped fund field research in Abuja, Plateau, Bauchi, Gombe, and Adamawa in 2016 – a trip that was made infinitely more educational and entertaining due to the good company and sharp mind of Matthew Page. (Our good friend Barkindo facilitated much of that journey.) The statistical tests in Chapters 4 and 5 would not have been possible without the continuous support and helpful tutorials from Assen Assenov, Dimitrije Tasic, and Angel Bogushev in American University's Center for Teaching, Research, and Learning.

Finally, the Office of SIS Research supported the book with a workshop, where Jennifer Raymond Dresdon, Kiki Edozie, Patrick Ukata, Sebastian Elischer, Peter Lewis, and my colleagues Gina Lambright and Claire Metelits, all provided detailed critiques of draft chapters. I received very helpful feedback on the Introduction from several other colleagues. Jonathan Fox offered valuable ideas for reframing the argument, especially for readers unfamiliar with Nigeria but interested in the broader issues related to democratization and consolidation. Stephen Tankel pointed me in the direction of relevant material about terrorism and helped me tighten key concepts. SIS Research also provided a Conference Travel Award that enabled me to present draft chapters at conferences, including the Midwest Political Science Association's Annual Meeting in 2018.

For my field research, I am indebted to a long list of people and I apologize for any omissions. In Port Harcourt, I have to thank Florence Kayemba-IbokAbasi, Chris Newsom, and Joseph Croft of the Stakeholder Democracy Network. I am also grateful for tutorials and help from Patrick Naagbanton, David Ugolor, Anyakwee Nsirimovu, Chukwumeka Eze of the APC, Justine Ijeomah, and Chucks Awasike. I am very much looking forward to my next dinner chat with Michael Uwemedimo and his colleagues at the Collaborative Media Advocacy Platform. I am in debt to the the University of Port Harcourt (UNIPORT) for the hospitality I received from the Vice Chancellor, Professor Ndowa Lale, and distinguished faculty, including Doris Chukwu and Henry Alapiki, who organized the public presentation of my analysis of the 2015 presidential campaign themes.

In Imo State, I have to thank Father AnthonyClaret Onyeocha for his generous hospitality and Emeka Ihedioha. During my brief stay in Anambra, I am in debt to Father Aniedi Okure and Father Sebastian Anokwulu, as well as several other individuals who shall remain anonymous. I also look forward to learning more about eastern politics from Nkolika Obianyo. Dr Jombo Ofo and Hon. Chidi Duru both provided critical interventions for me in Enugu. I'd like to thank Chime Asonye for inviting me to Abia State, and Chima Chuwu and Sam Hart for introducing me to the governor and taking excellent care of me. On this leg of the journey I also benefitted from advice from Daniel Jordan Smith, the staff at Amnesty International, and the superb navigational skills of my good friend Valentine Eke. In Abuja, I can always count on Ben Agande, Rotimi Fadeyi, Terver Akase, Ebere Onwudiwe, Idowu Bakare, C.J. Osman, Lateef Ibrahim, and many others for a home away from home. Jacqueline Farris at the Yar'Adua Centre always provides support and friendship. Idayat Hassan and the Centre for Democracy and Development kindly hosted a public lecture in Abuja in 2018, and Jibrin Ibrahim offered thoughtful feedback on my core findings.

At the American University of Nigeria, I want to thank Bill Hansen, Dauda Bello, Lionel Rawlings, Margee Ensign, Le Gene Quesenberry, and the brilliant students for their hospitality and probing questions about the political economy of corruption. For other segments of my road trip to Yola, I wish to thank Mohammed Bello, Seriki Adinoyi, and Ango Abdullahi. The Nigerian Institute of Policy and Strategic Studies (NIPSS) in Plateau State hosted Matt Page and I, where we shared an empirical analysis of the 2015 election closely related to the argument in Chapter 4 here. (That analysis was published in the *Review of African Political Economy*.) Thank you Jonathan Juma, Ambassador Tijjani Bande, Habu Gladima, and Celestine Bassey.

I reconsidered key ideas in Chapter 2 after fielding critical thoughts from John Campbell, who emphasized the military's ongoing influence in politics over time, and SIS Dean Emeritus Lou Goodman, who helped situate my analysis of pacting within relevant literature on Latin America and who has been an enduring source of support at American University. Todd Eisenstadt also deserves much credit for encouraging me to revisit the pacting literature in the first place during our collaboration on constitution-making. I received helpful feedback on Chapter 3 from Christopher Day and participants on a panel about "New Explorations on Violence in Africa" at the American Political Science Association's 2017 Annual Meeting. Ryan Dalton, Peter M. Lewis, and Princeton Lyman also provided input. The chapter is also much improved thanks to a workshop at Nairobi's Rift Valley Institute, organized by the African Conflict Location Event Dataset. Thank you Clionah Raleigh!

I presented a draft of Chapter 4 at the African Studies Association's 2017 Annual Meeting in Chicago at a panel on "Regional Security Concerns in West Africa." It also formed the basis of a presentation at APSA headquarters in Washington, DC in 2018, where I received excellent input from Jonah Victor, Dorina Bekoe, and others from the Africa policy community. In this regard, I consider myself very lucky to have been able to learn from helpful professionals at the State Department such as Dan Whitman, Bill Strassberger, Beth Lampron, Dan Mozena, Tobias Glucksman, and especially Sarah Aldrich. Alex Thurston provided feedback on Chapter 5, helping me rethink the political dynamics of Nigeria's presidency in 2015, as well as some of the micro-level influences of religion. The poem "Damsels of Gbaramatu" quoted in Chapter 6 is used with permission from the author, Patrick Naagbanton.

Each of these chapters benefited from truly exceptional research assistance. Yoonbin Ha constructed many of the early statistical models and Manuel Reinert helped us create (and understand) the data on violence. Jessica Walton painstakingly constructed the data on state-level debt, among other things, while Erin Kelly assisted with a broad range of tasks, including the presentation of data and statistical analysis. Her work on the index was nothing short of heroic. Last but not least, Arunjana Das deserves a thousand thanks for her work with Chapter 3's content analysis, including her valuable input into elements of the research design.

Finally, I acknowledge the support and ongoing understanding from my family, Monica, Thoreau, Emerson, my sisters Lisa and Allison, and my ever-hospitable Illinois in-laws. Among this family, I include Marcus Raskin from the Institute for Policy Studies – my mentor, collaborator, and co-conspirator since 1992. You are dearly and deeply missed.

1 | Introduction

In January 2015, Nigeria's ruling party was fighting for its life on two fronts. Politically, the elections scheduled for that month presented a daunting challenge as President Goodluck Jonathan's overall approval rating dipped to 29 percent from 43 percent just two years earlier (Loschky 2015). Dozens of disgruntled members of his People's Democratic Party (PDP) had defected and banded together to form a new "megaparty." The president faced an even more formidable fight on the military front. Boko Haram, once a small, isolated religious sect, had evolved into one of the world's deadliest insurgencies. During the previous year, its horrific kidnapping of 276 school girls in Chibok captured the world's attention, and it made steady territorial gains. Over a mere three months it attacked and looted over 200 towns across the northeast, and it took control of at least twenty local government areas across three states. The National Security Adviser said the military could not guarantee security for the elections in the northeast and the electoral commissioner decided to postpone the elections. Then, after pledging loyalty to the Islamic State, Boko Haram called for an election boycott and extended the reach of its terror as far as the city of Gombe (Agence France Press 2015). A military surge in the northeast proved too little, too late for the ruling PDP. Voters cast their lot with the newly formed All Progressive's Congress (APC) taking hold of the presidency, the House of Representatives, the Senate, and most of the governorships. Heading off a repeat of post-election violence in 2011, Jonathan's concession speech rose to the occasion, declaring, "Nobody's ambition is worth the blood of any Nigerian. The unity, stability and progress of our dear country is more important than anything else" (Nossiter 2015a).

This book dissects the 2015 presidential campaign and tells the political story of Nigeria's first "electoral turnover," tracing the origins of the PDP's vulnerability to deals struck during the transition to democracy in 1998–1999. The party internally (and informally) decided to alternate the presidency between north and south, geographically rotated other political offices by "zoning" them, and established an understanding that the party's first presidential candidate in 1999 needed to be Yoruba. Another agreement, between the military and elites more broadly, offered the outgoing authoritarian rulers various guarantees, paved the way for new career paths, and delimited the rules for elite political competition. After capturing power through these elite deals and elections of varying quality, the PDP controlled all levels of government, along with billions of dollars in oil revenue, for sixteen years. These agreements amounted to what the democratization literature refers to as "pacts," meaning "explicit (though not always public) agreements between contending actors, which define the rules of governance on the basis of mutual guarantees for the 'vital interests' of those involved" (Karl 1990, 9). As such, a pact indicates a "transition from above by authoritarian incumbents with sufficient cohesion and resources to dictate the rules of the game" (O'Donnell and Schmitter 1986c, 39). As constitutional crises, tensions over presidential succession, and suppressed internal competition weakened the transition's founding pact, the PDP became vulnerable to a new coalition of rivals under the banner of the APC.

The rise of the APC tacks closely with the transitional pact's decline. This means that the elements of successful democratic consolidation in Nigeria will ultimately differ from the conditions for successful democratic transition. This story is also important because although pacts were common in Latin American and Southern European transitions in the 1970s and 1980s (Stepan 1988), scholars have largely dismissed them in Africa, attributing the expansion of democracy in the 1990s primarily to popular pressures. Moreover, we have little comparative understanding for when and how pacts end (Diamond, Plattner, et al. 1997; Linz and Stepan 1996; O'Donnell and Schmitter 1986b).

How did the APC – a party less than two years old, cobbled together from regional parties and PDP defectors – defeat Africa's largest ruling party? I argue that its campaign on economic issues offered a broader electoral coalition than the PDP's traditional ethnoregional strategy, and the APC's emphasis on electoral integrity appealed to disgruntled politicians and voters alike. I demonstrate this through complementary analyses of elite rhetoric and electoral behavior, drawing on interviews in ten different states with nearly fifty individuals and extensive quantitative data. First, a content analysis of 2,390 news articles quoting the top officials from the PDP and the APC offers empirical evidence that the opposition systematically campaigned on the economy and corruption. Since several national surveys identified insecurity as voters' top concern, and the PDP could have credibly campaigned on economic performance, this strategy suggests that the opposition took a small gamble on its choice of issues. Given the consistent differences between the parties on all five issues I analyze, and the nearly consistent messaging by each party leader on each issue, my results also offer some evidence that African political parties can and do run on strategies calculated and calibrated by issue appeals. Second, a statistical analysis demonstrates that subjective evaluations of national economic performance, objective measures of economic conditions, and enthusiasm for the opposition candidate's economic promises systematically explain electoral outcomes across states. Even the level of violence proves a less reliable predictor of voting patterns. Since outcomes diverged from voters' stated priorities, this provides a building block for inferring that the APC "primed" citizens to engage in "economic voting" (Hart 2016). I also present evidence that campaigning on counter-terrorism played to the PDP's core supporters but meant less to APC voters, who were motivated by other issues. These tests remain robust after controlling for a range of potentially intervening factors, including economic conditions, gender, literacy, and ethnicity. Third, though 2015 electoral maps offer some encouraging signs of voting across ethnicity and indicate that political institutions do promote inter-ethnic electoral coalitions, statistical tests with individual-level data do provide evidence of co-ethnic voting. More alarming is the robust evidence of religiously motivated voting on both sides of the partisan divide. This tempers the "good news" about campaigning and voting on programmatic issues, and has important implications for how Nigeria will confront its most pressing challenges to democracy in the coming years.

I close the book by analyzing how the terrorism of Boko Haram in the northeast, a revival of Igbo secessionism in the southeast, and geographically dispersed farmer–pastoralist conflicts constitute "stress points" that challenge Nigeria's democratic institutions. I argue that electoral accountability will be essential but insufficient for resolving the nation's representational and distributional issues. The peaceful resolution of this stress through political institutions is undermined by lingering legacies of the elite deals struck during the transition. Pacts essentially are "antidemocratic mechanisms, bargained by elites, which seek to create a deliberate socioeconomic and political contract that demobilizes emerging mass actors," writes one critic (Karl 1990, 12). Thus, while the defeat of the PDP delivered Nigeria's first electoral "turnover" ever, marking an important political milestone, the undemocratic nature of the transition continues to haunt the nation's democratic development.

By adopting the term "stress points," I depart from the usual terminology on democratic "consolidation." On the one hand, the classic literature identifies the relatively uncontested legitimate use of force and the absence of serious secessionist claims among the minimum conditions for consolidation (Linz and Stepan 1996; Englebert 2009). These are useful benchmarks for analyzing the stress points above. On the other hand, consolidation as a concept problematically envisions the path to democracy as a linear process, beginning with discrete stages such as political liberalization and elite splits and culminating in electoral competition from which other essential features of democracy follow (Carothers 2002). The vast new literature on hybrid regimes and democratic reversion underscores the complex, multidirectional reality of post-transition politics around the world (Foa and Mounk 2017; Levitsky and Way 2010). Stress points are subnational case studies for examining whether a regime's institutions can weather extra-institutional pressures. Can radical demands for representation be channeled into party politics? Can federalism relieve tensions in disgruntled regions? Do state actors have the means and motives to render violent participation in politics both ineffective *and* irrational? By considering Nigeria's contemporary subnational stress points and empirically analyzing its electoral politics, this book provides a new way of thinking about regime transitions, when they end, and how they shape the democratic institutional capabilities.

Nigeria's contemporary violence seeks to destroy these institutions, and popular accounts of the PDP's defeat point the finger squarely at Boko Haram. This chapter therefore begins by identifying broader African conflict trends and relevant research on terrorism and electoral politics in order to situate Nigeria's insurgency within a comparative politics of violence. One dominant theme in this research focuses on identifying the causes of terrorism and how to defeat it. In its efforts to "counter violent extremism" (CVE) over the past decade, the US Department of Defense has spent over US$1.7 billion on counter-terrorism training and equipment for Africa, and another US$2 billion on counter-terrorism and stabilization for the African Mission in Somalia. Such figures do not include US$465 million (in Fiscal Year 2015–2016) through other budget accounts on training, equipment, and assistance to support CVE initiatives in Africa, or spending by the US Agency for International Development (Blanchard and Arieff 2016). Nor do they include spending by other bilateral and multilateral donors, or by African governments. Africa is on the frontlines of counter-terrorism, and with the fall of aging dictators in Zimbabwe and the Gambia, it is once again at the forefront of democratization.

In order to bring these two trends – democratization and violence – together, this book also engages research on the politics of violence through its detailed analysis of Nigeria's elections. Existing literature in this area typically focuses on the "triggers" or the timing of election violence. I ask instead about the broader political effects of terrorism on electoral democracy in order to understand how the presence of a violent insurgency impacts political campaign strategies, the party system, and voting behavior. These remain nascent areas of research for emerging democracies and pose urgent questions for Nigeria. Like numerous developing countries, it faces what I call the paradox of democratic counter-terrorism: less effective strategies might be more politically popular. This means that if citizens vote on issues other than insecurity, any incentives to build a national constituency for peace lose some appeal.

Next, this chapter introduces Nigeria for readers less familiar with this complex and important African country. Since the book focuses on the Fourth Republic, a period which spans from the 1999 democratic transition to the present, I provide some historical background, situating Nigeria's contemporary politics within broader concerns of colonialism, democracy and dictatorship, and complications of underdevelopment. I highlight three conditions that shaped the post-colonial political context: the precedent of military intervention and limitations on the ability of institutions to structure uncertainty; geopolitical realignments that internationally amplified Nigeria's strategic importance and domestically produced conflicting structures of interest aggregation; and the normalization of violence as these structures failed to moderate or mediate citizen demands.

I conclude with a succinct summary of the book's chapters, identifying my main findings and their principal implications for different areas of research. By describing the elite deals that facilitated the transition to democracy in 1999 and linking the weakening of that "pact" to new opportunities for opposition political parties, I offer a new account of how transitions end. Then, by systematically identifying rhetorical differences between competing presidential campaigns, I contribute to our understanding of how parties adopt different issue portfolios to distinguish themselves from each other and appeal to voters. Although religion and ethnicity remain important factors in Nigerian politics, as I will show later, the APC's strategy points to the promise of programmatic campaigns. In addition, by linking the APC's core campaign issues to electoral outcomes, I contribute to emerging comparative research that shows how party messaging can shift voter preferences by "priming" them to vote on particular issues. In Nigeria's case, the opposition effectively discounted the politics of fear fueled by Boko Haram's reign of terror and built a winning campaign on economic promise and electoral integrity. Nigeria's 2015 Presidential Election was certainly not perfect, yet these findings offer some "good" news for African democracy and advance important research agendas on party competition, African politics, and elections amidst terrorism in the developing world.

Terrorism and Electoral Politics

Terrorism such as Boko Harm's is a specific form of non-state violence that targets noncombatants in order to instill fear and achieve some broader political objective.[1] According to a seminal study by Enders and Sandler (2012), terrorist groups are 3.5 times more likely to be present in democracies than in dictatorships. Yet, we are still learning about how terrorism impacts elections, the principal feature of democracies (and many dictatorships too). Enders and Sandler's work, *The Political Economy of Terrorism*, mentions terrorism and elections only in passing, noting, "elected governments may lose the next election if

---

[1] The US Code of Federal Regulations defines terrorism as "the unlawful use of force and violence against persons or property to intimidate or coerce a government, the civilian population, or any segment thereof, in furtherance of political or social objectives" (28 C.F.R. Section 0.85).

domestic attacks are not curtailed" (Enders and Sandler 2012, 9). The overall number of terrorist attacks increased just prior to elections taking place in Western European democracies between 1950 and 2004. However "a relatively permissive electoral system makes the use of peaceful means a more favorable option" (Aksoy 2014, 911). Such findings constitute a marked departure from analyses prior to 9/11, when terrorism was often blamed on poverty, limited economic opportunities, or a demographic "youth bulge" (US Agency for International Development and Management Systems International 2009). By locating conditions conducive to terrorism in institutions, these findings also imply that, like other political actors, terrorists' behavior is shaped by the political context generating constraints and opportunities. By this reasoning, good counter-terrorism involves raising the costs of violence while reducing the barriers to entry into legitimate politics. Voters in Mali, Kenya, Niger, Algeria, Somalia, and Nigeria have all had to go to the polls while facing risks associated with terrorism with all of its spectacular, random, and deadly features. How do politicians campaign in the context of terrorism, and how do voters decide who to vote for?

In Mali, Wing finds that the government elected in 2013 repeatedly contradicted itself as rival politicians jockeyed for electoral constituencies. Some officials labeled groups terrorists in order to "frame" them as enemies, while other officials sought to accommodate them as legitimate players in the post-conflict context (Wing 2016). Similarly, Oates finds differences across countries in how politicians characterize terrorism. In Russia and the United States, a "show of strength" is central to campaign rhetoric, while in Britain, discussion of terrorism is "more rational and less emotional" during election cycles (Oates 2006, 426). She concludes that the impact of terrorism on elections is conditioned by this rhetoric and media coverage, not simply by the level of violence. Evidence from seventeen (primarily Western European) democracies over fifty years finds that parties will seek to form surplus coalitions in anticipation of terrorist activity, and if terrorism does occur, ideological differences fade (Indridason 2008). This "rally-around-the-flag" effect was especially pronounced in a study of France, Germany, Spain, the United Kingdom, and the United States between 1990 and 2006 (Chowanietz 2011).

Another area of research focuses on voters. How do they respond to framing and other efforts by political parties to motivate them?

Findings from one influential study of the 2004 US Presidential Election, the 2006 California Gubernatorial Election, and the 2008 Presidential Election further highlight the distortions generated by populism. Merolla and Zechmeister conclude, "conditions of threat cause strong leadership to take on a greater relevance to individuals which is then demonstrated by its changed effect within the candidate choice calculus" (Merolla and Zechmeister 2009, 597). Terrorist activity, according to this research, leads voters to prioritize leadership over traditional campaign issues such as the economy.

The most consistent finding is that terrorism increases electoral support for right-wing parties in more advanced democracies, deepening ideological polarization. Basing their analysis on areas that fall within the range of rockets sometimes used by Palestinians (and thus equating Palestinian violence with terrorism), Getmansky and Zeitzoff (2014) find that the right-wing vote share is 2 to 6 percentage points higher in localities within the range of rockets. In fact, the mere *threat* of an attack benefits right-wing parties. Other research on Israel similarly finds that a terror attack in a given locality before elections increases right-wing support by 135 percent. This means that "terrorism does cause the ideological polarization of the electorate," and, further, each fatality has significant electoral effects beyond physical location of the attack (Berrebi and Klor 2008, 279). A study of Turkey finds that support for right-wing parties that are "less concessionist towards terrorist organizations" increases where the government security services have suffered from Kurdistan Workers' Party (PKK) attacks (Kibris 2011, 220). In this view, terrorism is a bad tactic for achieving political objectives since it motivates voters to support hardline politicians. Rather than the rally-around-the-flag effect noted above, these studies suggest that terrorism contributes to political polarization.

Polarization of the electorate and narrow party appeals to the base contribute to what I call a paradox of democratic counterterrorism: less-effective strategies may be more popular with voters, thereby making "good" policy bad politics.[2] One study of Israel finds

---

[2] That idea evokes an insight (or debate) from the era of economic liberalization, when some scholars argued that optimal economic policies were politically irrational, that is, often not in the self-interest of politicians making policy (Bates 1989).

that political parties explicitly appeal to their core supporters rather than broader electoral constituencies. As right-wing parties tack right and left-wing parties go left, this ultimately means that "electoral incentives may induce democratic governments to select inefficient or suboptimal strategies around election time" (Nanes 2016, 171). Bueno de Mesquita argues that electoral pressures inspire governments to spend on visible counter-terrorism strategies that enable them to take credit. Unless the government's and voters' preferences are aligned, "the government will always allocate resources to observable counterterror in excess of the social optimum" (De Mesquita 2007, 11).

It is important to note that terrorism sometimes generates potentially positive "second-order effects" for democracy. For example, Blattman finds that forced recruitment in northern Uganda "leads to greater postwar political participation – a 27% increase in the likelihood of voting and a doubling of the likelihood of being a community leader among former abductees" (Blattman 2009, 231). Abduction, in this case by radical Christian extremists in the Lord's Resistance Army, does not impact nonpolitical social activity. One cross-national study points to another unexpected, positive result: voter turnout increases in democracies with recent terrorist attacks (Robbins et al. 2013).[3] In general, though, the research suggests that we know little about how terrorism influences parties and elections outside the developed world, and why politicians can so easily harness the public's passions.

A relatively recent rise in terrorism in Africa points to the need for a research agenda organized around the political logic of security in emerging democracies. After a decline starting in the mid-1990s that accompanied a wave of political liberalization, the overall number of incidents rose swiftly, as illustrated in Figure 1.1. Between 1990 and 2015, the Global Terrorism Database reports 9,804 separate incidents (National Consortium for the Study of Terrorism and Responses to Terrorism 2016). By another measure, conflict among African non-state actors contributed to at least 59,000 deaths in twenty-four countries between 1990 and 2009 (Williams 2016).

Of the 9,804 terrorist incidents in Sub-Saharan Africa since 1990 illustrated in Figure 1.1, nearly a third (29 percent, or 2,882 of the total) occurred in Nigeria. On the basis of frequency alone, Nigeria

---

[3] I am grateful to Jennifer Raymond Dresdon for pointing out this research to me.

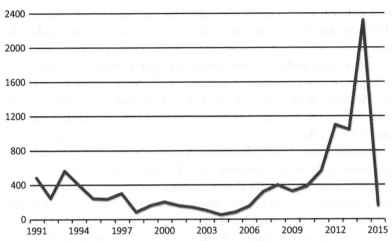

Figure 1.1 Terrorist incidents in Sub-Saharan Africa, 1990–2015.
Source: Global Terrorism Database

constitutes an important case for understanding violence on the continent. Figure 1.2 plots the incidents limited to Nigeria, illustrating a pronounced rise in violence following the 1999 transition to an elected civilian government, consistent with Enders and Sandler's (2012) generalization about democracies experiencing more terrorism. Another trend that stands out is the ups and downs in the years prior to 2015. Heading into March of that year, the country faced its most competitive election since 1979. Did Boko Haram see this as a political vulnerability that it could tactically exploit? And, even more interestingly, did the ruling PDP worry about how the spike of violence in 2014 would appear to voters?

This book seeks in part to situate this rise and decline of Boko Haram's violence in the broader context of democratic competition and political change. At one level, the growing possibility of electoral defeat increased the pressure on the PDP to do something differently. In November 2014, a military surge announced by President Jonathan began taking back the estimated twenty-one local governments held by Boko Haram across the northeast. When the election, scheduled for January 2015, was delayed by six weeks to allow the surge to advance, politicians and voters alike asked what the military could possibly accomplish in six weeks that it could not accomplish over the previous six years. The surge sounded like

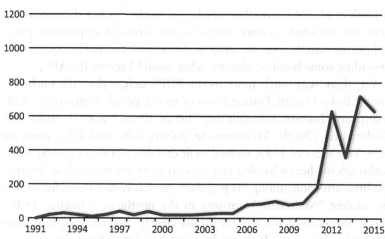

Figure 1.2 Terrorist incidents in Nigeria, 1990–2015.
Source: Global Terrorism Database

"demonstration counter-terrorism," a performance of sorts for voters. Two weeks before the election, the Army claimed to have retaken seventeen of the local governments (Mbah 2015). It was too little, too late for the PDP.

Criticism of the government's handling of Boko Haram took on a partisan tone well before the military surge. As the National Assembly debated a 2013 Anti-Terrorism Bill, opposition parties that had just begun negotiations to form the super-party that became the APC united in outrage against the proposed concentration of power in the National Security Adviser in the legislation. The bill charged him with formulating and implementing a "comprehensive counter-terrorism strategy," including leadership and coordination of all the relevant agencies: security, intelligence, law enforcement, and military services. The police, the State Secret Service, and the intelligence agencies all resented the concentration of authority, while senators expressed concern about the NSA's broad discretionary powers to "do such other acts or things necessary" for security. As the National Assembly debated the bill, a senator from the Congress for Progressive Change (CPC), for example, complained that the security agencies were not sufficiently justifying the huge increase in funds by showing results against insecurity; another senator worried about "a situation where security agencies appear to be competing for funds"

(Abbah et al. 2013). In other words, substantive policy disagreements over the national security infrastructure brought opposition party politicians together on an issue at the top of the public's priorities, providing some bonding glue for what would become the APC.

Yet, there was much more to the PDP's defeat than the mishandling of Boko Haram. During times of terror, people romanticize leadership and become nostalgic for "better times," write Merolla and Zechmeister (2009). Muhammadu Buhari, who had led a coup on New Year's Eve of 1983, seemed to fit this description in several ways. Although his heavy-handed response to petty crimes such as littering left little affection among the populace, he was remembered for ending the violent "Maitatsine" uprising in the northeast (Osaghae 1998). More importantly, his modest means clearly distinguished him from the hedonism of the PDP; he had not benefitted from the rampant corruption (Paden 2016). It established him as a man of the *talakawa,* the Hausa word for a commoner with weak ties to patronage networks and therefore more economically vulnerable (LeVan et al. 2018). In the early 1980s, during Buhari's tenure as a military head of state, a "talakawa nationalism" among the urban working class emerged to challenge traditional elite circles (Lubeck 1986). Combined with his (part-)Fulani heritage, which ensured his place among the traditional ruling elite, and these features with grassroots appeal, Buhari seemed the ideal candidate for bringing together conservative elements of the north and disaffected citizens who sought to end the PDP's long run.

However, Buhari was all these things when he ran and lost in the 2003, 2007, and 2011 presidential elections. The political climate in 2015 differed not simply because an electoral constituency for a new approach to counter-terrorism seemed to be emerging; it differed because the PDP itself had begun falling apart. In August 2013, 5 (out of 36) governors, 22 (out of 109) senators, and 57 (out of 360) members of the House defected to the newly formed APC (Okocha 2013). The mass defections put the PDP's control of the National Assembly at stake and raised a constitutional challenge to a party's authority over its members. Just prior to announcing they had switched parties, the defecting politicians sought to comply with obscure constitutional provisions requiring the formation of a faction or a merger following a party 'division' before joining another party. The relevant constitutional clause, Section 68(g), is meant to promote party discipline. But it had also facilitated PDP dominance by raising the political costs of defection. Members therefore decamped en masse, declaring themselves "New PDP." They wrote to the House and Senate leadership in December 2013, announcing, "We have merged with the APC according to Section 68 of the 1999 Constitution." They then sued the leadership, demanding that their seats should not be declared vacant. To show the "old" PDP it was serious, the APC members in the National Assembly threatened to vote against federal budget. The New PDP suffered a setback in 2014 when the Federal High Court in Abuja ruled that there is no faction in PDP, arguing that the defecting members owed their election to the party rather than to voters (Ikhilae 2014; Bernard 2014, 26–7).

In the end, political reality prevailed over the courts' legal contortions. The former PDP members joined forced with Buhari's Congress for Progressive Change (CPC), the southwest-based Action Congress of Nigeria (ACN), the All Nigeria Peoples' Party (ANPP) with its northern appeal, and several politicians from the southeastern All Progressives Grand Alliance (APGA). Buhari's personal qualities contributed to his choice as the new party's candidate, and his northern roots reassured northerners who felt betrayed by Goodluck Jonathan's election in 2011. After the APC won, Buhari's honeymoon was short-lived; Boko Haram's bombings returned, Buhari disappeared for several months to receive medical treatment abroad, and inflation and debts rose. Instead of rallying around the flag as in the Western cases noted above, Nigerians saw familiar factionalism reemerge. Buhari had spent very little time building the new party and, once elected, no time mediating the differences among the CPC and its new bedfellows (All Progressives Congress 2016). Despite these obstacles, Nigeria's party "turnover" marked a major milestone in the nation's political history by changing what politicians see as necessary to win and what its democratic citizens see as possible. In order to appreciate this milestone, the next section familiarizes readers with the nation's turbulent political history, from the broken promises of its dictators to the shallow hopes vested in its oil wealth.

Before Terrorism and Turnover: The Fourth Republic in Historical Context

Nigeria's experience with democracy got off to a rocky start in the 1960s, and its first two democratic regimes lasted a combined length of only ten years. This makes the endurance of the current regime in the face of deadly insurgency an important accomplishment, and the peaceful defeat of the ruling party all the more remarkable. A large body of excellent research already describes different periods of Nigeria's political history between independence and the historic 1999 transition. For example, Diamond (1988) and Sklar (2004 [1963]) detail the First Republic (1960–1966), Panter-Brick (1971) accounts for the slide into civil war, Oyediran (1979) analyzes the first long stretch of military rule from 1966 to 1979, and Falola and Ihonvbere (1985) explain the transition to the Second Republic in 1979 and its collapse in 1983. Books by Diamond et al. (1997) and Amuwo et al. (2001) discuss military regimes from 1985 to 1993 and then from 1993 until 1998, respectively. Osaghae's *Crippled Giant* (Osaghae 1998) authoritatively covers the period from independence until 1998, and my previous book analyzes political drivers of public policy performance from independence to 2007 (LeVan 2015a).

This section introduces Nigeria to readers unfamiliar with it. Most of the book concerns the present political era known as the Fourth Republic, which began with the election of a civilian president, the promulgation of a new constitution, and – most importantly – the exit of the military in 1999. In what follows, I briefly situate the present democratic regime in the nation's tumultuous history prior to the transition and reference relevant literature on Nigerian politics. Rather than presenting a chronology, I organize most of this historical information around three thematic post-colonial contexts that shaped the political structure of the transition. Readers already familiar with Nigeria may want to skip ahead.

For most African countries, political history follows a familiar series of challenges and themes. Colonialism affected every country in Africa except Ethiopia, leaving legacies that varied substantially based on the imperial power involved, the strategy adopted to resist colonialism, and domestic factors such as ethnic diversity and the structure of the economy. Ghana's independence set an optimistic tone in 1957, and Nigeria led a large cohort of new nations liberated from Europe's grip in 1960. The enchantment of political independence for this generation of hopeful leaders was, however, tempered by the reality that social transformations and imperial economic structures could neither be undone nor easily harnessed for nation-building.

Like their other colonies (and not to be confused with "settler" colonies such as Rhodesia or Kenya), Britain governed Nigeria through "indirect rule." Economically, this involved the creation of "marketing boards" that served as the *sole* buyers for various commodities such as ground nuts, cocoa, and palm oil. They paid farmers below the market value for their goods, leaving the government to reap the surplus of productivity and giving rulers an incentive to suppress the prices paid to producers. Small farmers formed the backbone of the economy, but this arrangement of government-run "monopsonies" kept the producers decentralized and disorganized (Forrest 1995). In the years following World War II, exports expanded and tax revenue increased, making the colony increasingly self-sufficient and thus achieving the underlying goal of indirect rule, which was to make colonies profitable, or at least not costly. While political constituencies back home in the United Kingdom were less willing to pay for the "civilizing" mission of imperialism or the exportation of Christianity, the third "C" of colonialism – "commerce" – remained a sensible goal. As pressure from Nigerian nationalists such as Obafemi Awolowo and Nnamadi "Zik" Azikiwe mounted, Britons hoped commerce would bind the countries and that carefully groomed Nigerian elites would remain sympathetic to their former rulers under any eventual "self-rule."

Nigerians, like other Africans, disrupted Britain's vision of this choreographed transition. For example, Zik in his speeches expressed support for treaties and trade relations with the "Anglo" world as the basis of lasting friendship, while warning "that in the next world war, we shall pitch our tent in any camp which by word and deed satisfies our national aspirations" (Azikiwe 1961, 160). As in other colonies under indirect rule, the British aimed to prepare Nigerians for self-rule through a gradual process. But for Zik and other nationalists such as Herbert McCauley, the process was not fast enough and the powers incrementally acquired through several constitutions were too limited. Decolonization was comparatively peaceful, but early anti-colonial activists suffered greater violence at the hands of Lord Lugard and his successors than many histories acknowledge (Falola 2009).

Once the handover to Nigerians finally occurred in 1960, the leaders of the First Republic soon realized that they had inherited a political structure more suited to colonialism's exploitative strategies of divide and rule than to national integration and sustainable economic development. The Westminster parliamentary system provided for a prime minister chosen by the majority party. As a practical matter, this meant that the overwhelmingly Muslim north, with its large population advantage, would dominate politics (Baba 2018). This led to other debilitating effects on democratic development. It generated incentives for politicians in each of the three regions created by Britain (North, East, and West) to appeal to ethnic and political minorities in the other regions (Sklar 2004 [1963]), and it ensured that population counts would become politically sensitive undertakings. The creation of the "Midwest Region" in 1963 was a tactic to weaken the Western-based opposition, and then the explosive reactions to the first independence-era census fulfilled these respective fears (Suberu 2001). Each of the regions retained their strong subnational powers, which generally undermined integration of the country's 300 ethnic groups into a coherent national identity. Moreover, the retention of the marketing boards gave each region's politicians a fiscal basis for independence from the federal government as well as incentives to continue exploiting agricultural producers (Bates 1981). As Ekeh notes in a classic essay, many African elites simply wanted to *replace* European elites (Ekeh 1975).

Colonialism's disruptive socio-economic impacts were also difficult to remedy through political independence. Women's movements that had inspired and led much of the early anti-colonial resistance found themselves on the margins of post-colonial political power. The south had a huge educational advantage since a British agreement with Fulani emirs kept Christian missionaries and their schools out of the predominantly Muslim north. In 1964, just a few years after independence, 192,127 students were enrolled in secondary schools across the south, while only 12,885 were enrolled in the north, despite similar population sizes (Federal Office of Statistics 1968). It would take a half-century, under Goodluck Jonathan's government, before the vast gender disparities in enrolments neared parity (since Muslim families were more reluctant to send daughters to school). Enrolment rates overall in the north remain low compared to the south. An individual living in the northwest or the northeast is four times more likely to have no education compared to someone in the Niger Delta, for example (African Development Bank 2013). Fulani elites successfully agitated for a "northernization" of the civil service, which improved ethnic balance but placed ill-prepared and undereducated staff in the

government (Dudley 1973). The Fulani continued to maintain disproportionate influence in the military.

A military coup in January 1966 and a swift counter-coup preceded
the descent into one of Africa's bloodiest civil wars in June 1967.
If the deck was stacked against democracy at independence, the
nationalists' dreams of peaceful prosperity soon faded. Dictators
governed until October 1979. The new democratic regime, the Second
Republic, got off on the wrong foot after the Supreme Court had to
pick the winner of the presidential election since no candidate met all
the constitutional requirements for victory. Inheriting huge budgetary
commitments from the outgoing Olusegun Obasanjo dictatorship
and declining oil revenues, the fragile democratic government soon
faced a fiscal crisis. The collapse of a multi-party coalition in 1981
accented tensions with the executive as well as ethnoregional political
alignments, and violence engulfed the 1983 elections (LeVan 2015a;
Falola and Ihonvbere 1985). On New Year's Eve 1983, then-General
Muhammadu Buhari brought back the military with the "primary
objective of saving our beloved nation from total collapse." Implying
that the military had all along remained the guardian of national
interest throughout the years of civilian rule, he also noted that the
1979 transition plan "was implemented to the letter" but politicians
had brought the country to a "present state of general insecurity"
(Soldiers Seize Power 1984, 7110).[4]

Depending on how one counts, the country experienced two more
successful coups, in 1985 and then in 1993, bringing the total to
five since independence in 1960. Chapter 2 will detail the transition
to democracy triggered by the dictator Sani Abacha's sudden death
in 1998, emphasizing how his decision to run for president proved
unpopular both inside and outside the regime. A group of prominent
elites called it "morally unjust and ethically dishonest for the chief
umpire of this transition programme to become the chief participant
in the electoral process" (Tijani 1998, 18). Most importantly, his candidacy would have left unresolved the fate of Moshood Abiola, the
apparent winner of transitional elections in 1993. The annulment of
those elections had brought the country to a standstill, and an Abacha

---

[4] Another less-known reason for the coup was the military's frustration with
civilian handling of Nigeria's border war with Chad (Africa Confidential 1984).

candidacy threatened a return to such paralysis. Even with Abacha out of the game, Nigeria's last transition still faced tremendous odds.

Post-Colonial Contexts of Nigeria's Last Transition

Several patterns and features of post-colonial politics shaped the 1998–1999 transition, and further serve to efficiently introduce the country's complex political history to readers. First, comparatively speaking, the precedent of military intervention is one of the best predictors of future military intervention (Cheibub 2007; Kandeh 2004). This meant that a cloud of uncertainty hung over the 1999 handover to civilians. Nigerians had come to doubt the military's promises, shaping how they interpret moments of political change. Transition plans became a recurring feature of politics, and when Buhari overthrew the democratic regime in 1983 he made clear that civilian politics depended on the ongoing goodwill of the military, which kept a watchful eye over civilians – instead of the other way around. Obasanjo's resume (a civil war hero who handed over power to civilians in 1979 and who again proved his democratic credentials by serving prison time under Abacha) made him an ideal candidate in 1999. But he also had to manage fractious elites, a military worried about retribution, and a public inexperienced in institutionalized participatory politics. In the nation's consciousness, coups, failed coups, annulled elections, and aborted transitions had undermined the credibility of government promises and grossly abbreviated people's "time horizon," the temporal frame of reference for behavior and decision-making. Surveys conducted in the years after the transition captured the problem of an abbreviated time horizon when 86.6 percent of Nigerians said they "anticipate being more satisfied in a year," with 58.9 percent expecting to be "much more satisfied." The Obasanjo Government thus faced seemingly impossible expectations: 70.8 percent said they expected the government to fulfill its promises within four years – meaning before the end of his term (Lewis and Bratton 2000). Surveys also measured "patience with democracy" through a series of questions. In 2000, 79 percent of respondents agreed that "our present system of elected government should be given more time to deal with inherited problems." Only 17 percent agreed that "if our present system of government cannot produce results soon, we should try another form of government." By 2005, patience had dropped to 55 percent and impatience had increased to 39 percent. Similarly, those satisfied or "very satisfied" with democracy had dropped from 84 to 25 percent, and those "not very satisfied" or "not at all satisfied" increased from 14 to 71 percent (Afrobarometer 2006).

When the Berlin Wall fell in 1989, and pressure for democratization mounted across Africa, Ibrahim Babangida had already inched toward a "permanent transition." With an endless series of public consultations, new political agencies, and plans to transition to democracy, the Babangida regime (1985–1993) seemed to make the process of political reform, rather than any particular reform outcome, its governing strategy (Diamond, Oyediran, et al. 1997). When he annulled the June 12, 1993 election, the jig was up and the country could only be "saved" from a descent into total chaos by a new military ruler, Sani Abacha. While democratic optimism swept the continent and much of the world in the 1990s, Abacha's regime swam against the tide, throwing pro-democracy activists in prison. The hanging of playwright Ken Saro-Wiwa along with eight of his ethnic Ogoni colleagues shocked the world and mobilized new support for sanctions with the hope that they would increase pressure on the regime and give a boost to civil society (Lewis et al. 1998). The problem was that the demand for oil exceeded the love for democracy in the West, and the sanctions that were put in place accomplished little (Sklar 2001).

A second post-colonial context relates to a geopolitical realignment. One dimension was domestic. At home, oil transformed the logic of federalism and the social contract between citizens and policy-makers. Oil had been discovered in the Niger Delta in the 1950s, but it initially played a small role in the post-independence economy. Starting in 1946, states (at that time known as "regions") and local governments were responsible for sales tax, property tax, and personal income tax, while the federal government collected taxes on imports, exports, excise, business, and natural resources. These tax authorities remained relatively stable. But subnational dependence on central revenue allocation increased dramatically as oil revenue increased. For example, in the 1953–1965 period, states received about 56 percent of their revenue from the federal government. By the 1970s, this figure had risen to approximately 80 percent (Suberu 2001). Later in the book, I show

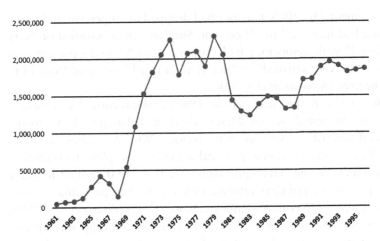

Figure 1.3 Barrels of oil exported, 1960–1997.
Source: Nigerian National Petroleum Corporation (1998)

how debt rather than this revenue is an increasingly important source of the center's leverage over subnational politics.

The surge of oil revenue coincided with the entrance of Nigeria's autocrats, and huge export revenue in the 1970s contributed to massive postwar reconstruction, increasing international influence, and corruption on a grand scale as Dutch disease contributed to an overvalued naira and cheap luxury imports (Ahmad Khan 1994; Ikein and Briggs-Anigboh 1998). Figure 1.3 illustrates the dramatic rise in oil exports, which by the time of the 1999 transition accounted for approximately 90 percent of export revenue. Like other African countries in the 1980s, Nigeria underwent structural adjustment programs (SAPs) that attempted to liberalize the public sector. With the decline of oil prices, Nigeria found itself with little revenue or leverage against external pressures (Olukoshi 1993). SAP also realigned state–society relations, creating new alliances among labor, students, market organizations, and new human rights organizations with transnational ties (LeVan 2011b; Edozie 2002). Unlike earlier civil society organizations focused on community development or cultural practices, this "Second Wave" of organizations rose to challenge the state and defend prodemocracy and labor activists from human rights violations (Kew 2016).

A corresponding trend with the rise in oil revenues was the steep reduction in the "derivation formula" that returns a share of profits back to the state of origin if the federal government owns the rights to the source of those profits. With minerals such as tin in the country's Middle Belt region, these profits were relatively small. But as the economy shifted to oil, the derivation formula declined from 50 percent under the independence constitution, to 25 percent in 1977, to its nadir of 1.5 percent under the Buhari Government in 1984, before reaching its current level of 13 percent under the 1999 Constitution. A study of the nearly two-dozen formulas used since the 1940s found that changes to the derivation formula were strongly related to "regional control of the political process" (Mbanefoh and Egwaikhide 1998). Some studies claim that the north received more than its share of revenue allocation between 1968 and 1981 (Adesina 1998), contributing to resentment about northern power and southern frustrations over the negative externalities (notably massive pollution) associated with oil. By 1991, 70 percent of revenue generation came from the south (Okoye 1999), deepening resentment against a long string of northerners who had governed almost uninterrupted since the counter-coup in 1966.[5] In the 1950s and 1960s, it was northerners who hinted at secession; by the 1990s it was southerners in the oil-producing Niger Delta venting their frustration. Perhaps above all, oil revenues introduced patronage on a grand scale. Today, there is some evidence that clientelist networks are weakening. For the PDP, this has precipitated a particular crisis as a party built on an inclusive philosophy of patronage. "They have no federal government or structure in hand, which is the one thing that is going to patronize and oil the party," explained one APC politician (Lamido 2016).

The geopolitical effects of oil also had an international dimension for Nigeria, interacting with the logics of domestic politics. Oil made the economy vulnerable to price shocks. When prices were comparatively low, as in the 1980s, the new regime struggled to live up to democracy's promises. Then when prices were high, oil helped incumbents consolidate power internally and project power internationally. For the military regimes in the 1970s, this meant a more assertive foreign policy in line with the rise of the Organization of

---

[5] The exceptions being the brief five-month period after the first coup, and then the three-year military regime of Obasanjo.

Petroleum Exporting Countries. For Abacha's dictatorship, it insulated the regime from external pressures. For the new democratic regime in 1999, steady oil revenues provided an indigenous source of development, and for a period during Obasanjo's second term, the country was virtually debt free. Nigeria positioned itself as a new global power, embarking on a campaign for a seat on the United Nations Security Council. When the US Department of Defense announced plans for a new military command for Africa, Nigeria critiqued the plans. The transitional government in 1998 appreciated this geopolitical rebalancing from the start.

A third important post-colonial context is the "normalization of violence." The different types, geographical dispersion, intensity, and frequency of violence in Nigeria are startling, even if one sets aside the civil war from June 1967 to January 1970 in which at least a million people perished. The violence – including state violence – has been a fundamental feature of politics, regardless of whether autocrats or democrats are in charge. Largely lost to history is the violence that accompanied the 1999 transition; the day power was handed over to civilians in May, 200 people died in Ijaw–Itsekiri clashes. In July, 60 people died in the "Shagamu riots," and in August another 200 people died in Ijaw clashes, this time with Ilaje communities (Sandra 2005). Later that year the military, under the command of the former dictator-turned-civilian-elected president, bombed the village of Odi in Bayelsa State, killing hundreds. A large conflict analysis literature organizes such violence into categories such as "ethnic conflict," labels that can easily become so inclusive as to obscure the variety of conflict drivers. For example, the Ijaw–Istsekiri clashes in Delta State were triggered by disputes over local government, and conflicts in Plateau State between Fulani and ethnic minorities such as the Berom are significantly rooted in legalized discrimination against "settlers" by "indigenes" (Higazi 2016). In the more ethnically homogeneous eastern part of the country, conflicts are rooted in land pressures, chieftancy disputes, or simple political differences (Ibeanu 2003). When the ethnic groups in question belong to different faiths, the violence may take on a religious color even if religion was not necessarily the source of tension. When religious reformers rose to question or challenge secular state power, as the "Maitatsine movement" did during the Second Republic and Boko Haram has done in the Fourth Republic, the security services have responded with overwhelming force (Adesoji 2011; Thurston 2018).

The normalization of violence means that democratic politics has lost some of its luster as an institutional and behavioral means for resolving conflict through procedural participation. Citizens resort to organized violence because they feel the government no longer represents their interests, shares resources fairly, or accommodates multiple centers of power. When one survey asked Niger Deltans "how justified is violence if peaceful demands [are] continually ignored?" 43.0 percent in Akwa-Ibom, 33.8 percent in Delta, 32.7 percent in Rivers, and 43.3 percent in Ondo said it was either "justified" or "well justified" (Alapiki et al. 2015). The conflict resolution organization Search for Common Ground in 2017 reported similarly alarming figures in the northeast, even among activists who self-identify as peacebuilders. Meanwhile, the state utilizes violence because there are no judicial or political consequences for doing so. Police officers and soldiers are not convicted for abuses – even serious ones. The public thus embraces a kind of cognitive dissonance: supporting a heavy-handed approach as a way to reduce insecurity, while continually signaling its mistrust in the security services and, increasingly, organizing their own local self-protection through vigilante groups (Okenyodo 2017). "Violence is not only used as a political instrument by ruthless political entrepreneurs," explains Mehler (2007, 194), "it can be an established mode of competition."

These three broad themes represent only one way of grappling with Nigeria's complex post-colonial experience, and they are not meant to obfuscate other implicit and relevant factors. For example, ethnic politics and religion deserve attention, and Chapters 4 and 5 will dwell on those cleavages. But these three post-colonial experiences discussed above – distorted time horizons and high levels of political uncertainty, domestic and international geopolitical realignments, and the normalization of violence – are all useful devices for understanding the context and content of the 1998/1999 transition.

Overview of the Chapters

When and how do transitions end? How did an upstart opposition, barely two years old, defeat Africa's largest political party? And now that citizens know that they can actually vote out a party as powerful as the PDP, can democratic competition increase the resilience of the nation's political institutions? These are important questions not just for Nigeria, but for a whole range of countries with dominant parties, terrorist threats, or elites aging out of regime changes that unfolded in the 1990s.

Chapter 2, "The End of a New Beginning: Nigeria's Transition, 1999–2015," discusses how the classic democratization research identifies the end of a transition, sometimes pegging the final moment when the new regime organizes its first free and fair elections, or perhaps when the previous regime's power brokers, such as the military, lose control over policy-making. I argue that Nigeria's transition from dictatorship to democracy did not end until the defeat of the ruling PDP in 2015, sixteen years after the handover to civilians. I take 2015 as the critical historical moment not simply because the country experienced its first "party turnover" with the PDP's defeat at the polls, but because the election expressed a new weakness of elite agreements that had facilitated the 1999 transition.

The transition's pact included agreements to alternate the presidency between north and south, rotate various offices among different parts of the country through "zoning," and an understanding that the party's first presidential candidate in 1999 needed to be Yoruba. As my co-authors and I explain elsewhere (Eisenstadt et al. 2017), it also produced a democratic constitution through undemocratic means. Drawing on interviews with politicians, retired military officials, and civil society leaders, I show how the PDP's founding principles were congruent with broader demands from the outgoing regime's elites. In 1998, the military found itself without explicit veto power, as in many Latin American transitions. But it did secure important exit guarantees, similar to other transitions in Africa. Once in power, the PDP reassured the departing military with a little-noticed wave of promotions and opened up new career paths for those who left the military. Borrowing a concept from research on coups (Powell 2012), I also document how President Olusegun Obasanjo's administration "spoiled" the Ministry of Defence with large spending increases and other perks. Such policies helped keep the transition on track, but they also interfered with the Fourth Republic's democratic restructuring. The resounding electoral defeat of the PDP in 2015 dealt these elite bargains a blow.

To document this pact's unraveling, I highlight a generational shift that put the PDP out of touch, and rendered military experience less politically relevant. More importantly, I detail how principles of rotating power tore the party apart internally. "Power shift" and "zoning" weakened links to voters, generated opacity by virtue of their informality, and suffocated ambitious politicians. These institutions to rotate power based on ethnoregional identity generated widespread resentment among politicians. The party's crude disciplinary measures deepened this resentment, contributing to mass defections to the newly formed APC in 2013–2014 (LeVan 2018). The present historical moment highlights how the traits of a successful transition differ from the features of a successful democracy. Nigerians also have a new opportunity to reconsider representation and accountability in a new deal grounded in elect-oral politics.

The title of Chapter 3, "The Rational Counter-Terrorist? Economic Policy and Insurgent Insecurity in Nigeria's 2015 Presidential Campaign," is an intentional play on words. It asks when it is in a politician's self-interest to campaign on a platform of counter-terrorism, a question rooted in both academic research and political discourse. After the attacks of 9/11 on the United States, President George W. Bush rhetorically asked, "Why do they hate us?" In a speech before a joint session of Congress, he answered, "They hate our freedoms: our freedom of religion, our freedom of speech, our freedom to vote and assemble and disagree with each other ... These terrorists kill not merely to end lives, but to disrupt and end a way of life" (Bush 2001). In the social sciences, Bush's comments set off a debate: are terrorists irrational fanatics or is there some calcula-tion behind the chaos? In an early study, Robert Pape shows that nearly all suicide terrorism is driven by a broader strategic goal, and most of it is not linked to Islamic fundamentalism; the crude characterization of terrorists as irrational therefore misses the mark (Pape 2006). But politically, casting terrorists as irrational arguably worked for Bush's re-election in 2004. So why didn't it work for the PDP in 2015? And did the victorious APC actually campaign on counter-terrorism?

I answer these questions in three separate chapters, culminating in a comprehensive account of the ruling party's historic defeat. The first step, in Chapter 3, empirically examines what the parties talked about and finds that insecurity as an issue played a smaller role in the campaign than expected. I provide context for the election by describing President Jonathan's unusual route to power though the death of President Umaru Musa Yar'Adua, and I summarize existing explanations for the PDP's loss. I then show how the opposition APC opted for a campaign strategy centered more on the economy than on terrorism. I demonstrate this through a content analysis of 929 comments by party officials, drawn from a search of 2,390 news articles. I code party leaders' comments and quotations into five thematic categories, based on claims made in qualitative research about the election. APC politicians overwhelmingly focused on economic issues, with 284 references compared to 72 references by the PDP. The APC also emphasized electoral integrity and reform to a surprising degree – exceeding even the references to terrorism and insecurity. Though social issues were less prominent in the campaign, I find that the APC discussed them twice as often as the PDP. My key findings are triangulated through interviews with state-level PDP and APC officials.

Some readers might assert that campaigning on the economy is not surprising and thus my argument is premised on a "straw man." However, I cite several statistically sampled national surveys in which voters identified insecurity as a top priority or criticized the government's handling of Boko Haram. Importantly, these surveys show very similar levels of concern in the north, where Boko Haram's violence has been concentrated, and the south. Moreover, though the economy grew significantly over the previous ten years, Nigeria is a poor country with a highly unequal distribution of wealth and significant corruption. The economy is therefore always an issue in political campaigns, so we need to ask how 2015 was somehow different. Complementing my quantitative analysis with interviews, I conclude that the APC took a calculated risk by not focusing on fears of terrorism. Instead, it identified economic growth, anti-corruption, and electoral integrity as the programmatic basis of a winning electoral coalition.

These findings have important implications for foreign aid and democracy promotion. Between 1985 and 2015, the US Agency for International Development spent at least US$643 million in eighty-five countries on narrowly targeted "democracy and governance" programs for legislators, political parties, and democracy advocates in civil society.[6] Evidence that APC successfully campaigned on this

---

[6] This information is based on calculations from an unclassified US Agency for International Development database. The total includes assistance to at least three entities, such as the Andean Parliament, which are not countries.

issue means that an electoral constituency for free and fair elections and internal party democracy is emerging, and politicians have taken notice. This also contributes to research on the Lindberg hypothesis, which claims that the repetition of elections has democratizing effects by educating voters (Lindberg 2009; Edgell et al. 2017). This chapter thus provides new information about the mechanism that makes voting pedagogical and not just procedural.

While the first part of my answer to the question of why the PDP lost focuses on elite behavior, the next part empirically examines voting outcomes across thirty-six states (plus the capital of Abuja). In Chapter 4, "Voting against Violence? Insecurity and Economic Uncertainty in the Presidential Election," I summarize the literature on voting behavior in Africa. I also describe my dataset, which is constructed from original variables measuring state debt, internally generated revenue, the incumbent party's margins of victory, and voter turnout. It also draws on surveys commissioned by the US Government that explore voting intentions, economic conditions, ethnicity, religion, and other relevant variables. My dependent variable (the outcome I am seeking to explain) is the change in the ruling party's vote share between the 2011 and the 2015 Presidential Elections. Next, a "national in/security" hypothesis finds that proximity to actual violence did not systematically impact voting patterns. The statistical tests also show that while PDP supporters fervently believed that "extremist attacks" would increase if Buhari was elected, the issue of terrorism mattered less to APC supporters. In short, Jonathan played to his base on the issue of insecurity. But the APC pivoted to issues of the economy and corruption. As tests of an "economic voting" hypothesis demonstrate, this generated a broader electoral coalition. Citizens voted not just based on their own wallets but on their assessments of past and future national economic conditions. I find strong statistical evidence that Buhari's promises to improve the economy were critical; where people believed he could improve economy, they overwhelmingly voted for the APC. Finally, control variables in all models indicate that states with weak economies and higher debt levels were overwhelmingly risk-averse, voting to keep President Jonathan.

Taken together, Chapters 3 and 4 suggest that voters responded to campaign rhetoric – though I am cautious about fully making that inferential leap. Voters cast their ballots based on the same issues emphasized by the APC, suggesting that voters were "primed" to vote on the economy, shifting from their own self-declared priorities. People do not simply vote on the economy because they are poor, they respond to information cues (Hart 2016) and, in this case, an effective political campaign that shaped the rhetoric on the economy. These findings engage an emerging literature showing that African voters increasingly vote on evaluations of policy rather than ethnicity or candidate personality (Gibson and Long 2009; Bratton 2013b). The stark differences between the issues that the parties campaign on should be read alongside statistical tests that fail to find systematic evidence for a patronage strategy in 2015 (LeVan et al. 2018). Clientelism may be common in Nigeria. But, like elsewhere in Africa, it can be an ineffective electoral strategy (Weghorst and Lindberg 2011).

However, if Chapters 3 and 4 offer some "good" news for African elections, Chapter 5 tempers that optimism by revealing the persistence of ethnic and religious cleavages. Shifting my dependent variable from patterns of electoral outcomes across states to individual-level voting behavior, I find support for an "ethnic affinity" hypothesis and even stronger statistical support for a "religious referendum" hypothesis. I explain Nigeria's electoral system that promotes inter-ethnic cooperation by requiring a geographical distribution of electoral support. Consistent with recent research on African elections, I suggest that ethnicity remains relevant, but by itself it is not a very effective electoral strategy. This is an encouraging institutional story. Religion appears to be a bigger problem. It appears to undermine rather than reinforce incentives for cross-ethnic coalitions. The year after the 2015 election, the United States Commission on International Religious Freedom called on the State Department to add Nigeria to a list of nine countries designated as "Countries of Primary Concern," meaning the "government engages in or tolerates particularly severe violations of religious freedom that are systematic, ongoing and egregious" (US Commission on International Religious Freedom 2017, 1). This is cause for concern. Nigeria's electoral laws that require a geographical distribution of votes in presidential elections do help. But depoliticizing religious cleavages and extending the inter-religious messages of peacebuilding beyond the war against Boko Haram and its potential recruits will be critical challenges for democracy. Unless religion is disincentivized as the basis of shared political interest, these challenges could be exacerbated by party competition.

In Chapter 6, I explore Nigeria's political future. In the classic democratization literature, a transition is a temporary process for transferring authority from one regime to another as a country moves toward democracy. By these standards, Nigeria's Presidential Election in 1999 was a "founding election" and the defeat of an incumbent party in 2015 indicates a step toward democratic "consolidation." However, this literature overstated the linear nature of democratization, failed to anticipate the present global wave of illiberal regimes, and generally underestimated the level uncertainty after a transition ends. The erosion of the transition's pact and the defeat of the PDP has increased rather than institutionalized political uncertainty in Nigeria. I analyze three "stress points" that test the ability of Nigeria's democratic institutions to weather extra-institutional tensions: the terrorism of Boko Haram in the northeast, threats of Igbo secession in the southeast, and farmer–pastoralist conflicts. Features of the transition's pact, including impunity and the political saliency of sectarianism, have exacerbated each of these conflicts. I argue that electoral accountability will be essential but insufficient for resolving the representational, distributional, and cultural components of these challenges.

The concluding chapter discusses how, over the long run, the possibility of losing power promotes elite accountability. It generates a constructive sense of insecurity in politicians by binding their behavior to voters. But the conclusion also advances the argument that this no substitute for a rule of law that thus far remains elusive and that must accompany the representation-based remedies to Nigeria's nation-building woes. To defeat terrorism, facilitate fair political competition, and improve public policy outcomes, Nigeria will need rule of law. This is the task for a new generation of democrats.

2 | The End of a New Beginning: Nigeria's Transition, 1999–2015

The unexpected death of the dictator Sani Abacha in June 1998 ended a long reign of dictatorships that began on New Year's Eve 1983, when then-General Muhammadu Buhari (now president) staged a coup that ended the short-lived Second Republic. It also set in motion the nation's most successful transition, climaxing when Olusegun Obasanjo took the oath of office as an elected president in May 1999. The transition was remarkable not only for its successful transfer of power, but for its swiftness. Within a year, a Provisional Ruling Council (PRC) released dissidents from jail, removed state military administrators, oversaw the formation of new political parties, promulgated a constitution, and organized elections at the local, state, and federal levels. Nigerians had learned from past mistakes; the elaborate plans of Ibrahim Babangida's dictatorship (1985–1993) to hand over power had amounted to no more than a theater of consultation. The process became known as a "transition without end" (Diamond, Oyediran, et al. 1997). Abacha's transition plans followed an even more dubious commitment to the transfer of power. When five political parties formed, they all endorsed him as their presidential candidate. "You can put up anybody you like. But the presidential candidate is me" he told one such party, the Coalition for National Consensus (Aminu 2010). "The pro-Abacha campaigners seem to be living in a world of illusion," another party official recalled Abacha saying. "They have embarked on a massive propaganda campaign that implies that the transition programme is not a reality but a ploy to perpetuate the military in power" (Constitutional Rights Project 1998d, 22).

By definition, transitions involve a formal transfer of power from one regime to another, with "regime" referring to the rules of governance and not just the individuals occupying office (LeVan 2015a). There is a long debate over what causes transitions and a large literature on what makes them successful, with some recent research emphasizing that transitions do not necessarily mean a transfer of power *to democracy.*

There is also a debate over whether change comes from below, through grassroots pressure, or from above through "pacts" resulting from elite negotiations over the terms of the transition. Such pacts bring together major stakeholders to establish new rules of governance and a route to get there by offering mutual guarantees (O'Donnell and Schmitter 1986c; Colomer 1994). Civil society organizations and other actors often weigh in on these deals but "pacting" is an inherently undemocratic process (Karl 1990). Our understanding about when transitions end is more limited, and it largely derives from research on democratic "consolidation" (Linz and Stepan 1996), a term that remains common despite its association with optimistic assumptions about the linear direction of regime change and other flaws (Carothers 2002; Diamond et al. 2014b).

In this chapter, I outline the key terms of Nigeria's transition negotiated by elites. These deals provided members of the outgoing military junta a smooth exit, resolved the legacies of the aborted transition in 1993, and explicitly but informally established some criteria for competition among politicians. Nigeria's pact facilitated a successful transfer of power to democracy and helped hold the ruling party together for sixteen years. I do not attempt to provide a comprehensive historical overview of political events during this period. Instead, I describe the declining political saliency of the transition's pact from shocks that fractured the PDP and facilitated the country's first party turnover with the defeat of an incumbent political party in 2015. I argue that this turnover formally ended the transition. But weakening the pact also generated new uncertainties about Nigeria's political institutions; the conditions for successful democracy will differ in important ways from the terms of a successful transition. I highlight these problematic conditions later in the book.

First, I review existing literature that provides the analytical tools for assessing the political meaning of the PDP's defeat in 2015 as a political juncture in relation to the military's exit in 1999. This discussion places Nigeria's transition within a comparative understanding of democratic struggles in Africa since the 1990s and in the Arab world since 2011. I also compare different thresholds for when transitions end, elaborate on the conceptual meaning of "pact," and explain why we should consider 1999 Nigeria's only successful transition.

Second, I detail the terms of the transition. With Abacha dead, the regime quickly picked someone to shepherd the process. Once liberal reformers successfully pushed the interim head of government to abandon core elements of Abacha's transition plans, the PRC settled on several compromises with the military, including professional rewards that provided opportunities for career advancement, no consequences for looting government money, and impunity for human rights violations. Importantly, these exit guarantees in the PRC's pact with the outgoing military regime overlapped with the founding principles of the PDP, which went on to win the presidency, control of the National Assembly, and most of the governorships in the transitional elections.

In the third section, I identify an informal agreement within the PDP to alternate the presidency between north and south known as "power shift," rotate offices to different parts of the country through "zoning," and an understanding that its first presidential candidate had to be a Yoruba, the dominant ethnic group in the southwest. Yorubas harbored lingering resentment from the annulled 1993 Election, and from a 1979 Presidential Election narrowly decided by the Supreme Court. Once in power, President Olusegun Obasanjo embarked on a wave of firings and forced retirements in the military. However, rather than holding the generals accountable for human rights violations or making public the truth of their many abuses, the PDP generated new career paths in the party and in the private sector for those who left the military. For those who stayed in the military, the party embraced a policy of "coup proofing" with a massive increase in military spending and a little-noticed wave of promotions at the end of Obasanjo's first term. In sum, the outgoing military found itself with ample exit guarantees. And by adopting founding principles congruent with the PRC's pact, the PDP extended and embraced the basis of the transition, ruling for the next sixteen years.

Fourth, I demonstrate how elite rivalry and grassroots democratic pressure weakened the pact, creating new political space for rise of the opposition All Progressives Congress. I provide evidence of a generational shift that put the PDP out of touch with an increasingly youthful nation. More importantly, I detail how principles of rotating power tore the ruling party apart. Power shift and zoning weakened links with voters, who were unable to reelect well-performing politicians rendered ineligible for office by virtue of their ethnicity. Power shift and zoning also suffocated ambitious politicians, whose annoyances with the party's disciplinary measures led to mass defections to the

APC in 2013, shortly after its formation. The conclusion mentions how the legacies of the transition affect contemporary politics. As a new generation looks beyond the milestone of electoral turnover in 2015, it must grapple with the ghosts of Nigeria's transition and distinguish its elite pact from the vision of a vibrant democracy powered by participation and accountability.

Literature Review on Transitions

A seminal study by O'Donnell and Schmitter (1986a) defines transitions as the interval between one political regime and another, where "regime" refers to a set of rules for deciding who governs, how to allocate resources, and how to limit state power. Transitions often emerge from liberalization reforms by an incumbent regime that extend civil and political rights, protecting groups and individuals from state abuses. In this conceptualization, democratization more broadly refers to a process whereby the incumbent regime loses its hold on power and a new regime takes shape. For O'Donnell and Schmitter, transitions are thus discrete political processes that outline the roadmap for changing the underlying rules of politics. Transitions fix the boundaries of debate during this period, often by placing certain issues off the table. They also define the actors eligible to participate in post-transition politics and specify their roles in the new system.

In Latin America and Southern Europe during the 1970s and 1980s, change came "from above" as elites divided over questions of political liberalization resolved their differences. In these classic models, transitions resulted from compromises between "hardliners" who support the old regime or "softliners" who favor democratization (O'Donnell and Schmitter 1986c), while their allies outside the regime are "radicals" and "reformers," respectively (Przeworski 1991). When these various forces see the costs of democratization as lower than the costs of the status quo, they seek mutual reassurances through a pact. For example, in Chile, supporters and opponents of democratic reforms within the military junta formalized an agreement that gave the exiting dictator and his supporters a guaranteed presence in the Senate, while at the same time embarking on multiparty electoral competition and launching a truth commission (Barros 2002). Brazil attempted a similar "controlled" and gradual democratic opening negotiated by elites, including the military retaining control of its own military promotions (Huntington 1991). Spain's elites exercised less control over the transition but conservatives still protected their interests, and the former authoritarian regime continued to enjoy sympathy after its exit (Colomer 1994). An alternative conceptualization of pacts suggests that they are not necessarily the distinct and delimited historical moments. Higley and Gunter define a pact as "less sudden than an elite settlement, this process is a series of deliberate, tactical decisions by rival elites that have the cumulative effect, over perhaps a generation, of creating elite consensual unity" (Higley and Gunther 1992, xi). Thus, rather than arriving at a mutually beneficial understanding about how to govern in a single stroke, elite agreements in their view emerge from an iterative process, opening up the possibility – or necessity – to renegotiate the terms of governance.

The fall of the Berlin Wall in 1989 ushered in a vast expansion of electoral democracy around the world that seemed to render pacts less relevant. The post-Cold War transitions differed from the patterns and generalizations in at least four ways. First, proponents of modernization theory had long argued since the 1950s that certain preconditions were necessary for democratization. One variant claimed that democracy required a shift in cultural mindset (Almond and Verba 1963), and that this is difficult in countries that have not reached certain socio-economic thresholds (Lipset 1959). By the 1990s was it clear that poor countries could successfully transition to democracy, even if they had trouble staying democratic (Przeworski et al. 2000). Second, transitions from Africa and the former Soviet Union provided compelling evidence that grassroots pressure "from below," rather than pacting "from above," led to democratization. Popular protest, labor movements, and mass-based guerrilla organizations fought for democracy (Bratton and Van de Walle 1997; Bunce 2003; Wood 2000). Third, Huntington and others, hung up on modernization theory's assumptions about a unidirectional march toward Western-style democracy (Fukuyama 1992), assumed that few "intermediate" regimes would emerge (Huntington 1991). By the early 2000s though, democratic "backsliding" made clear that many regime transitions were not transitions *to democracy*. Many were in fact transitions from democracy to authoritarianism, or from one type of authoritarian regime to another (Elkins et al. 2009). Many regimes were not merely temporary setbacks in a hopeful democratization process; they constituted "electoral authoritarian" (Schedler

2006), semi-authoritarian (Ottaway 2003), or hybrid (Tripp 2010) regimes that proved resourceful and resilient.

The pacting model has retained relevance, even if it originally possessed a crude over-determinism. In Africa, different modalities of multiparty competition in some two-dozen countries today have roots in elite deals struck in the early moments of their respective transitions as exiting autocrats sought reassurance (Riedl 2014). In the Middle East, evidence from the Arab Spring suggests that the democratic revolutions initiated by popular protest arguably failed in every country except Tunisia (Brownlee et al. 2015; Diamond et al. 2014a). Across the region, new "ruling bargains" have preserved elite deals and limited political reforms (Kamrava 2014). Finally, pacting has been utilized as a tool for analyzing phenomena other than democratization, such as constitutional reform processes (Eisenstadt et al. 2017). Comparative research often seeks to interact the structure of politics with the elite agency implied by pacts, for example, demonstrating that many transitions are triggered by distributive gaps rather than mere levels of development suggested by modernization theory (Haggard and Kaufman 2016).

The term transition has retained its relevance too, even as the large number of countries at the turn of the century to which it was applied (arguably up to 100) highlights the concept's fuzziness. Not only did many countries deviate from the theorized sequence of political opening (liberalization), democratic "breakthrough" and then consolidation (Carothers 2002), where democratic roots did take hold, identifying the end of a transition remained murky. One solution is to establish minimum conditions, such as a successful "founding election" organized by the transitional government or simply the successful transfer of power from one regime to the next (Bratton 1999). A slightly higher threshold is one where the new regime successfully organizes its first free and fair election. This task entails implementation of the new regime's institutions (O'Donnell 1997).

Most analyses adopt a higher threshold whereby free and fair elections are a necessary but insufficient condition for ending a transition; the government in question must also, for example, exercise both *de jure* and *de facto* powers over policy-making (Linz and Stepan 1997). "A democratic transition is completed only when the freely elected government has full authority to generate new policies," writes Larry Diamond, "and thus when the executive, legislative and judicial powers generated by the new democracy are not constrained or compelled by law to share power with other actors, such as the military" (Diamond 1997, xix). This constituted a corrective for important cases where pacts protected old regime elites, and generally allowed for very limited civilian control over the military. As already noted, the military in Chile retained significant control over policy throughout the 1980s. Burma's constitution, promulgated during the transition, enshrines significant protections and policy authority for the military; this pact enabled the transition but is now holding back democracy (Diamond et al. 2014a). In Ecuador, the military stipulated the transition would take no less than three years. While on its way out, the generals secured obtuse candidacy requirements, including one that eliminated the previous incumbent. And in Peru, the military controlled ministerial appointments concerning military affairs. In general, in Latin America's transitions from the 1960s through the 1980s, the military "endeavored, to the best of their ability, to fix the subsequent rules of the game" and seek "a permanent right to supervise ensuing political decisions" (Rouquie 1986, 121).

This literature on transitions, pacting, and exit guarantees relates to this book's analysis of Nigeria in several ways. For starters, Nigeria has experienced at least three political processes that qualify as a transition. Decolonization could count as the first transition. After World War II, Nigeria followed a calculated process gradually expanding the franchise, legislative powers, and indigenous control over economic resources (Suberu 2001). Once the nationalists won the day, federal elections in 1959 led up to independence in 1960, and then graduation to status as a full republic in 1963. Tragically, over the next three years the new nation witnessed ethnic pogroms, electoral violence, a declaration of a State of Emergency, and finally its first *coup d'etat* in 1966 (Diamond 1988). By June 1967, the country had descended into a full-scale civil war that killed over a million people. The second transition began in 1975 with Murtala Muhammed's coup, overthrowing the military regime of Yakubu Gowon. Gowon had abandoned his transition plans in 1974, alarming moderates in the regime and infuriating politicians from the First Republic who planned to contest. From Gowon's perspective, elites (notably Obafemi Awolowo) "started really doing things that were a repeat of the first crisis we had in 1965," by stoking the kind of paranoia that led to the first coup (Gowon 2010). The transition process carried out by Muhammed and his successor entailed drafting a new constitution, which included a delicate compromise on Islamic law and the formation of new parties, and culminated with elections that swore in Shehu Shagari as president in October 1979 (Laitin 1982). But that democratic regime also fell prey to a coup after suffering a violent Islamic rebellion in the north, the collapse of a fragile coalition government, and elections in 1983 that degenerated into riots (Falola and Ihonvbere 1985; Diamond 1984).

The establishment of both the First (1960–1966) and Second (1979–1983) Republics involved liberalization, the formation of new parties, and the promulgation of a new constitution (Odinkalu 2001). But beyond the organization of a founding election, neither of them satisfied the criteria for a complete transition according to the literature. The 1998/1999 process could therefore be viewed as Nigeria's *only* completed transition. The pact between the Provisional Ruling Council, which oversaw the transition, reduced the military's fear of exit and shaped political competition. "Although the country did succeed in shifting peacefully from military to civilian rule, this was the result of a pact among leaders seeking to maintain their power and privileges inside an ostensibly democratic structure. The broader society was hardly involved," says one analysis (Coleman and Lawson-Remer 2013, 9). "The elites – not a middle class or the poor – orchestrated the 1998–99 transition from military to civilian rule and were the beneficiaries of the new regime, as they had been of the previous one," says a study by the former US Ambassador to Nigeria (Campbell 2013b, 210). The 1999 pact is also important because rather than evolving, as Higly and Gunter anticipate, it decayed.

In the next section, I outline the broader political circumstances following the death of the dictator Sani Abacha, and dive into detail about the terms of the pact. Nigeria's military lacked the sort of veto authority obtained by the generals in some of the cases mentioned above. But they did enjoy an unofficial immunity and continued to exercise considerable influence over politics through a visible presence in the People's Democratic Party. Keeping the military content imposed both economic and political costs on the new democracy. It was not until the PDP's ability to uphold this pact began wavering that the elite basis of the transition's successful transfer of power became evident. Thus, rather than ending in 1999 with the founding elections, or in 2003 with the first elections organized by the new regime, I pinpoint the end of the transition later than the literature would suggest: in 2015 with the electoral defeat of the ruling PDP.

A Dictator's Demise and a Swift Transition

Nigeria's last dictatorship began when Sani Abacha took the reins of government in August 1993, after three tumultuous months of unrest precipitated by Ibrahim Babangida's annulment of the June 12 election. Unofficial results showed Moshood Abiola, a Yoruba from the southwest, had won (Omoruyi 1999; Suberu 1997). This victory worried northern elites and military officers who had dominated politics since 1960 (Osaghae 1998); his substantial wealth also provided him with a measure of independence from this ruling coalition (Okoye 1999). Abacha's initial government included a broad cross-section of political elites, including some impacted by the annulled election. At the same time, he also dismissed Babangida's allies, known as the "IBB Boys," from the cabinet and he later systematically purged them from government (Amuwo 2001; LeVan 2015a). Babangida's decision to "step aside" thus bore close resemblance to a bloodless coup.

Abacha's coalition government did little to ease tensions within the regime regarding how to handle the aborted transition, the blame for which stood on the shoulders of Babangida and hardliners in his government suspicious of handing over power to a Yoruba. "We were selfish and without foresight," recalls a National Republican Convention (NRC) member of the National Assembly at the time. Like others, he aligned with the military out of fear of a southern president (Wada 2004). Another NRC party leader put it this way: "The north dominated the military and they were afraid he [Abiola] was going to clean out the army. The army is their compensation for the 1966 coup" (Ebri 2010). Abiola fled abroad and declared himself the winner; upon his return to Nigeria he immediately found himself in prison. This further complicated the basic issues at stake in any transition. Not only did Abacha's government need to chart a course for political reform after discarding Babangida's elaborate program, it needed to decide whether it would honor the 1993 election results. Divisions within the pro-democracy movement worked in favor of a transition by procrastination. Civil society organizations such as the National Democratic Coalition, the Campaign for Democracy, and the Nigeria Labour Congress broadly united around opposition to the military.

But they disagreed about the role of external assistance, protest tactics, and most importantly whether a transition plan should honor the June 12 election results or call for new elections (Edozie 2002; Akinterinwa 1997; LeVan 2011b).

In 1997, Abacha's tight grip on power weakened as several factors worked in favor of the pro-democracy movement and moderates within the military. In particular, his decision to run for president openly clashed with the expectation that he would not participate in elections he was responsible for organizing. His ambitions seemed to receive a blessing from President Bill Clinton though. During a visit to South Africa, Clinton said of Abacha, "If he stands for election, we hope he will stand as a civilian. There are many military leaders who have taken over chaotic situations in African countries, but have moved toward democracy. And that can happen in Nigeria; that is, purely and simply, what we want to happen" (Clinton 1998). Abacha bragged to his cabinet, "All these pro-democracy activists run to America to save them. But the US president is himself calling me 'sir.' He is scared of me" (Cohen 2009).

The pro-democracy movement felt deeply betrayed by Clinton's comments, and the media continued to skewer Abacha for his "self-succession" bid (Amuwo 2001; Constitutional Rights Project 1998d). But more importantly, the self-succession campaign forever cast Abacha's commitment to a transition in a dubious light. Barely a month after President Clinton's comments, the US State Department in April 1998 changed course, declaring, "The current transition process appears to be gravely flawed and failing. We do not see how the process, as it is now unfolding, will lead to a democratic government" (Constitutional Rights Project 1998b, 8). Pope John Paul II, during a visit to Abuja in March, called for the release of all political prisoners. "The world was becoming increasingly impatient with military administrations in developing countries, especially in Africa," recalls a state governor (Ikpeazu 2017). Domestic opposition also mounted as thirty-four prominent politicians, led by the Second Republic's vice president, known as G34 (or the "Group of Patriotic Nigerian Citizens") condemned the five parties' endorsement of Abacha (Badejo 1997; Constitutional Rights Project 1998b). "It had to be cloak and dagger," explained a member; "you would send your driver to an intermediary who would tell you where to go, and who could therefore alert the others if the military showed up" (Aminu 2010). In effect,

Abacha's refusal to exit contributed to the opposition's unity, enabling it to focus on obtaining a transition to civilian rule rather than resolving the June 12 question.

Abacha also seemed to overreach with a crackdown on an alleged coup plot in December 1997. A Special Investigation Board interrogated 144 persons, more than half of whom were detained in connection with the investigation. The arrests included Lieutenant-General Oladipo Diya, a prominent Yoruba moderate within the regime sympathetic to the June 12 cause. But the Chief of Army Staff, Major-General Ishaya Bamaiyi, who had supposedly proposed the coup to Diya, was absent. Pro-democracy organizations and others saw this as compelling circumstantial evidence of a set-up by Abacha to eliminate critics of his self-succession plans (Constitutional Rights Project 1998a). Shehu Musa Yar'Adua, who was Obasanjo's second-in-command during the 1970s (and brother of the president elected in 2007), died in prison that same month. Activists maintained that he had been denied medical care because Abacha had wanted to get rid of him ever since he had warned the constitutional conveners in 1994 that the regime did not intend to carry through with the transition (French 1998). Amuwo (2001) cites a secret memo calling for his elimination due to Yar'Adua's opposition to the self-succession plan.

The Provisional Ruling Council dealt with the question of succession immediately following Abacha's death, most likely by assassination. Lieutenant-General Jerry Useni, a minister with Abacha at the time of his death, emerged as one possible successor. He claims the PRC did not pick him due to protocol (Abdallah and Machika 2009). This makes little sense, though, since he was next in command. Other information points to Abacha's widow quickly intervening to oppose Useni. She brought Babangida to the presidential villa to weigh in and deployed Hamza Al-Mustapha, Abacha's notorious security chief, to physically block Useni, who was known as a hardliner. Useni had also previously shown interest in joining party politics, which could lead to a repeat of the self-sucession problem – a dictator seeking to transform himself into a civilian politician through elections (Niboro 1998).

After a brief meeting in Kano, the PRC quickly settled on General Abdulsalam Abubakar. Muddling his fresh start, his opening speech declared "we remain fully committed to the socio-political transition programme of General Sani Abacha's administration and will do everything to ensure its full and successful implementation" (Abubakar

1998a, 14). Like other civil society groups, the Constitutional Rights Project (CRP) immediately criticized the interim administration's commitment to Abacha's transition program. "Clearly, what is needed at this time is for all the political parties to be dissolved, the sham elections conducted so far, set aside, new and independent parties allowed to form" (Constitutional Rights Project 1998c, 5). The National Democratic Coalition (NADECO), the G34, and various elites called for a government of national unity (GNU). But even this was difficult to envision since the existing five parties had thoroughly discredited themselves by previously endorsing Abacha (Niboro 1998). Picking a successor to Abacha who could lead the transition settled a big question. But the status of the parties, the possibility of a GNU, and what to do about the annulled June 12 election were even thornier. The sudden death of Abiola (the election's apparent winner) while still in prison softened this difficult dilemma. Up until then, Abubakar's position was by no means clear; he had met with foreign officials to urge them to abandon the international community's insistence on honoring the June 12 election results (Olowolabi 1998b).[1]

Abubakar quickly advanced a comprehensive vision for the transition that jettisoned his initial commitment to Abacha's plan and that took a step toward resolving June 12 and Abiola's future. In a speech entitled "The Way Forward," he declared that "cancellation of the flawed transition programme which we inherited is necessary to ensure that we have a true and lasting democracy as demanded by the majority of our people" (Abubakar 1998b, 13). He promised to release all political detainees and withdraw pending political charges. He dissolved the political parties and said, "every Nigerian citizen has equal opportunity to form or join any political party," in line with guidelines to be determined by a new, civilian electoral commission. This eliminated the idea of a GNU whose "composition could only be through selection that would be undemocratic," he explained in reference to the Abacha parties. "We will not substitute one undemocratic institution for another" (Abubakar 1998b, 14).

With the GNU off the table, the question of June 12 still lingered, even with Abiola's death. Opposition to honoring the June 12 mandate with a Yoruba presidency was not limited to conservative northerners such as the Sultan of Sokoto. Many Igbos, including Abacha's Secretary

---

[1] Though it remains unclear who these foreign dignitaries were.

for Education, Ben Nwabueze, and Secretary for Information, Uche Chukwumerije, wanted to neutralize the influence of the Yoruba (Omoruyi 1999). One of Abacha's military governors pointed out that some Igbos in the east also shared resentment for Yorubas not enabling the eastern secession attempt through the civil war from 1967 to 1970 (Nmodu 1998). Abubakar said of the annulment and massive protests, "we cannot pretend that they did not happen," but he also urged the country to not dwell in the past (Abubakar 1998b). This announcement committed Abubakar to a punctual transition schedule that increased his credibility with the pro-democracy movement.

Abubakar also delivered on the promise of a new constitution, though it had virtually no public participation (Eisenstadt et al. 2017). In November 1998, he introduced a drafting committee. By the following month it had submitted its report, which supposedly reflected ideas from 405 memoranda (Ojo 2004). However, the PRC could not prevent the security services from repeatedly injecting themselves into the constitution-making process. For example, according to a former governor, they screened political candidates (Ebri 2010). Even more poignantly, the PDP's Secretary General later said in an interview that the military vetoed constitutional provisions – supported by Abubakar – to limit the president to one term and rotate the office among six geopolitical zones (Nwodo 2010). The promulgation of the constitution just a few weeks before the handover of power on May 29, 1999 kept the transition on track. But it offered few illusions of public input despite long, hard popular struggles for democracy.

The transition elections also proceeded as promised, but they clearly reinforce the interpretation of the transition as orchestrated from above by beneficiaries of the pact. The first set of elections took place across Nigeria's 774 local governments in December 1998, which was intended to help the new parties build up a grassroots base and also to qualify parties for higher-level elections.[2] Gubernatorial and State Assembly elections took place in January 1999, followed by National Assembly elections on February 20 and the Presidential Election on

---

[2] To participate in the state and federal elections, parties were required to obtain at least 5 percent of the vote in twenty-four states during local government elections. Since this had been reduced from 10 percent, the electoral commission further specified that at least three parties would advance to the later three rounds of elections.

February 27. These processes whittled down the playing field from nine parties competing in the local elections to three parties at the state and federal level. The PDP's candidate, former dictator Obasanjo, prevailed over Olu Falae, a joint candidate of the southwest-based Alliance for Democracy (AD) and the All Peoples Party (APP) by a margin of 18 million to 11 million votes. When Chief Falae immediately called the entire process "a farce" and announced his intention to appeal, an international election observation mission led by the former US President Jimmy Carter revised its previous statement characterizing the electoral process as flawed but acceptable. After additional analysis from field observers, Carter now castigated the "wide disparity between the number of voters observed at the polling stations and the final results that have been reported from several states. Regrettably, therefore, it is not possible for us to make an accurate judgment about the outcome of the presidential election" (Carter Center and National Democratic Institute for International Affairs 1999, 11–12). After convincing Falae to take his appeals to the courts, the final joint report with the Washington-based National Democratic Institute concluded that the low quality of the elections cast doubt upon the integrity of the process overall and therefore the legitimacy of those elected. The report praised Abubakar for his role but also downplayed his influence, noting "from the onset, a compressed time-table and top-down structure controlled by the very military officials it intended to replace affected the process" (Carter Center and National Democratic Institute for International Affairs 1999, 32). Reinforcing the profoundly undemocratic features of the transition, one human rights group complained that the military decrees governing the process were nowhere to be found – even after the elections (Legal Defence Centre 2000).

The transition also proved largely beyond Abubakar's control when it came to delivering on his promises to release pro-democracy activists or to rein in hardliners such as Jerry Useni[3] and Abacha's Chief Security Officer, Hamza Al-Mustapha. More than three months after the "Way Forward" speech, Abubakar had yet to release most of the 291 political prisoners, including moderates such as General Diya. The Constitutional Rights Project (CRP) asserted that Abubakar "may

---

[3] *This Day* ran an expose on Useni on August 2, 1998, describing him as the mastermind behind Abacha's refusal to hand over power.

in fact, not really be in control of the government" (Constitutional Rights Project 1998e). "If there's one thing Abubakar still has to do, it is to quash the proceedings of the trial of Obasanjo, Diya and co. Declare them a nullity" said a former military governor (Nmodu 1998, 35). At a press conference in Lagos, Abubakar repeated many of his promises. But since he had not yet delivered on them, the press greeted the statements with cynicism (Olowolabi 1998a). Abubakar did not pardon Obasanjo until September 30 (Godwin 2013) and Diya remained in prison until 1999.[4]

Bargaining for Democracy: Civilian Concessions and Military Demands

The peaceful transition of power from military generals to civilian elites on May 29, 1999 came at the cost of transparency, accountability, and legitimacy from a public largely cut out of the process. This was by design, often despite Abubakar's best efforts. He put in place provisions that prevented members of the security services (as well as traditional rulers) from belonging to a political party. However, the military did obtain commitments to ease the generals' departure and pave the way for lasting influence after the handover to civilians. Retired military generals argued their case for such guarantees at a meeting with Abubakar in October 1998. The meeting included former heads of state Yakubu Gowon and Ibrahim Babangida, as well as Theophilus Danjuma and Murtala Nyako, wealthy retirees who became major power players in the PDP. Obasanjo did not attend, mostly likely because he had by then signaled his interest in running for president (Adekanye 1999).

Three essential compromises emerged from the military's meeting with Abubakar that would form the basis of an elite pact. One involved the promotion of prominent (and controversial) Abacha loyalists. The transitional government promoted Zakari Biu, who as Assistant Police Commissioner led a security unit that tortured Abacha's opponents; he became chair of the lucrative Federal Petroleum Monitoring Unit (Adeyemo 1999). He was forcibly retired after the transition, then reinstated and fired twice (including once for an incident where he was

---

[4] This became news briefly in 2013 when President Goodluck Jonathan claimed to pardon them in an effort to generate Yoruba support in the southwest.

accused of assisting a Boko Haram escapee) before being reinstated for an honorary retirement in September 2015 (Obi 2015). In the early weeks of the transition, in 1998, CRP complained about the "juicy military appointments" of General Bamaiyi, who had allegedly entrapped Diya, as well as other hardliners such as Abacha's Chief Security Officer, Al Mustapha, and Major General Patrick Aziza (Constitutional Rights Project 1998e). Another human rights group also complained about the promotions, adding that forty-three "obnoxious" military decrees remained on the books, including one (Decree No. 2) that gave the PRC the power to jail opponents, though Abubakar may have retained it in order to check the hardliners (Adeyemo 1999).

Abubakar's reluctance to intercept or expose money stolen by Abacha and his family amounted to a second compromise with the exiting military. By January 1999, the transitional PRC had recovered over 60 billion naira (approximately US$690 million) from the former dictator. But when investigators interrogated Abacha's powerful National Security Adviser, Ismaila Gwarzo, they released him; Abubakar said he should not be held liable for taking orders from his boss. Then Abacha's finance minister, trying to position himself for electoral politics, attempted to take credit for informing on Gwarzo (Adeyemo 1999). The disclosures of stolen money infuriated ethnic Ijaws just as they were starting to drift toward militancy in the Niger Delta (Umanah 1999). Much of "Abacha's loot" is still in the process of being discovered and recovered. In 2014 for example, the US Department of Justice announced a forfeiture of US$480 million from banks around the world where Abacha stashed his money (US Department of Justice 2014).

A third compromise with the military concerned the transition government's approach to human rights violations under previous military regimes. Around March 1999, as the handover neared, Abubakar was being squeezed on one side by softliners such as Mike Okhai Akhigbe, Chief of General Staff, who insisted that transition proceed, and on the other side by hardliners such as Bamaiyi who thought the incoming civilian administration should make the decision about Diya's fate. As Abubakar managed these two factions, regime softliners possibly contemplated a palace coup against Abubakar in order to keep the transition on track (Ayonote 1999). They also wanted the transitional government to get credit for doing right by Diya. The softliner argument won out and politicians from president-elect

Obasanjo's party, who were meeting at an Abuja hotel, greeted Diya's release with "jubilation" (Agekameh 1999). Around the same time, the top candidate for spearheading a human rights panel died. Tunde Idiagbon, the feared deputy of Muhammadu Buhari during the short-lived dictatorship (1984–1985), had stayed out of politics since 1985. Abubakar's National Security Adviser, who was from the same town, summoned him to Abuja. He died immediately after returning home of suspicious symptoms, precipitating theories that hawks in the junta had dispatched him to prevent a powerful military figure from overseeing any investigations into human rights violations by the military (Mumuni 1999; Semenitari 1999).[5] In the final weeks before the handover, the regime also decided not to move forward with prosecution of the dreaded security chief Al-Mustapha, in military detention, leaving such a tough choice for the incoming civilians.[6] The reformers were released from prison, while Abacha's hardliners eventually got off the hook.

The People's Democratic Party Unfolds a "Big Umbrella"

The exit guarantees regarding career advancement, tepid anti-corruption measures, and impunity for human rights violations constituted the core features of the pact agreed upon by Abubakar and the military. In this context, a new generation of elites joined what was left of the old-guard democrats (after all, nearly seventeen years had passed since the end of the Second Republic) to form new parties. The INEC ban on members of the military or security services from joining parties meant that many officers, who had seen the military as a route to politics for at least a generation, now had to resign in order to follow such a path. The PDP's umbrella logo offered an apt metaphor for the moment, welcoming many former military officers. The

[5] One of President Obasanjo's former aides who served during that era also told me that he was convinced Idiagbon was poisoned before he left Abuja.

[6] In 2004, senior prison officials were sanctioned for a major security breach by allowing Al-Mustapha external communications. This immediately led to speculation that he was exploring the possibility of a coup, and twenty-eight people whom the presidency called his "apparent civilian collaborators" were detained for questioning (Nwosu and Onuorah 2004; Madunagu and Olufowobi 2004).

idea, says a PDP governor, was to "conglomerate ideas and politicians in one boat so that they were able to present a front that was capable of receiving power from the military administration" (Ikpeazu 2017). For PDP elites, inclusion thus meant not just the usual ideas of ethnic representation but also a military that could be happy in the barracks. "Unless you convince the military that it is a credible arrangement," recalls a PDP founder, "they might not go" (Aminu 2010). The principles that brought the party together shared a congruence with the Abubakar's compromises, thus extending and operationalizing the transition's pact.

The PDP struck on three founding principles. First, party elites settled on a Yoruba presidential candidate. "Who would represent the dominant class better than a retired General Obasanjo who had engineered the 1979 handover of power to a bourgeois party, the NPN [National Party of Nigeria]?" (Braji 2014, 103). Importantly, many Yorubas did not trust Obasanjo for precisely that reason; the presidential contest in 1979 was so close that the Supreme Court decided in favor of the NPN's presidential candidate from the north, and Obasanjo let it stand (Akinterinwa, 1997). Thus, with the nullification of the 1993 election, many Yoruba felt that they had been denied the presidency twice – in 1979 and again in 1993 – generating a "Yoruba debt" (LeVan 2015a). Ironically, this history contributed to northern trust in Obasanjo. Babangida, the former dictator, became influential in the PDP during this period, forming a "military wing" of the party composed of retired officers (Mosadomi 2017). This influential voting bloc within the PDP offered decisive support for Obasanjo's candidacy (Agbaje 2010). A politician from the rival All Nigeria People's Party (ANPP) recalled the military's insistence on a southwestern candidate went beyond mere meddling. "Politicians had no choice. They had no input. They were formed or sponsored by the military," says Umar Lamido, later a member of the Gombe State Assembly. "Nobody was going to be given any chance. Except the southwest" (Lamido 2016). Naturally, this meant that primaries mattered little – a flaw in the party that came back to haunt it, as we shall see in the analysis of the elections in Chapter 3 and also with the Igbo secessionist revival explored in Chapter 6.

The party settled on Obasanjo, but only after shoving aside Alex Ekweume, a seasoned Igbo politician who served as Vice President during the Second Republic. One reason appears to be that the military simply did not trust him, according news accounts and PDP leaders who were present (Nnaji 2017). Demands for "military restructuring" had ranked high on civil society's agenda once Abacha was gone. Ekueme's campaign provocatively took out advertisements portraying him as the candidate for "truly civilian rule," in contrast to Obasanjo, who was merely a "civilianized general" or "the military in *babanriga*," meaning civilian robes rather than military uniform (Adekanye 1999, 196). A founding member of the PDP from the north says that few in the north trusted him (Aminu 2010). The feelings were mutual; several Igbo participants at the PDP convention, which took place in Jos, recall Hausa politicians brazenly telling them to stop campaigning for Ekwueme because the north would never trust him (Emeana et al. 2017). Even today, Igbos across eastern Nigeria remain widely committed to the perception that northerners in the PDP railroaded their candidate. "Alex Ekueume, who was clearly the frontrunner, suddenly lost his followership on the basis of an agreement to bring Obasanjo back," says John Nnia Nwodo, President-General of Ohanaeze Ndigbo, the pan-Igbo organization. "The basis for it was a necessity to contain the dismemberment of Nigeria on account of Western Nigeria's dissatisfaction with the handling of Abiola's election annulment." Ekueme became "easy prey to sacrifice" (Nwodo 2017).

A second founding principle of the PDP was an agreement known as "power shift." In order to reassure northern elites, the party agreed to alternate the presidency between the north and south every eight years, after two presidential terms. This was necessary in light of the broad agreement that the 1999 presidential candidate should come from the south. But as a governing principle, it has roots in Nigeria's underlying geopolitical bargain that emerged from the colonial amalgamation of the north and south in 1914. By the 1950s, as the country prepared for "self-rule," ensuring a balance of power between north and south became a reality of representative governance (Paden 1997). Quotas and efforts to ensure representation of other major geographical differences then became important following the Civil War, when, after the Igbos' failed war of secession, the dictatorship of Yakubu Gowon initiated policies to reintegrate them back into the military and the civil service (Ekeh 1989; Afigbo 1989). This practice of "federal character" is enshrined in the constitution and guarantees some

ethnoregional balancing within the cabinet and the civil service –
though it has hardly insulated any administration from charges of
ethnic bias.[7]

An important difference between ethnic balancing as envisioned
through federal character and as practised through zoning (or power
shift) is that the latter involves taking turns at power, rather than dividing authority into smaller pieces shared at any given moment of
time (Ayoade 2013). Zoning emerged from proposals for a rotational
presidency during a failed constitutional reform conference in 1995
(Nwala 1997; Akinola 1996). One complication with rotation is that
dividing the country into north and south is inadequate if various
segments within each region are to have a shot. This led to the idea of
six geopolitical "zones" (Sklar et al. 2006). Conceptualizing rotation
across six zones rather than two regions meant that if the presidency
was limited to one six-year tenure, each zone would have to wait thirty
years for its chance to rule. Moreover, a single deviation due to death
in office or any variety of reasons would inspire deep mistrust and
uncertainty.

Neither the single-term limit nor the division of the country into
zones made it into the 1999 Constitution. According to one PDP leader
from the north, "What we did is because the constitutional conference
of Abacha which accepted the idea of rotation." Speaking in a 2010
interview, he said "After 2015 or even from 2011, it could be decided
by the whole country that we will not be zoning anymore," but the
important thing at the moment is to honor the agreement that exists,
even if it alienates many politicians who are "rotated out" of office
(Aminu 2010). Rotation causes the same problem at the state level,
where the governorship and legislative leadership offices rotate among
the constituencies defined by the three senatorial districts. A reduction
in the number of units (i.e., from six national zones to three senatorial districts in each state) and hence the time to wait for office does
seem to reduce the sense of frustration. And at the local government
level, evidence suggests inter-ethnic and inter-religious trust are higher
and violence is lower where power-sharing principles are practised,

---

[7] President Jonathan, for example, was often accused of relying on an inner circle
of advisers from the Niger Delta. Many southerners see President Buhari as the
embodiment of northern bias. "Buhari's plan is Islamicization of Nigeria," said
one Catholic priest active in MASSOB's leadership (Onuorah et al. 2017).

compared to places where they are not (Vinson 2017). All of these practices serve to institutionalize an informal institution and invest political communities at different levels in principles of power shift, power-sharing, and leadership rotation.

Finally, the PDP sought to weaken the military's appetite and institutional capacity for politics. According to Senator Joseph Waku, the Vice Chair of Arewa Consultative Forum, an organization of northern elites, "both the conservatives and the progressives all agreed to team up for the purposes of assuring the military exit from governance … let's form a formidable political party that the military will find out is strong, it pulls people together" (Waku 2010). Although northerners feared losing control of the military for the first time since Obasanjo's tenure in the late 1970s, public opinion was on the PDP's side. A survey found that 62 percent of the nation expressed deep mistrust in the military, concluding that "protracted army rule and the repression and corruption under recent dictatorships has tarnished the image of the military" (Okafor 2000).

The new party began with the imprisonment of hardliner Bamaiyi, breaking with the transitional government's reluctance to reign him in. He stayed there throughout Obasanjo's two terms (1999–2007) during an investigation and (ultimately unsuccessful) prosecution for his role in the assassination of a prominent newspaper publisher, Alex Ibru (Sahara Reporters 2008). This seeming progress came at a cost to the pro-democracy movement since his replacement as Army Chief of Staff was Victor Malu, now promoted to Lieutenant-General. The promotion angered the human rights community since Malu had chaired the military tribunal that condemned Diya (the softliner) to death (Agekameh 2001). Obasanjo's next steps were more encouraging for pro-democracy activists. Within a month, the government identified more than 100 officers who had served at least six months in any previous military government, and immediately retired them (Siollun 2008). This provided some continuity with the decision by the Independent National Electoral Commission during the transition under Abubakar to ban military participation in politics. Formulating a clear policy with a bright line helped reduce anxiety in the military.

Next came a thinning of the bloated ranks. The swift military growth during the civil war from 10,000 in 1967 to 200,000 in 1970 brought in thousands of unqualified and under-trained soldiers who had few options after the war (Adebanjo 2001). Murtala Mohammed and

Olusegun Obasanjo made significant cuts from 1975 to 1979 (Gboyega 1989). "They destroyed the civil service and the military as well as the police," said their predecessor, General Yakubu Gowon, in retrospect (Gowon 2010). But the military remained large, in part because it had become a route to professional advancement and other careers (Africa Research Bulletin 2000). At the time of the 1999 transition, the armed forces still included at least 80,000 soldiers and officers.

In January 2000, Obasanjo retired 150 air force officers, prompting several northern emirs to urge the National Assembly to intervene to keep their kinsmen in the ranks (Okolo 2000). "The first thing he [Obasanjo] did was fire all the military officers who had held political office," says a PDP state leader. "He then weakened the power of the north so the military would not belong to any one section of the country" (Olotolo 2017). Yet, northerners remained palpably nervous throughout Obasanjo's first tenure. Hausa-Fulani had dominated the military for decades and were nervous about losing it as a lever of power under Obasanjo, a born-again Christian from the southwest (Agekameh 2002). The purging thus added a strong ethnoregional element to the precarious civilian hold on the military. When Obasanjo met with northern governors in 2000 shortly after twelve states had passed Sharia law, the administration allegedly became concerned that Sharia was really a potential pretext for a coup led by northerners (Agekameh 2000).

When Obasanjo's Chief of Air Staff retired thirty-seven more officers in September, ten were singled out for "over ambition" and "plotting to change the present social order" (Okafor 2000, 30). To be effective, Obasanjo had to consider ethnicity, military service, and rank; many officers had acquired influence beyond their rank by accumulating wealth in political positions under previous dictatorships. It was these officers who feared they had the most to lose as civilian government cut off their traditional routes to wealth and status, and who were retired for "over ambition" in January 2001 (Agekameh 2001). A high-level wave of retirements hit in April when Obasanjo dismissed all three service chiefs. The last straw for Lieutenant-General Malu, after his declaration of faith to the previous military regime, was his public criticism of new bilateral ties between the military and the United States (Africa Research Bulletin 2001).

As it took office, the PDP faced a dilemma between alienating officers who had signaled a willingness to give civilian government another chance and, on the other hand, undermining the credibility of the ongoing transition by angering voters, human rights groups, and the international community. Under President Obasanjo, a hero of the 1967–1970 Civil War, the party resolved this dilemma by adopting a dual strategy, complementing the purges with a series of less-visible measures that reassured the exiting military that the PDP's "umbrella" (its logo) would be big enough for them too.

The PDP's Dual Policy: Impunity, Promotions, and Pathways to the Private Sector

The PDP took four steps to reduce the military's anxieties, which demonstrate how it adapted and implemented the transition's pact to a post-military regime. First, it established a truth commission that enabled victims of the nation's dictatorships to vent grievances, but this generated few confessions by perpetrators and no successful prosecutions. The terms of reference for the newly minted Human Rights Violations Investigations Commission charged Justice Chukwudifu Oputa with investing human rights abuses dating back to the coup that ended the Second Republic on New Year's Eve of 1983. President Obasanjo further tasked the Commission to identify individual or organizational perpetrators, ascertain state culpability, and make recommendations for redress (Constitutional Rights Project 2002). Despite hopeful comparisons of Oputa to Desmond Tutu in South Africa, the government never released the "Oputa Panel's" findings nor successfully prosecuted the major culprits of abuses under Abacha (1993–1998), Babangida (1985–1993), or Buhari (1984–1985). The newly appointed Chief of Army Staff Malu appeared on television before the Panel to insist Diya actually had been plotting a coup. Malu also repeatedly proclaimed his own loyalty to Abacha: "I feel proud wearing the badge of Abacha. I will wear it again, if I am given any," exclaimed Malu (Agekameh 2001, 31). The following year Obasanjo fired him, but he also received numerous commendations; he later told a group of northern elites that he regretted not staging a coup against Obasanjo (Mamah and Ajayi 2006).

Civil society's miscalculations, or shifting organizational self-interests, may have midwifed this miscarriage of justice with Oputa. Immediately after the transition, frontline human rights groups such as the Civil Liberties Organisation (CLO) announced that it had to change apace with the times. It participated in activities such as election monitoring but "it failed to act against the executive lawlessness of the state actors" (Mohammed 2010, 133). "We thought that the major problem would be driving the military out. We found that we should have organized much, much better after the handover from the military" recall activists involved with the Transition Monitoring Group. "Because we did not organize, civil society became broken into parts" (Ndigwe 2017). Donors compounded these problems of fragmentation amidst shifting priorities at this critical moment during the transition. Competition over new grants and contracts undermined efforts to agree on shared reform agenda groups. It also created incentives for groups to reorganize more hierarchically so that leadership could cultivate relationships with big funders; this naturally weakened ties to their respective grassroots bases (Kew 2016, 333). In the end, Nigerians obtained neither truth nor accountability.

A second source of reassurance for exiting military officers was that they had ample opportunities for new careers. Many joined the ranks of the PDP. For example, four senior retired military officers embraced their civilian status and won seats in the new National Assembly: Major-General Nwachukwu, Brigadier Jonathan Tunde Ogbeha, Brigadier David Mark (who went on to become Senate President), and Nuhu Aliyu. According to one study, retired generals such as Major-General Ali Mohammed Gusau and Lieutenant-General Danjuma constituted the backbone of the PDP's fundraising apparatus. During previous, failed transitions, military involvement was seen as an "aberration." But, by 1998, officers were more comfortable with politics, and many had resigned themselves to the role of "big money" in politics. Most importantly, Adekanye documents the expansive involvement of the military in the economy over the previous two decades; this in effect gave many officers a more concrete stake in stability and the external legitimacy (i.e., for attracting foreign investment) that a civilian government would offer (Adekanye 1999, 184). "Since 1999, the retired generals have dominated political activities," writes Braji in a similar study. "The ruling PDP has become subservient to the dictates of the retired generals" who have successfully reduced the influence of the original G34 leaders who formed the party (Braji 2014, 179).

Many former military officers moved into the private sector, typically building on contacts and investments they had already established during active duty under the military regimes. For example, those who went into agriculture, including President Obasanjo himself, had already acquired land during their previous forays into politics during military rule. Abubakar transformed his small family farm into a massive operation, with over 300 laborers during harvests. The ex-military also had more access to capital due to policy changes engrained within the transition. Just days before the handover to civilians, Abubakar issued a decree outlining the procedures and policies for privatization, thus saving the incoming civilian regime from getting stuck with a contentious issue – and generating new opportunities for newly unemployed generals. "President Obasanjo's policy on the recapitalization of banking and insurance sectors gave the retired military officers the opportunity to appropriate weak private and state-owned financial institutions" (Braji 2014, 161). In the transportation sector, Abacha-era power brokers such as Brigadier General Yakubu Muazu moved into the airline business (thriving because the roads are so bad and the oil boom expanded the middle class) immediately after Obasanjo retired him. Ibrahim Babangida, the former dictator, purchased Nation House Press and several other media outlets. A long list of former generals, including T.Y. Danjuma, went into manufacturing or the oil sectors, while others capitalized on the construction boom with engineering ventures. Importantly though, the ex-generals in each of these sectors cultivated close ties to politics, since they needed access to government spending for capital and government power to avoid regulatory roadblocks (Braji 2014). Obasanjo's revocation, early in his term, of oil block rights held by many military officers underscored the importance of maintaining ties to politics. After the transition, senior civilian bureaucrats moved into directorship positions within multinational subsidiaries, though few had capital on the scale of Ahmed Joda, a former Federal Permanent Secretary.

Third, President Obasanjo and the PDP reassured soldiers who opted to stay in the military by increasing the military's resources and benefits. In a comparative study of civilian control over militaries, Powell (2012) characterizes such decisions to "spoil" the military as "coup-proofing." While public estimates are probably understated, available data show that Nigeria's military budget increased from US$793 million in 1998 as the transition began, to over US$2.2 billion (in constant 2015 US dollars) by 2002 (Stockholm International Peace Research Institute 2016). These trends are illustrated in Figure 2.1.

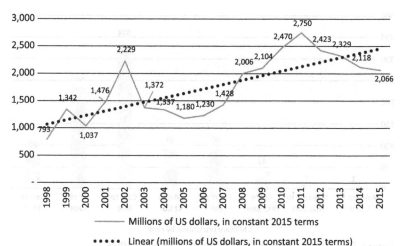

Figure 2.1 Military spending, 1998–2015 (in constant USD).
Source: Stockholm International Peace Research Institute

This was a substantial sum of money for a military that had shrunk after the 1999 transition and that faced no serious external or internal threats.

The ranks slowly grew to about 100,000 in 2010 after various peacekeeping deployments. There was some resentment within the military for these deployments. But they facilitated what Huntington identifies as a critical step for depoliticizing militaries by keeping them focused on military missions rather than developmental or domestic policing operations. Similarly, he suggests moving the troops away from the capital to "relatively distant unpopulated places." Finally, Huntington advises spending on militaries as insurance against a praetorian uprising. "Your military officers think that they are badly paid, badly housed, and badly provided for – and they are probably right" (Huntington 1991, 252). Civil society observers and the National Assembly alike acknowledged such frustrations in the military after the 1999 handover (Fayemi 2002). An American contractor reported that 75 percent of the army's equipment was damaged or unusable, fewer than ten of the navy's fifty-two vessels were seaworthy, and only a handful of helicopters and planes in the air force were combat-ready (Africa Research Bulletin 2000). The spending also gave Nigerian military hardware a needed boost.

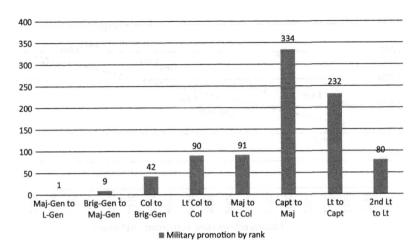

Figure 2.2 Military promotions announced in May 2003.
Note: Figures include at least twenty-five executive commissions converted to
promotions.
Source: *Federal Republic of Nigeria Official Gazette,* May 15, 2003

Fourth, the PDP government approved a massive wave of 879 military promotions[8] a mere two weeks before Obasanjo was sworn in
for his second term in 2003. These promotions by rank, illustrated
in Figure 2.2, have received far less attention than the dismissals and
forced retirements discussed earlier. They provide further evidence of
the PDP's dual policy toward the military, pointing to "coup-proofing"
strategies in order to avoid the sort of military frustrations that
Huntington warns about.

In sum, the PDP's founders agreed upon an understanding that
their presidential candidate needed to be Yoruba in order to bury the
lingering resentment over the annulled 1993 election once and for
all. The party also borrowed from ideas of power rotation discussed
during the failed 1995 constitutional convention and consistent with
the federal government's policy of federal character, in place since the
postwar years. "Power shift" would alternate power between north
and south, while "zoning" would rotate offices across six geographical areas at the national level, across three senatorial districts within
each state, and typically across different neighborhoods within each

---

[8] It appears, though I have been unable to confirm, that many of these
promotions took effect retroactively.

of the 774 local governments. In settling on Obasanjo and marginalizing Ekueme in its primaries, though, the PDP established lingering resentments among eastern Igbos – a hazardous legacy I return to in Chapter 6.

Most importantly, the PDP squarely confronted the dilemma of civilian control of the military through its dual policy. President Obasanjo purged the ranks of officers who had played a role in politics, linking such efforts to a broader policy of professionalization that colored the dismissals as reform rather than retribution. This reflects the advice of one study at the time: "civilian control should not be seen as a set of technical and administrative arrangements that automatically flow from every post-military transition, but, rather, as part of overall national re-structuring" (Fayemi 2002, 119). The PDP also reduced military anxiety by increasing military spending, limiting the Oputa Panel's terms of reference and depriving it of prosecutorial powers, and promoting nearly 900 officers in the final days of Obasanjo's first term. Finally, the party generated career opportunities for retired military officers. A new post-transition generation of retired officers rose within the PDP after 2003, including ex-military elites who had not previously been involved in forming the PDP or forcibly retired as part of the transition. Their absorption into the PDP means that the party had institutionalized the military's influence, and that the transition's pact with the military had survived those initial years of transition. "This attests to the political ingenuity of the military retirees who are able to conspire and take control of such an influential party" (Braji 2014, 180).

Eroding the Transition's Pact and Defeating the PDP

The vast research on pacting and democratization discussed in the literature review has little to say about why pacts collapse. In their massive volume, O'Donnell and Schmitter only briefly list factors such as secularization, social mobility, and market vulnerability, which make it difficult for elites to control their followers – the pact beneficiaries. Voters eventually become more "free floating in their preferences," and parties without a history within the pact may form. In much the same vein, associations may demand more autonomy from partisan or other controls on behavior. "Under these circumstances, it will become increasingly difficult to hold the elite cartel together" (O'Donnell and Schmitter 1986c, 42). They also note that cartels easily rot from within over time. Guaranteeing elites a seat for political participation, a share of the economic spoils, and protection from outside competition makes them lazy, undermines their accountability to voters, and eventually leads to corruption.

This section explores how such factors undermined the transition's pact. Elected politicians who looked less and less like the youthful population, ambitions frustrated by zoning and power shift, and an expanding middle class (described in the next chapter) with "free-floating" preferences all contributed to the PDP's electoral defeat. "The incumbent PDP president did not understand the danger signs," explains one PDP governor. By 2015, "the binding factors that held the PDP [together] began to fall apart, and the people started moving across lines without his noticing it" (Ikpeazu 2017).

One source of change in the PDP concerned subtle shifts in its composition. By 2011, the party had more candidates and officers coming from non-military backgrounds. For a party rooted in the transition's pact with the military, these social and demographic trends impacted the coherence of its founding principles. As the years went by, there were simply fewer and fewer who had lived through or fought for the transition. Heading into the 2015 elections, PDP elites faced a striking demographic dissonance. On the one hand, the country's mean age declined with rapid population growth. With an overall population growth rate of between 2.5 and 2.6, Nigeria is one of the fastest-growing populations in the world. According to the World Bank's estimates, in 2013 about 44.1 percent of the population was under the age of fifteen, a figure that had steadily increased since 2000. On the other hand, the average age of politicians elected to the House and Senate increased over the same period. The 1999 transition elections produced nine senators under the age of forty; the 2011 elections yielded none. The House had 132 members under forty in 1999, and only 34 members in 2011. As the country was getting younger, PDP politicians were getting older (LeVan 2015b). Figure 2.3 illustrates this latter trend.

A second, larger problem in the PDP concerned the party's internal rules to rotate power and limit eligibility for positions based on one's ethnographic background. The PDP had implemented "zoning" of political offices at national, state, and local political levels. As the transition progressed, the informality of rotational principles left the nation

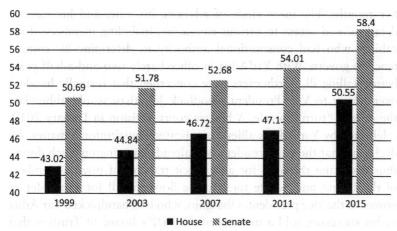

Figure 2.3 Average age of a National Assembly member, 1999–2015.
Source: The Lawmakers (Anyanwu 1999, 2003, 2007, 2011)

unprepared for unexpected contingencies. The resulting deviations gradually undermined the pact's relevance.

An example of the confusion generated by the informality of zoning arose when Obasanjo ran for his second term in 2003. Igbos, led by Governor Orji Uzor Kalu of Abia State, pushed back, insisted that the presidency had been zoned to the southeast for 2003–2007. Naturally, Obasanjo used the PDP machinery to punish Kalu later by removing his party allies in the state (Obianyo 2013). This reflected a minority interpretation of power shift, but it also would have been consistent with its guiding assumptions, since the presidency would remain in the south (the east being a part of the south in Nigerian geography) for the period of two presidential terms. It would also mean that the PDP would have opted to not run a relatively successful incumbent. The collective interests of the party prevailed, in part because few party leaders seemed to share Kalu's understanding of how power shift relates to internal party zoning; he was apparently still interpreting power shift through the eyes of the 1995 constitutional convention (which envisioned a single term).

The informality of power shift presented an even more explicit challenge to the PDP's hegemony when it contradicted the constitutional provisions for presidential succession, further eroding the pact under Obasanjo's successor. In November 2009, President Umaru Musa Yar'Adua fell ill and disappeared from public view for over five months. His inner circle of advisers, his wife, and his security detail refused access to various emissaries, including members of his cabinet who had constitutional authority to determine his competence to govern. With Yar'Adua in office barely two-and-a-half years before falling ill, northerners were concerned that formally handing over power to Vice President Goodluck Jonathan would abbreviate the north's "turn" to rule. A bizarre court decision in January 2010, celebrated by Yar'Adua's allies, complicated constitutional matters by declaring that the vice president was already carrying out such duties, thus obviating the need for an explicit transfer of power. Members of the House and Senate took to the floor to call for a transfer of power to the vice president. Obasanjo, who had handpicked Yar'Adua as his successor, told a meeting of the PDP's Board of Trustees that the court's judgment was plainly inconsistent with the Constitution. More urgently, he said "there is no commander in chief and the vice president has no power. Some people cannot see the danger, so let me make it very clear by asking: what if there is a military coup?" (Adeniyi 2011, 204). For the final three months before Yar'Adua's death, Jonathan served as acting president, authorized by the National Assembly on February 9, 2010 under the controversial "Doctrine of Necessity" (Campbell 2013c). The Senate President, David Mark, said the situation had not been contemplated by the Constitution (Adeniyi 2011). Obasanjo's coup fears seemed entirely real when Yar'Adua finally did return from treatment in Saudi Arabia and a large military detail met his plane in the dark of the night without informing the top defense officials (LeVan 2015a).[9]

The nation survived the constitutional crisis but then the party faced a new dilemma with the 2011 Presidential Election around the corner: should Jonathan run with all the advantages of incumbency, or should the PDP honor power shift? The PDP sent mixed messages, sometimes suggesting that Jonathan would run and other times implying he would step down, thus giving northerners hope that the party would uphold (Kendhammer 2014). When the PDP's Board of Trustees met after Yar'Adua's death on May 5, 2010, northerners, led by Governor Babangida Aliyu of Niger State, argued that the party should respect rotation or renegotiate it. Some northerners seemed to

---

[9] In the weeks before Yar'Adua's death, and while serving as acting president, Jonathan managed to fire many of the top national security officials.

belittle Obasanjo's 1999 candidacy, saying they he became the candidate "to put June 12 behind us," referring to the Yoruba frustration with the annulled 1993 election (cited in Ayoade 2013, 36). Others, under the banner of the Northern Political Leaders Forum (NPLF) took a harder line, declaring, "Northerners have all it takes to win free and fair elections without special arrangements" (ibid). These elites argued that Jonathan violated power shift, and if he wanted to run in 2011, he would have to leave the party. Former Vice President Atiku Ababakar of Adamawa State emerged from a NPLF pool of northern contenders that included former dictator Ibrahim Babangida, Jonathan's National Security Adviser Aliyu Gusau, and Kwara State Governor Bukola Saraki. In the end, "incumbency was a critical factor in favour of Dr. Jonathan," argues a study of PDP's internal dynamics at the time, though fear of a rise in Niger Delta violence also played a role should the first president from the region be denied the chance to run (Ayoade 2013, 38).

With rotation of power no longer a sacrosanct principle, politicians further chipped away at it inside the National Assembly. In 2011, the PDP had zoned the position of Speaker of the House to a member from the southwest and the Deputy speaker to the northeast. But then Emeke Ihedioha, a powerful Igbo politician from the southeast, built a large enough voting bloc to support his election to the Deputy Speakership in return for supporting Aminu Waziri Tambuwal, a politician from the northeast, for Speaker. Both positions thus violated the party's internal rules of power shift, with predictable consequences; when Ihedioha vied for the Imo State governship in 2015, party leaders said he "should not be given ticket to return or go for higher position" of governorship (Afolabi 2014). Tambuwal, seeing his ambition similarly blocked by the rules of power shift, eventually left the PDP and went on to win the governorship of Sokoto State under APC's banner. As the PDP repeatedly turned to traditional mechanisms of party discipline by suspending members, it frustrated the ambition or more and more politicians.

Some PDP leaders today, including Governor Ikpeazu of Abia State, believe that leaving leadership rotation out of the constitution was a mistake that generated inconsistencies between the formal rules of politics and the PDP's role in carrying out the terms of the transition. "Within the party, there was this understanding that zoning was important," yet the 1999 constitution left it out (Ikpeazu 2017).

A member of the constitutional drafting committee who drafted provisions related to Federal Character says this omission was deliberate; they always hoped power shift would become irrelevant. The problem with power shift and zoning, he explains, is that "people do not believe that power comes from the electorate" (Ebri 2010). In several cases, voters have apparently demonstrated discomfort with zoning when it imposes arbitrary constraints on their choices. In Imo State, party stalwarts such as Ikedi Ohakim and Senator Ifeanyi Ararume adamantly opposed the choice of Rochas Okorocha because he was from the Orlu zone of the state, when it was the Okigwe zone's turn according to the "Charter of Equity" (as the state's rotation agreement was known). Ararume later left the PDP because former President Obasanjo interfered with his re-nomination as retaliation for not supporting Obasanjo's third term. Okorocha similarly abandoned the PDP for a minor party in 2011 (and decamped again in 2013 for APC). In neighboring Abia State, Governor Orji Uzor Kalu unsuccessfully argued against returning Uche Chukwumerije to the Senate for similar reasons (Obianyo 2013).

Zoning and rotation impaired internal party democracy in ways that ultimately undermined both member loyalty and (as the next chapter demonstrates) the PDP's electoral fortunes. "The issue about parties that most concerns the public since the return of democracy in 1999 is their lack of internal democracy," argues Egwu (2014, 193). Moreover, shortchanging internal democratic processes alienated several cohorts of politicians who wanted to run for re-election (and whose constituents may have wanted them to). "The dominant trend is that parties hold internal primary contests, but then proceed to select their nominees for offices without regard to those primaries" (Egwu 2014, 193). Candidates "imposed" from above for this or other reasons often block ambitious politicians seeking to rise up through the party. For example, the Abuja PDP rammed Nuhu Ribadu's nomination for governor through the Adamawa State party primaries over the protests of local political leaders. In Enugu State, the party undertook parallel primaries, making it difficult to determine who the candidate was at all. Outgoing Senator Ayogu Eze failed to prevail as the candidate as the PDP split into rival state factions, which held competing primary conventions (Olotolo 2017). Courts later rejected the results of at least two gubernatorial primaries previously certified by INEC, in effect certifying the problems with primaries (though PDP was not alone in these imperfections). Aside from the question of the quality of primaries, though, the larger point is that such frustrations fueled the defections from the PDP into the nascent APC. "If you don't have transparent primaries, you will have a lot of disenchanted members," the APC spokesperson told a Washington audience in 2014. "So you need internal democracy for your own self-survival" (Muhammed 2014).

In sum, feelings about power shift and zoning are mixed; at the national level, voters see it as a useful mechanism for limiting regional dominance, while politicians see their ambitions blocked by arbitrary qualifications. The Congress for Progressive Change, one of the parties that formed the backbone of Buhari's APC in 2014, has displayed its dislike for rotating offices: "we don't believe in the principle of zoning because it is against the tenant of democracy" (Ayoade 2013, 37). In the words of Governor Amaechi of Rivers State, who managed Buhari's presidential campaign, the PDP designed power shift "to serve the elites in power," as a means of "sharing resources in a manner that will not represent the interests of the poor. That's in-house corruption." After defecting to the APC, he said, "we believe in power shift in terms of class, in terms of – even within the elites – in terms of merit." Unlike power shift's role in the 1999 transition, "I don't know whether it is fundamental now" (Amaechi 2014). Significantly, the APC left power shift and rotation out of the party's constitution. The spokesperson for "New PDP," the defectors who joined the APC, says that power shift and rotation unnecessarily eliminates qualified politicians from the pool of potential candidates (Eze 2014). Since its 2015 loss, the PDP has come to recognize the problem. One state party leader bluntly echoed Amaechi's complaints about the effects of rotation on merit: "Zoning does not promote people to work hard" (Olotolo 2017).

Conclusion

According to one study, "The PDP lost the elections largely because the party failed to manage a stable elite consensus" (Owen and Usman 2015, 470). In this chapter, I detailed the basis for that consensus during and after the handover of power to civilians, referring to it as a "pact." In the democratization literature, pacts are the result of elite bargaining between those in favor of reforms and those who have the most to lose from them. After showing how Nigeria's pact facilitated a successful handover to civilian rule, and explaining how the PDP adapted and implemented it, I argued that the weakening of the pact undermined the PDP's hold on power. This fills in an important gap in the study of elite bargaining during democratic reform by tracing how a pact expires – despite its apparent success. I also argue in later chapters that the terms of a successful transition will differ in important ways from the institutional basis for a robust democracy.

I first identified the elements of the pact as a bargain struck by the Provisional Ruling Council in 1998–1999, starting with the selection of Abubakar to oversee the transition and concluding in less than a year. The military received several exit guarantees pertaining to career advancement, controversial promotions for regime hardliners, protection from corruption prosecutions, and impunity for human rights abuses. Next, I described how the PDP arrived at its own internal bargain congruent with the transitional government's pact. By selecting Obasanjo, the former dictator trusted by the military and the Hausa-Fulani, as its presidential candidate, the party effectively paid off the "Yoruba debt" triggered by the annulment of the 1993 election, when Abiola was denied the presidency. Party elites further agreed to alternate the presidency between north and south, and to establish zonal rotation of offices. A potential setback for the PDP, largely lost in the dustbin of history, was the party's failure to obtain a government of national unity (GNU), which would have limited electoral competition even further by building an explicit elite consensus across parties. After the transition was in motion, hardliners such as Bamaiyi, Useni, and Al Mustapha exercised significant influence over constitutional reforms and the scope of judicial investigations. Others received promotions.

Once in office, President Obasanjo implemented the transition's pact by adopting a "dual policy" that carried out a wave of military dismissals and then taking several steps to offset military anxiety that hardliners cultivated publicly. The PDP reassured the military by continuing the Abubakar Government's subtle embrace of impunity; to this day, the Oputa Panel's findings have not been published. Then the PDP generated opportunities within the party and in the private sector, where many officers already had economic investments. Finally, the administration promoted nearly 900 officers in the final days of

Obasanjo's first term. He gave the military a large down payment on democracy, "spoiling" them for staying out of politics.

The pact did not evolve over time as Higley and Gunther (1992) would expect. Instead, the elaborate bargain, promulgated swiftly in the 1998–1999 period, decayed. The pact's undoing and the road to the PDP's defeat began with slow demographic and professional changes within the party, including a rise in the average age of its politicians as the nation grew younger. But, more importantly, power shift and zoning suffocated political ambition. Politicians at the federal, state, and local levels saw their candidacies blocked if it was not their geographical region's "turn" to rule. The informality of this rotation mechanism further opened it up to occasional deviations when it suited the party's interests, as occurred with the nomination of Goodluck Jonathan for the PDP's presidential candidate in 2011 and in numerous gubernatorial contests.

After a meeting with the PDP leadership in 2017, Babangida expressed relief that the party defeated in 2015 is rebuilding. Hinting at the pact that facilitated the 1999 transition, he called the PDP an acceptable party for Nigeria because it had been accepted from "top to down [sic]" (Mosadomi 2017). The defeat of the PDP ended the transition but now the nation must contend with the legacies of this top-down process. In Chapter 6, I will show first how the transition's impunity for human rights violations continues to undermine the rule of law, and has undermined effective security strategies against Boko Haram's terrorism. I also explore how a new (and inexperienced) generation of elected politicians in 1999 inherited the illegitimate legal legacies of over sixteen years of dictatorships. Military decrees meant to empower subnational authoritarian administrators now undermine effective resolution of conflicts such as tensions between pastoralists and settled agriculturalists. Finally, the nation in general still must address deep resentment over its neutralization of the Igbo politician Alex Ekueme in the PDP's 1999 presidential convention. Despite the provisions for rotation of power and zoning, the east has not had a "turn" to rule since 1966, a historical observation at the center of new secessionist movements. "Westerners and northerners hijacked the party and organized it against the Igbos," say members of MASSOB, the Igbo secessionist organization, regarding the PDP (Onuorah et al. 2017). Secessionist agitators see Ekueme's sidelining as just one more example of a continuous marginalization of Igbos since the Civil War.

"With the election of 1999," said IPOB activists in an interview, "we all know that Ekueme won, but they robbed him of his right because he is from the wrong tribe. He is not from the north" (Indigenous People of Biafra 2017).

Looking back on the end of the PDP's rein and his new responsibilities, the APC's Speaker of the House Yakubu Dogara said, "it had not been part of our history that the opposition defeated the party that had the power of incumbency … but it happened" (Odebode 2017). The next three chapters tell the story of how this occurred. Chapter 3 categorizes and analyzes the content of political rhetoric in order to understand what parties campaigned on, highlighting important differences between the PDP and the APC on the economy, insecurity, and electoral issues. Chapter 4 turns to electoral outcomes across states, utilizing a statistical analysis of the presidential election to provide additional evidence that the economy and electoral integrity played a larger role in the election than insecurity. Then Chapter 5 analyzes voting behavior using individual-level data to show how ethnicity and religion remain powerful influences in electoral politics, even as issue-based politics rise. Read as follow-ups to this chapter, these three chapters suggest that the PDP lost by mistaking the transition's pact for institutionalized democracy, and the APC won by capturing a new constituency for economic and electoral reform.

3 | The Rational Counter-Terrorist? Economic Policy and Insurgent Insecurity in Nigeria's 2015 Presidential Campaign

The PDP's big umbrella had opened up after the death of Abacha, and the party's effective implementation of the pact with northern elites and outgoing military rulers kept the transition on track. The 2003 elections were the first organized by civilians that did not lead to a coup, and the 2007 elections resulted in the first peaceful transfer of power from one civilian to another (Omotola 2010; LeVan et al. 2003). As the 2011 elections earned praise for freeness and fairness, the nation enjoyed an economic growth spurt (European Union Election Observation Mission 2011; Akhaine 2011). These were positive but modest milestones, though, and the PDP remained deeply entrenched in power at all levels of government.

The party's fortunes began to shift prior to 2015 as Nigeria's economy flagged and Boko Haram's violence raged. The PDP had weathered difficult storms before, though. It had survived bitter infighting between President Obasanjo and his vice president, Atiku Abubakar. It had brushed off corruption scandals of cabinet ministers and successful impeachments of its National Assembly leadership. Its presidential candidates had defeated Muhammadu Buhari three times; in 2003 Obasanjo received 62 percent of the vote, in 2007 Yar'Auda won handily with nearly 70 percent, and in 2011 Jonathan secured 59 percent despite reservations from northerners who wanted power to "shift" back to their region. The inchoate nature of the opposition All Progressives Congress (APC) also seemed to favor the PDP. Even though the APC's loose coalition of parties managed to agree on Buhari as a presidential candidate, the new party had less access to state resources and had little time to put party infrastructure on the ground for mobilizing voters or recruiting candidates. So how did the APC defy the odds and prevail over Africa's largest political party?

In this chapter, I provide the first part of my answer to this question. I show how, faced with a choice of issues to campaign on, the APC opted for a strategy centered on economic issues, giving counter-terrorism somewhat lesser prominence. First, I provide some context for the election by briefly describing President Jonathan's unusual route to power. I summarize existing explanations that attribute the APC's sweeping victory to corruption, economic decline, improved electoral management, and a significant rise in violence. General insecurity and political violence were not new to Nigeria's electoral cycles; riots and ethnic killings of Igbos had followed the 1964–1965 elections, and violence was so widespread following the 1983 elections that much of the nation welcomed (then-General) Buhari's coup as a restoration of peace. Boko Haram's violence ravaging Nigeria gave the 2015 elections a different tone, though. Voters feared not just riots or political thugs but organized and deadly terrorism, thus making national security stand out as a different kind of issue. In the wake of suicide bombings, attacks on schools, churches, and highly protected government installations, as well as the horrific kidnapping of 276 school girls from Chibok, insecurity topped voters' concerns. I present qualitative and quantitative evidence to back up this claim.

Second, I explain my research design to analyze the comments of political elites in order to understand what the two major parties actually talked about during the presidential campaign. I focus on three senior figures from each major party, chosen due their respective powers and vetted by experienced Nigerian journalists who covered the presidential election. A search of three independent daily newspapers during the campaign period between August 2014 and March 2015 yields 2,390 distinct news articles. I code party leaders' comments and quotations into five thematic categories, drawing upon the existing qualitative research about the election. I then break each category into sub-themes.

Third, I use NVivo software to conduct a content analysis. This analysis of 929 coded references empirically demonstrates that insecurity and terrorism played a smaller role in the presidential election than previously appreciated. APC politicians overwhelmingly focused on economic issues, with 284 references compared to 72 references by the PDP. The APC also emphasized electoral integrity and reform to a surprising degree – exceeding even the references to terrorism and insecurity. Though social issues were less prominent in the campaign, I find that the APC discussed social issues twice as often as the PDP.

This empirical approach enables me to establish the campaign priorities of each party.

The APC took a small political risk by focusing on the economy instead of on widespread fears of terrorism. The prominence the party gave to electoral integrity suggests that four rounds of voter education, electoral observation, and massive civil society organizing since the transition has paid off.

While the analysis of campaign strategy and rhetoric here explicitly focuses on elites, Chapter 4 focuses on electoral outcomes at the state level and Chapter 5 analyzes individual-level voting behavior. The evidence suggests that voters responded to the campaign rhetoric. Nigerians engaged in "economic voting," subjectively assessing their pocketbooks alongside broader objective measures of economic policy performance. Taken together, these chapters thus contribute to a growing body of research that questions portraits of African elections as centered on ethnicity or parochialism and devoid of issue-based campaigning.

President Jonathan's Record and the APC's Victory in Electoral History

A cloud of dubious legitimacy hung over Goodluck Jonathan's presidency from the start. Unlike the flawed and corrupt elections that brought his predecessor, Yar'Adua, into office (Ibrahim and Ibeanu 2009; Human Rights Watch 2007), Jonathan emerged as an "accidental president" in 2010 following Yar'Adua's illness and disappearance for medical treatment. For over five months, starting in November 2009, Africa's most populous country governed without a president. No one, other than his wife and a few intimate advisers, saw him. Cabinet ministers who travelled to Saudi Arabia were denied access, and the cabinet collectively declined to assess his health condition, which would have established a temporary transfer of authority based in the constitution (Adeniyi 2011). "Eventually," writes the former US Ambassador to Nigeria, "the National Assembly extra legally by resolution designated Jonathan as acting president, to international approval and domestic acquiescence" (Campbell 2013c, 136). As a Gallup poll giving Yar'Adua a 38-percent approval rating (in April 2010) signaled, the nation desperately wanted some sort of end to the crisis. When the law failed to provide a solution, the National

Assembly stepped up. Jonathan finally took the oath of office in May 2010 following Yar'Adua's death; overall confidence in the government quickly increased to 55 percent. By mid-2011 that number had soared to 81 percent (Crabtree 2012).[1] However, three years later, as the Presidential Election campaign kicked off in 2014, public confidence in Jonathan had plummeted to 29 percent (Loschky 2014). What happened?

Post-election analyses converge on five broad factors that contributed to Jonathan's defeat: government corruption, declining economic conditions, increased autonomy and administrative competence of the electoral commission, the impressive conduct of the APC's party primaries, and a rise in Boko Haram-related violence (Owen and Usman 2015; Siollun 2015; Lewis and Kew 2015). Discussing each of these issues efficiently provides a summary of the climate headed into the 2015 elections. This analysis does not aim to provide a full account of Jonathan's five years in office. Nor does it describe the story of the APC itself. Instead, it puts the election in context and serves as the basis for the five issue categories utilized in my subsequent empirical analysis.

Corruption

A first factor in the PDP's defeat is corruption, which is common at all levels in Nigeria. Citizens are simultaneously resigned to it, paying petty bribes at police check points or paying fees to "expedite" government services, and resentful of it (Smith 2007). In 2012, 94 percent of Nigerians said they believed that their government was corrupt. That extraordinarily high figure only came down slightly, to 91 percent, in 2013 and 86 percent in 2014 (Loschky and Sanders 2015; Crabtree 2012). Transparency International's Corruption Perception Index gives us yet another gauge for public feelings about corruption. Out of 175 countries analyzed in 2016, Nigeria ranked as the 136th-least corrupt country. "Pray, whatever happened to the Economic and Financial Crimes Commission, EFCC, and the Independent Corrupt Practices and Other Related Offences Commission, ICPC?" the APC's spokesperson rhetorically asked during the presidential

---

[1] Another company, NOI Polls Ltd, tracked similar trends, reporting Jonathan's approval rating as 42 percent in mid-2013 (Olaleye 2013).

campaign. "Were they not institutions specifically created for the purpose of tackling corruption, but which the Jonathan administration chose to castrate?" (Usman and Agande 2015). While anti-corruption investigations are common and anti-corruption rhetoric is ubiquitous, high-level convictions are very rare.

Jonathan's administration lived up to this generalization through decisions that seemed to punish whistleblowers, protect political allies, and defang the above-mentioned anti-corruption commissions whose investigations slowed to a snail's pace. Jonathan's pardon of a corrupt former governor further tarnished his reputation on the issue. In the first corruption conviction for a senior politician in the nation's history, Governor Diepreye Alamieyeseigha of Bayelsa State had been sentenced to two years in the United Kingdom for stealing millions of dollars. The case was followed closely around the world since he had previously (in 2005) managed to skip bail and return to Nigeria disguised as a woman. Nuhu Ribadu, who as head of the EFCC had prosecuted him, called the pardon "shocking and unbelievable" and said it would undermine the fight against corruption (Cocks 2013). Jonathan also seemed to have little interest in investigating allegations of corruption in the military. Despite the huge increases in the defense budget documented in Chapter 2, soldiers on the frontlines against Boko Haram often lacked basic equipment as money disappeared through inflated procurement contracts and budgetary slush funds known as "security votes" (Page 2016). By buying off the military to prevent a coup and stabilize civil–military relations, Nigeria's defenses had been hollowed out.

Though Nigerians experience corruption at all levels of society, much of it originates in the oil sector, which accounts for nearly 90 percent of the country's export earnings. A 2015 report by the Natural Resource Governance Institute found that mismanagement of the Nigerian National Petroleum Company (NNPC) had worsened since 2010. One account managed by NNPC to feed Nigeria's refineries was discretionarily spending US$6 billion per year between 2011 and 2013, while sending only about 58 percent of its total value to the Federation Account. Between 2010 and 2014, the NNPC also funneled US$35 billion in "swap deals" prone to corruption by exporting crude and importing refined oil (Sayne et al. 2015). A government investigation into the fuel subsidy exposed the inner workings of such exchanges; at least fifteen fuel importers collected more than US$300 million in

2010 without actually importing any fuel. When leaks to the press revealed that various schemes to scam the government amounted to US$6 billion, civil society groups took to the streets in outrage. A long-serving member of the House of Representatives, Farouk Lawan, led an ad hoc committee that revealed the inner workings of fuel subsidy corruption, naming names and identifying billions of dollars gone missing (House of Representatives Ad-Hoc Committee 2012). He was accused of accepting a bribe from those he was investigating.[2]

Missing oil money was also at the center of tensions that erupted between Jonathan and Central Bank Governor Lamido Sanusi in early 2014. *Forbes* Magazine named Sanusi "African Person of the Year" in 2011, in part for reforms requiring new auditing procedures in banks and imposing limits on CEO tenure. He testified before a National Assembly Committee in January 2014 that the Ministry of Petroleum and the NNPC failed to remit over US$20 billion to the Federation Account. The Jonathan administration was swift to react, detailing a long list of accusations against Sanusi, including violations of the Procurement Act and wasteful spending (Idowu et al. 2014). However, since the Central Bank Act of 2007 does not give the president the authority to fire the Central Bank governor without a two-thirds vote of the Senate (which was keenly interested in the missing money), Jonathan reverted to a technical "suspension" instead of a dismissal. The drama energized anti-corruption activists, such as the Socio-economic Rights and Accountability Project and the Zero Corruption Coalition, a partner of Transparency International. The international business community also condemned Sanusi's removal; the naira immediately dropped in value and the stock market declined.

Jonathan seemed to sum up his anti-corruption approach when he said on national television in May 2014 that most allegations were "politically motivated." More controversially, he later regretted saying, "Over 70% of what are called corruption (cases), even by EFCC and other anti-corruption agencies, is not corruption, but common stealing" (Udo 2014). Good governance advocates swiftly reacted with sarcasm. Looking back on the election, one prominent civil society organization said, "there were many corruption cases like the Pension Scam, the Subsidy Fraud, and other scandals which the outgoing administration

---

[2] He was never tried in court, but he later lost his primary in Kano State.

handled with kid gloves and which led to its eventual fall" (Africa Network for Environment and Economic Justice 2015).

Improved Electoral Integrity

The quality of Nigeria's 2011 elections raised expectations, making electoral integrity a second prominent theme in the 2015 presidential contest. On the one hand, the 2011 elections were considered free and fair, and thus an improvement over elections in 2007 and 2003 (Akhaine 2011; Obi 2011). Much of the credit for this went to the appointment of Attahiru Jega as electoral commissioner, who took over shortly after the National Assembly passed an electoral reform bill. As one international election observer delegation noted, "the appointment of Professor Attahiru Jega as chairman of the Independent National Election Commission (INEC) in June 2010 increased public confidence and raised expectations among Nigerians that the serious flaws of the 2007 elections would not be repeated. INEC generally met this expectation with an increased level of transparency and responsiveness to voters' needs" (National Democratic Institute for International Affairs 2012, 7). A nationwide poll after the election reported that 76 percent of Nigerians described INEC as prepared, 72 percent said it was impartial, and 87 said they were satisfied with its overall performance (Onwuemenyi 2011). On the other hand, post-election violence killed over 800 people, primarily in northern opposition strongholds that voted for Buhari (Human Rights Watch 2011; Federal Republic of Nigeria 2011).

These hopes and fears simultaneously informed the public's expectations for 2015. Afrobarometer reported that 50 percent of respondents feared political intimidation or violence in the current election environment, a dramatic increase from 34 percent in 2013 (Nengak et al. 2015). The Assistant Inspector General of Police threw gasoline on the fire when he said he would not shoot first, but, "if one of my men is killed, I shall kill 20 of them" (Adeosun 2015). Gallup reported in 2014 that only 13 percent of Nigerians said they believed in the honesty of their elections – the lowest of all thirty-two African countries surveyed (Loschky and Sanders 2015). A few months later, in January 2015, Afrobarometer observed mixed views of INEC. Overall trust in the institution was limited, with only 32% saying they trust the INEC "somewhat" or "a lot." At the same time, almost two-thirds (64%) said INEC was "ready to hold credible free and fair elections."

Despite serious irregularities in pockets of the Niger Delta, President Jonathan's home turf, observers and scholars alike concluded that the 2015 elections were a milestone for Nigeria (Owen and Usman 2015). The administrative independence complemented an experienced civil society, which had monitored four previous elections and enjoyed significant international support (Lewis and Kew 2015). INEC also operated a civil society liaison office that simplified administrative tasks associated with election monitoring and clearly embraced transparency and participation as operational principles (largely the opposite of 2007). But again, Jega as an individual received much of the credit. "The former university lecturer exuded calm authority and integrity," writes Siollun. "He has painstakingly prepared for the task over the past four years by studying the rigging methods used in previous elections, implementing an elaborate system of voter registration, training thousands of electoral staff, and introducing biometric readers to identify voters by reading their thumbprint" (Siollun 2015).

Jega's integrity faced an unexpected test when President Jonathan's National Security Adviser made an offhand remark in January 2015 that the security services could not guarantee voters' safety. With terrorism raging in the northeast and the administration still reeling from the embarrassment of the #BringBackOurGirls campaign (discussed below), the military announced that it could not divert soldiers from a new military offensive in the northeast. Cynicism was swift and widespread, especially among voters in the region, who had little sympathy for the PDP to begin with. "Nigeria's security services have failed to defeat Boko Haram in five years," said a news report from Borno State. "Some are asking how they will do it in six weeks"(Ndege 2015). Civil society organizations and intellectuals immediately worried that the electoral delay could be a stealth effort by Jonathan to extend his tenure, using instability in the northeast as a pretext for undermining opposition politicians (Oyeyipoa 2015). The Situation Room, a high-profile coalition using technology and a nationwide network to track electoral preparations, called the postponement from February 14 to March 28 "blackmail" and demanded the resignation of the security chiefs (N-Katalyst 2015).

While Jega publicly declared he was "not being forced by anybody" to delay the election, a military loyal to the president in the midst of his waning campaign could have put voters at risk without a full commitment to security on polling day. When the National Council of State met to deliberate on the matter, Jega insisted, "INEC is substantially ready for the general elections as scheduled" (Jega 2015b). In retrospect, Jega later conceded to a Washington audience, "we were prepared but it would not been have good." The extension enabled INEC to do more training and distribute more voter cards, he said, which were huge tasks since Nigeria had adopted a complicated ballot system and costly biometric voter identification cards. Jega also said that President Jonathan "deserves credit" for leaving the commission alone and supporting INEC's budget requests (Jega 2015a).

Internal Party Governance

A third important context for the 2015 elections was that improvements in parties' internal democracy had helped level the playing field for political competition, lowering the "barriers to entry" for candidates. Up through at least the 2003 election, INEC maintained that it had limited jurisdiction over the conduct of internal party affairs (LeVan et al. 2003). The 2010 Electoral Act (still in effect in 2015) raised the standards for internal party democracy and transparency. One important reform, upheld in the Supreme Court Case *INEC* v. *Musa*, stated that INEC can deny a political association (i.e., a party) recognition if it violates the constitution's criteria for registration, for example, by including ethnic content in its name or symbol (Datau 2014). Also important was a new requirement for parties to have primaries or caucuses. This was as much a response to public expectations as it was meant to remedy disasters such as the PDP's primaries for the 2007 election, which locked out Obasanjo's vice president, Atiku Abubakar (Herskovits 2007; Ibrahim and Ibeanu 2009). Heading into 2015, the PDP operated as if nothing had really changed since 2011. As noted in Chapter 2, it overcame the hesitation of northerners who saw the selection of Jonathan as a betrayal of the "power shift" principle; it was still the north's "turn" to rule. But party leaders knew that running an incumbent was a safer bet for holding on to the presidency. In return, Jonathan supposedly agreed to not run for re-election in 2015 in order to return power to the north (Ayoade 2013).

Even with the legal reforms, INEC's efforts to advance internal democracy encountered several obstacles. There was such discord within the PDP that INEC often did not know who to liaise within the party. INEC also faced a slew of confusing court orders interfering with its work. Most importantly, incumbents encouraged "widespread misinterpretation" of a clause in the Electoral Act that seemed to suggest that INEC was obligated to accept the names of candidates provided to them by parties – ignoring other sections that make candidate selection contingent upon democratic electoral processes (Ibeanu 2014). At the state level, informal power-brokers known as "godfathers" did more than just financially support and politically endorse candidates – they interfered with the selection process itself. In some states, politicians who ran disappeared from the ballot, in others, those who did not participate in the primary appeared on the ballot (Obi 2011; Fashagba 2015). "Whether it's manipulation or support or whatever, it's all done locally within the state," says the former Deputy Speaker of the Plateau State Assembly under the PDP. "The national party has given so much power to the governors, and it has affected the political party negatively because if you are not in the good book of the governor, there is the possibility you might not go through" (Rapnap 2016). Scholars express the same sentiment; a collection of essays on parties recently concluded "all of the authors have also pointed out the lack of internal democracy in all of Nigeria's political parties" (Ibrahim 2014, 10).

Things had begun to change with electoral reforms and the appointment of Jega to run INEC. But even so, a lack of internal party democracy is arguably difficult as an issue to translate to voters. Even if voters personally have little access to party machinery or notice the disappearance of their preferred candidate from the ballot, the arcane laws are often opaque, with clauses that appear contradictory or in conflict with the constitution (Ibeanu 2014). So while issues of internal party governance were entirely "legitimate," whether parties would campaign on them with the hopes of winning over voters was hardly certain in 2015.

Insurgency and Insecurity

Insecurity in the oil-producing Niger Delta had declined under Jonathan's watch, potentially giving the PDP a success story to run on. A government amnesty program launched in 2009 brought militants out of the creeks and into retraining programs and reintegration camps. With the oil boom in full swing at the time, the government could afford to pay for peace. In a region devastated by poor infrastructure, environmental destruction, and few job opportunities, cash from the government generated a powerful draw (Asuni 2009). Upwards of 35,000 young men claiming to be militants enrolled in the program. A steep decline in insurgent activity and violence catalogued as "militant" soon followed.[3] But then many of the amnesty's programs flopped. For example, while militant leaders received lucrative contracts, young people who had gone through vocational training could not find jobs, leaving the program doing little more than providing monthly stipends (Alapiki et al. 2015; Abidde 2017).

However, violence from Boko Haram in the northeast moved in the opposite direction. The Nigeria Security Tracker attributes at least 11,709 deaths to Boko Haram, 5,165 to state security services, and 10,747 to some combination of the two during the period from May 2011 and the presidential election in March 2015 (Council on Foreign Relations 2017). These figures correlate closely to other data sources, providing some measure of validation (Serrano and Pieri 2014). Even so, the figures are conservative since they are based on media reports. Few Nigerian reporters were willing to travel to the region, and those who did were closely watched by the military. For example, Ahmad Salkadi, one of the few journalists to have interviewed Boko Haram's leader, was detained repeatedly. Such harassment grew as human rights groups documented widespread abuses by the security services (Amnesty International 2014; Human Rights Watch 2012). Some analysts mistakenly attribute the rise in violence to the handover from a northerner to a southerner following President Yar'Adua's absence and then death. However, "these analyses ignore Boko Haram's genesis and violence under Presidents Obasanjo and Yar'Adua" (Thurston 2016, 204). Terrorism had actually begun to increase before Jonathan took the oath in April 2010. As discussed in Chapter 6, the turning point in Boko Haram's tactics and violence corresponded with the 2009 extrajudicial execution of its leader, Mohammed Yusuf, by the police (LeVan 2013; Adesoji 2010; Thurston 2018).

The spike in violence was overwhelmingly concentrated in Borno, Adamawa, and Yobe, three northeastern states. But there was serious violence in other states, including attacks on police stations and

---

[3] Other categories, such as intercommunal and gang violence, increased around 2013 (Partnerships in the Niger Delta 2017).

prison breaks in Bauchi, a car bomb at the National Police Force Headquarters in Abuja, a suicide bomber at the United Nations head-quarters, and bombings in Kano State. Even though many southerners treated the violence with some detachment, given cultural differences and the physical distance between the north and the south, Boko Haram was clearly a problem that was national in scope. In 2014, polls showed that two-thirds (67%) of Nigerians said the government was "not doing enough" to effectively fight terror. Respondents were asked, "Do you believe that Boko Haram poses a major threat, minor threat, or no threat to the future of Nigeria?" Fully 95 percent called the terrorist group a "major threat," with a virtually indistinguishable difference between the predominantly Christian south and the largely Muslim north (Loschky and Sanders 2015).

In the minds of Nigerians, fear of the horrific violence was only part of the story. Boko Haram's kidnapping of 276 girls from a school in Chibok[4] had been a great national embarrassment, and it created a huge credibility gap between the military's professed progress and the situation on the ground. It triggered a social media campaign, making #BringBackOurGirls one of the biggest hashtags ever on Twitter; within two weeks it had been tweeted over two million times (Olin 2014). Organized by a former minister and a broad coalition of civil society organizations, its online response put the Jonathan administration under the microscope.

In the months that followed, a series of communication blunders by the administration deepened public cynicism about President Jonathan and damaged his credibility. First, the military said they had rescued the Chibok girls in April 2014, infuriating the girls' parents (Ameh et al. 2014). The military also provided different numbers of those kidnapped, contributing to confusion and conspiracy theories about how the administration might benefit from the kidnapping (Smith 2015). For example, one theory posited that the girls provided a pretext for a further power grab by the federal government in key opposition-held states in the northeast. The second communications blunder unfolded a month later when the Chief of Defence Staff Alex Sabundu Badeh said that the government knew where the girls were. This only intensified public frustration and demands for a rescue

---

[4] According to some reports, Boko Haram originally kidnapped 329 girls but 53 quickly escaped.

operation or additional military action (Jones 2014). General Chris Olukolade made a similar stumble later that year in September, when he declared that some of the girls were safe in a military barracks – but then retracted that statement (BBC 2014). Third, as international attention hit its peak, President Jonathan was filmed at a wedding celebrating, thus creating the impression of detachment or apathy. Fourth, as the #BringBackOurGirls movement held peaceful rallies in visible locations in Abuja, the police commissioner for the Federal Capital Territory banned the gatherings. "I cannot fold my hands and watch this lawlessness," he declared (Rhodan 2014). The immediate embarrassment and scandal prompted a swift retraction by police leadership (Nnochiri et al. 2014). Fifth, some military officials told newspapers that ten generals and other military officers had been convicted by court-martial for providing arms to Boko Haram. At the same time, a Ministry of Defence spokesperson disputed those reports (Faul 2014).

Several months into the crisis, the president still had not met with the girls' parents or traveled to Chibok. By the end of July, #BringBackOurGirls had been mentioned on Twitter over four million times, including a prominent retweet by American First Lady Michelle Obama (Querouil 2014). A sixth public relations blunder unfolded when, in July, Jonathan refused to meet with some parents who wanted to be accompanied by #BringBackOurGirls leaders, who had paid the parents' way from Chibok for the meeting (Agande 2014; Mutum and Onochie 2014). Finally, the administration repeatedly sent mixed messages about its willingness to negotiate with Boko Haram or whether it had agreed upon a ceasefire. On a few occasions, intermediaries reported that Boko Haram was willing to trade hostages for prisoners (Matfess 2017). According to a member of the Northern Elders Forum, a group of elites and traditional rulers in the region, Jonathan "never wanted to negotiate. Israel releases prisoners all the time in swaps; why shouldn't Nigeria do the same?" he asks. Instead, Jonathan and the PDP "wanted to keep the turmoil going because it had political value for them" (Abdullah 2016).

In short, under Jonathan's watch, the security situation had objectively deteriorated in the north and his administration had perpetrated enough mishaps in the mishandling of the Chibok girls that its claims of progress in counter-terrorism lacked credibility heading into 2015. Violence in the Niger Delta had declined, but that violence had also been qualitatively and quantitatively different; there were far fewer overall deaths at the peak of the insurgency. The APC, a party that had never won an election, would have to persuade voters that it could do better.

Economic Decline

When Jonathan took the presidential oath of office in 2010, the Gross Domestic Product (GDP) was expanding at 8 percent per year. Throughout 2011, growth outside of the oil sector ranged between 8 and 9 percent, suggesting that Nigeria could be breaking the "oil curse." Mismanagement, corruption, and policy missteps soon left their marks, though. For starters, Jonathan's economic team inflated peoples' expectations for perpetual growth; it was as if no one had lived through the oil crash in the late 1970s that left the Second Republic with huge commitments for spending and declining revenue (LeVan 2015a). "Between 2013 and 2015, the economy is expected to grow in real terms at over 7 percent given the constraints experienced in 2012," the government optimistically predicted (National Bureau of Statistics 2012b, 4). By the following year, the government tried to moderate expectations. "The Nigerian economy faced numerous challenges which impacted overall economic activity in 2012," said a government report. "Declines in the real growth rates of economic activity were experienced in both the oil and non-oil sectors. Oil production was less than expected due to security challenges, and floods which occurred in the latter part of the year," while weak consumer demand hit the non-oil sectors (National Bureau of Statistics 2013, 5).

The Jonathan administration also misstepped in 2012 when it suddenly announced cuts to the fuel subsidy, instantly sending the price of petrol (gasoline) through the roof along with the cost of public transportation, food, and other essentials. Since he had met with the International Monetary Fund a few weeks earlier, it also left the impression that the president was kowtowing to foreign advice. According to news accounts, protests against the cuts, loosely aligned with the "occupy" movement spreading from Wall Street around the world, were massive (Nossiter 2015c). "The placard-carrying protesters made up of students, market women, civil society groups commercial vehicle and motorcycle operators, civil servants, business men and women poured into the streets every morning rallying behind leadership of the organised labour and civil society" (Idonor 2012). Public pressure forced the presidency to backpedal but not before the week-long national strike crippled the economy with an estimated US$3.8 billion loss (Ogah et al. 2012).

The administration also suffered a steady stream of criticism when, despite high economic growth rates, government statistics revealed that poverty had been rising. In 2004, half of all Nigerians lived in absolute poverty but, by 2011, six in ten did. Relative poverty was even worse, rising from 54 to nearly 72 percent in the same period (National Bureau of Statistics 2012a). The inverse relationship between economic growth and socio-economic poverty widened a new credibility gap for the administration among citizens. Two Nigerias were emerging: one with high growth rates and macroeconomic indicators rolled out to foreign investors, and another one with rising poverty and low school enrollments. After raising expectations, the economy slowed while objective social conditions deteriorated outside of the lavish lifestyles led in Abuja and other metropolises with access to PDP power.

Then the price of oil plummeted. During a long boom beginning with the Iraq War in 2003 and ending in 2011, the Organization of Petroleum Exporting Countries basket price of crude tripled to US$107. The steep decline in 2014 inconveniently coincided with Jonathan's campaign, with the price dropping below US$50 in early 2015. This drop is illustrated in Figure 3.1. Adding to the sense of panic, the United States had ramped up its domestic production and, in summer 2014, did not import a single barrel from Nigeria for the first time since the 1960s. The Jonathan administration responded much like previous administrations that experienced an exogenous price shock – it borrowed money. Many governors followed suit. For sure, there was bad management, but Jonathan also had some bad luck.

Research Design for Identifying Issue Priorities in the Presidential Campaigns

The 2015 election outcome suggests that citizens did indeed vote on the PDP's record, and the next two chapters will statistically test that proposition. Before turning to voting patterns, though, this chapter focuses on *elite* behavior. More precisely, through a content analysis of hundreds of speeches and public comments, I examine what politicians said in order to distinguish their party from the rival party

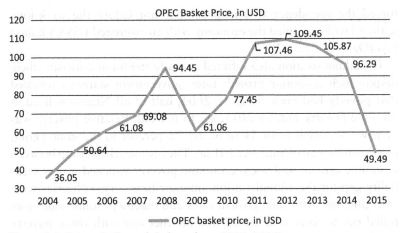

Figure 3.1 Price of oil on global markets, 2004–2015.
Source: Organization of Petroleum Exporting Countries. www.opec.org (accessed February 3, 2017)

and to appeal to voters. I organize their rhetoric into categories, based on the issues identified above by existing research as fundamental to the APC's victory: in/security, electoral integrity, internal party governance, and the economy. For reasons I will explain, corruption is included as a sub-category of the economy. I add "social issues" as a fifth category because political leaders did sometimes discuss topics such as health, education, and women's rights that fall under this heading. Perhaps more importantly, this extra category serves as a way of checking the explanations outlined above; in other words, one of the parties could have campaigned on these issues more than has been noticed by the existing literature. It is also useful to include social issues since they are a traditional staple of parties in Africa.

Methodology

In order to compare the strategies and messaging by each campaign, I conduct a content analysis of approximately 1000 pages of campaign rhetoric by the top three officials from each party during the period between August 2014 and the March 2015 Presidential Election. Though informal campaigning begins early in Nigeria, this period coincides closely with the official political campaign season as well as the formation of the APC. The PDP officials included in the analysis are Goodluck Jonathan, the incumbent president (2010–2015); Doyin Okupe, the Senior Special Assistant on Public Affairs to President; and Adamu Mua'zu, PDP National Working Committee Chairman. The APC officials included are Muhammadu Buhari, the presidential candidate; Lai Mohammed, National Publicity Secretary; and Chibuike Rotimi Amaechi, Director-General of the Presidential Campaign. I chose these six individuals because of their comparable roles and respective power within their parties. For example, a party leader in Amaechi's home state bragged about the former governor's impact on the campaign, saying "Buhari's emergence was at least 60 percent due to Amaechi's input," otherwise the former Vice President Atiku would have prevailed as the party's candidate (Finebone 2017). To interpret such claims and settle on comparable figures in each party, I consulted Nigerian journalists from *Vanguard*, *PUNCH*, and *This Day* newspapers who had covered the presidential election. This provided both an insiders' perspective as well as an independent vetting of my selections for analysis.

The project compiled articles from three major Nigerian daily newspapers: *Vanguard*, *This Day*, and *Daily Trust*. *This Day* and *Daily Trust* have very large circulations and reputations for independence dating back to the military years. A search for the above individuals yielded 2,390 separate articles. The data were then analyzed for direct or indirect quotes from said politicians using NVivo software for content analysis. Approximately 480 articles were eliminated due to duplicate quotes or content that had nothing to do with the presidential campaign. Examples of topics that prompted elimination of articles included coverage of weddings, social engagements, op-eds by others about Jonathan, or speeches discussing Nigerian history (i.e., predating the Fourth Republic). This paring-down of articles not relevant to campaign rhetoric is important because afterwards there were more references to the APC than the PDP in the sample overall. This in itself is an interesting side note on the content of the campaigns; the PDP tended to discuss superficial or more marginally relevant information, relying on familiar routines of campaigning.

Next, a pilot study produced a coding matrix with five nodes, which I refer to as "themes": economy, electoral integrity, party politics, security and insecurity, and social issues. The coding groups in Figure 3.2 identifies each sub-theme under these broader themes. References to the economy include comments about inflation, job

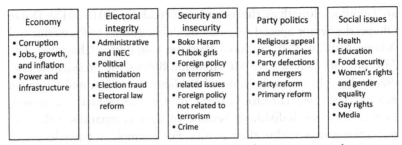

Economy	Electoral integrity	Security and insecurity	Party politics	Social issues
• Corruption • Jobs, growth, and inflation • Power and infrastructure	• Administrative and INEC • Political intimidation • Election fraud • Electoral law reform	• Boko Haram • Chibok girls • Foreign policy on terrorism-related issues • Foreign policy not related to terrorism • Crime	• Religious appeal • Party primaries • Party defections and mergers • Party reform • Primary reform	• Health • Education • Food security • Women's rights and gender equality • Gay rights • Media

Figure 3.2 Coding groups for content analysis of campaign appeals.

creation, or the macroeconomy, as well as discussion of infrastructure (roads, power supply, etc.) Electoral integrity includes references to INEC, including Jega's leadership, as well as proposals for systemic electoral reform or complaints about electoral fraud or intimidation. Security as a category includes mentions of Boko Haram, the kidnapped Chibok girls, and foreign policy in general (distinguishing between terrorism and foreign relations concerns). Comments related to internal party governance, as discussed above, were few in number and closely related to general comments about parties. I therefore grouped them with party politics, a theme covering religious appeals, and discussions about primaries or efforts to reform them, as well as the numerous comments about defecting politicians. Finally, social issues include health, education, food security, gender rights, and a few comments about media coverage. The analysis yielded a total of 929 coded references in the dataset.

I took several important steps to probe the validity of the thematic categories. For instance, I made every effort to code each reference into a specific sub-theme. In the few cases where no sub-theme was relevant, I labeled the text under the primary theme. In addition, some references could be interpreted in different ways or a single sentence might discuss more than one theme. When it was not practical to avoid overlap, phrases were coded more than once. This also occurred in instances when the actual content of the rhetoric by a particular politician was seemingly driven by political or strategic concerns that were different from the literal interpretation of the content. Occasionally, there were multiple interpretations of text too. As a *content* analysis rather than a *discourse* analysis, I therefore coded for the most literal meaning of the text rather than the potentially more opaque interpretation. These standards are consistent with well-known guidelines for qualitative analysis, particularly where the researcher wants to identify the "constituent elements" of a broader phenomenon, as I do here. Simultaneous coding is a standard approach with modestly sized samples, and it generally acknowledges that language is contextual and not simply occurring as isolated units (Saldaña 2015). Some readers might also wonder about my use of newspapers in a country with modest levels of literacy, especially across much of the north. In this regard, it is important to reiterate that this chapter focuses on elite analysis by studying what politicians said (the medium through which people heard the message is therefore less important).

Figure 3.3 provides a helpful visual for understanding the coding process by breaking down frequency through non-numerical representation. It shows the themes and sub-themes with their degree of physical proximity in the chart being directly proportional to the word similarity prevalent in the text coded under said nodes and sub-themes. In other words, the themes and sub-themes that display the greatest similarity of words in terms of text coded under them show the greatest physical proximity in the chart. For example, the economy and the sub-theme of corruption share the greatest degree of word similarity in the chart. This make sense since economy and corruption were typically linked together in political rhetoric. Political violence is specifically mentioned in connection to elections, more closely resembling the idea of intimidation. This is important because it visually illustrates a difference between physical intimidation by party thugs, for example, and Boko Haram's violence. This clustering validates my decision to *not* code electoral tensions with the broader category of insecurity. Moreover, at a conceptual level, most Africans experience electoral violence as intimidation rather than the more spectacular violence resulting in deaths that tends to get more media attention (Burchard 2015; Strauss and Taylor 2012). Nigerian law reflects these realities by including verbal intimidation, hate speech, destruction of property, and disinformation in its definition of electoral violence (Federal Republic of Nigeria 2011, 8).

Campaigning on Counter-Terrorism? Analyzing the Issues and Parties

Which themes came up the most during the presidential campaign? Did the parties choose to emphasize different issues? With insecurity

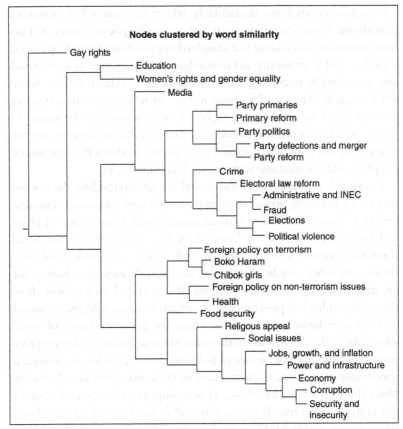

Nodes clustered by word similarity

- Gay rights
- Education
- Women's rights and gender equality
- Media
- Party primaries
- Primary reform
- Party politics
- Party defections and merger
- Party reform
- Crime
- Electoral law reform
- Administrative and INEC
- Fraud
- Elections
- Political violence
- Foreign policy on terrorism
- Boko Haram
- Chibok girls
- Foreign policy on non-terrorism issues
- Health
- Food security
- Religous appeal
- Social issues
- Jobs, growth, and inflation
- Power and infrastructure
- Economy
- Corruption
- Security and insecurity

Figure 3.3 Thematic categories, clustered by word similarity.

foremost in voters' minds, did the PDP campaign on counter-terrorism? This section answers these questions through an analysis of the rhetoric of top figures from the two major parties. The very idea that parties campaign on issues at all would be an important milestone in Nigeria's democratic progress. Much of the literature on Nigerian parties says they do not run on issues (Okoye 1999). One study of Nigeria's political parties shortly after the transition concluded, "so far, there is little sign of an ideologically coherent party system in the country" (Simbine 2002, 56). Another one asserted, "The parties as they currently stand are bereft of concrete ideologies," arguing that even the parties created by the dictatorship in 1993 were better because they had different ideologies and platforms (Aina 2004, 93). During an interview, one party leader in Rivers State lamented, "our politics do not really have a strong ideological ethos. What you see is more of people coming together to do the fundamental thing politicians do – get power" (Finebone 2017). A recent book on parties declares, "there is often an absence of issue based campaigns" in the primaries, and, "there may be a general poverty of issues" (Datau 2014, 158–9).

In order to determine if the choice of campaign issues mattered, I need to do more than describe what the parties talked about, however. I need to establish meaningful differences between the issues emphasized by each party. I therefore empirically compare comments by three leaders in each party. If all three leaders in each party chose to discuss each issue with similar levels of frequency, this would provide some evidence of effective coordination of messaging within the party's campaign. I also sought to triangulate the data with an open-ended question posed to state-level officials and politicians: what issues did your party think were most important in the 2015 election? I then disaggregate the results in order to demonstrate that the APC overwhelmingly campaigned on the issue of economic performance. By doing so, it took a small, calculated political risk given voters' stated concerns about insecurity. Together, these findings form the first step in inferring that campaign rhetoric shaped electoral outcomes.

Stage 1 Tests: Which Issues Came Up the Most in the Presidential Campaign?

There were compelling reasons to expect that security and insecurity would dominate the presidential campaigns. Boko Haram brought Nigeria its bloodiest wave of violence since the civil war (1967–1970). The kidnapping of the Chibok girls had embarrassed the Jonathan administration and introduced an intense new level of civil society mobilization via social media. Finally, as noted above, Gallup had earlier reported that 95 percent of Nigerians saw Boko Haram as a "major threat" to the nation. In a different poll that ranked citizens' priorities a few weeks before the election, 41.6 percent of respondents put security first – above creating jobs (26.1 percent), reducing corruption (15.1 percent), and several other issues (US State Department – sponsored poll 2015). However, the evidence demonstrates – somewhat surprisingly – that neither party gave security primacy in its campaign appeals.

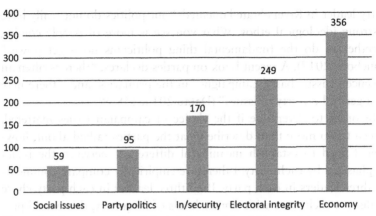

Figure 3.4 Issues mentioned during the presidential campaign.

Figure 3.4 provides a breakdown of issues mentioned during the campaign period. The economy is the most frequently mentioned thematic category, with 356 references. Corruption is the most frequently referenced sub-theme under economy, with 71 references, followed by the sub-themes of power and infrastructure, and jobs, growth, and inflation. The second-most referenced theme is electoral integrity, with 249 references. This included sub-themes (in order of frequency) of political intimidation, administrative and INEC-related issues, and election fraud, followed by electoral law reform. In/security turned out to be the *third*-most referenced theme, with 170 references. This includes sub-themes (in order of frequency) of Boko Haram, Chibok girls, foreign policy on terrorism-related issues, foreign policy on non-terrorism issues, and crime. Although the fourth-most referenced theme is party issues, with 95 total references, including themes and sub-themes, this is due to sub-topics mentioned under this theme (in order of frequency): religious appeal, party primaries, party defections and mergers, party reform, and primary reform. Finally, there are 59 references to social issues, which cover references to health, education, food security, women's rights and gender equality, and media (in order of frequency). There were no mentions of sexual minority rights, which would have been coded under social issues.

One important finding to emerge from this initial, broad analysis is that the economy and corruption were even more important in the campaign than expected. As I demonstrate in the next stage of tests, the

PDP did have a case for economic progress and the need to sustain its "growth agenda," while the APC decided to run against the Jonathan administration on corruption and slowing growth. This evidence will also shape the formulation of tests in the next chapter. It could harbor good news for Nigerian democratic culture if citizens actually voted on these terms instead of clientelism, ethnicity, or other factors traditionally credited with mobilizing African voters. Another key finding concerns the large number of references to issues coded as electoral integrity (249), which even exceed references to Boko Haram and in/ security. Some readers might remain skeptical of my decision to code electoral intimidation and violence under "electoral integrity." If such references are coded under "in/security" (which, as I demonstrated through the word cluster analysis, does not reflect an appropriate contextual representation of those textual references), then in/security ranks second, with 232 references. But the 187 references to electoral integrity are still striking and consistent with my overall conclusions.

Stage 2 Tests: Did the Parties Campaign on Different Issues?

The best strategy for an inchoate opposition party – whose candidate had been defeated in the three previous presidential contests – was not obvious. Should the APC campaign on insecurity, perhaps presenting an alternative counter-terrorism plan? Would it be too risky to run on the economy, since the downturn under Jonathan was so recent? What if the strategic choice is not dichotomous, and the opposition needed just the right mix of issues in its platform? If so, which issues would mobilize voters? I answer these questions in figures that follow by visually illustrating the number of references that each political leader made to each thematic issue. Not only do important differences *between* the APC and PDP emerge, the evidence demonstrates that political leaders *within* each party made similar strategic choices about which issues to discuss during the campaign. I briefly identify how each party campaigned on each issue, for example, contrasting how APC highlighted economic decline while the PDP emphasized economic growth and diversification. The end of the chapter provides a snapshot of the divergence between the two parties. The evidence strongly suggests that the substance of the parties' campaigns differed, and the significant divergences on four out of five issues suggests that the APC struck on a winning portfolio of themes.

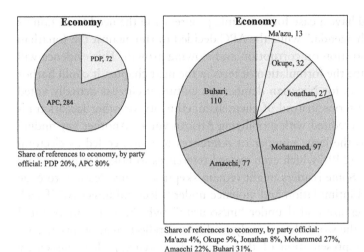

Share of references to economy, by party
official: PDP 20%, APC 80%

Share of references to economy, by party official:
Ma'azu 4%, Okupe 9%, Jonathan 8%, Mohammed 27%,
Amaechi 22%, Buhari 31%.

Figure 3.5 References to the economy, by party and party leaders.

First, I examine references to the economy. According to an Afrobarometer survey administered less than three months before the election, 71 percent of Nigerians said the government was managing the economy "very badly" or "fairly badly." But only 13 percent said economic conditions in the country were "much worse" compared to a year ago (Afrobarometer 2016). No less important for the PDP's hopes was that Nigeria had emerged as the largest economy in Africa, following a much-overdue recalibration of its GDP (Dalby 2014). "Nigeria has declared itself the biggest economy in Africa. Overnight, with the wave of a statistical wand, it has added 89% to its GDP, exceeding South Africa's net worth," wrote *The Economist.* "The GDP revision is not mere trickery," cautioned the editorial, "it provides a truer picture of Nigeria's size by giving due weight to the bits of the economy, such as telecoms, banking and the Nollywood film industry, that have been growing fast in recent years" (*The Economist* 2014). In short, the economy really had grown, and the international business sector had noticed. Figure 3.5 compares the total number of references to the economy (including corruption) by the APC and the PDP, and then breaks down the overall figures according to the political leaders from each party.

A dramatic difference is visible between the parties; PDP leaders mentioned the economy only 72 times, while the APC mentioned it

284 times. The APC highlighted slowing growth, persistent poverty, massive corruption, and rising government debts and inflation. Former President Obasanjo, a founding member of the PDP, famously tore up his membership card while blasting President Jonathan on the economy: "I left a very huge reserve after we had paid all our debts. Almost $25 billion was kept in what they called excess crude, including excess from the budget we were saving as a reserve for rainy days. When we left in May 2007, the reserve was said to have been raised to $35 billion. But today, that reserve has been depleted!" Borrowing money weakened the currency in the face of the country's declining credit rating. With the election just around the corner, the elder statesman urged citizens to evaluate the Jonathan administration's policy performance. "It is now left to you to decide who you cast your vote for ... Find out the track records of achievements of those you want to vote for. What they have achieved in the past and not what they have said" (Olatunji 2015).[5]

Next, I analyze references to election-related issues under the "electoral integrity" category. These references relate to expectations about fair elections and commitments to electoral reforms. There were fears of violence as in 2011, as well as some doubt that the nation would take a step backwards to 2007, when elections failed to meet even minimum standards of credibility (Omotola 2010; Human Rights Watch 2007). Here, we would expect the opposition to highlight the PDP's poor record of organizing elections, and to raise doubts about the ruling party's willingness to let INEC do its job. Figure 3.6 illustrates the total number of references to electoral integrity by the APC and the PDP, and then breaks down the overall figures according to the political leaders from each party.

Once again, there is a significant difference between the parties; APC political leaders mentioned issues related to elections and electoral integrity 162 times, while the PDP brought them up only 87 times. After allowing for a fair playing field, at least in terms of electoral administration, the PDP did not seem take credit for it – even though citizens clearly valued non-interference with INEC. When President Jonathan did not question INEC's budget requests, as noted earlier in Jega's comments, the PDP would have been better served by more

---

[5] See Bamiduro and Oshewolo (2014) and Okonjo-Iweala (2012) for discussion of the debt payoff.

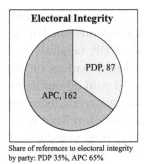

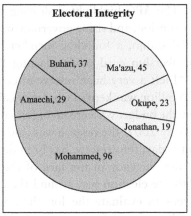

Share of references to electoral integrity, by party official:
Ma'azu 18%, Okupe 9%, Jonathan 8%, Mohammed 38%,
Amaechi 12%, Buhari 15%

Figure 3.6 References to electoral integrity, by party and party leaders.

explicitly identifying this as evidence of its public commitment to electoral integrity. Another lesson seems to be that the hard work of civil society and international electoral assistance has paid off. After four rounds of elections (1999, 2003, 2007, and 2011), the nation has high expectations for electoral conduct and citizens are increasingly savvy about electoral manipulation. More than previously appreciated by the literature, parties recognize electoral integrity as an important issue to campaign on (and apparently, the media sees it as a newsworthy item with a market for readership). This finding supports Lindberg's (2009) claim that even imperfect elections contribute to democratization. They generate expectations of participation and educate citizens about the workings of democracy. The APC's effective use of electoral integrity as a campaign issue helps disaggregate Lindberg's findings, by showing how such expectations were "politicized" (when they became a campaign issue) in a "good" way. Democratic citizens demanded a fair playing field and the parties responded. This increased voters' confidence that a ballot cast for opposition would count. The evidence in Figure 3.7 below, comparing references to party politics, is more mixed but generally consistent with this claim. Again, the figure includes the overall references by party, and then breaks down each party by party leaders.

The PDP referenced issues coded as party politics 47 times, while the APC mentioned them 48 times. As explained in Chapter 2, the PDP

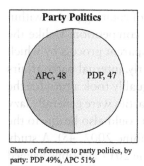

Party Politics

APC, 48   PDP, 47

Share of references to party politics, by
party: PDP 49%, APC 51%

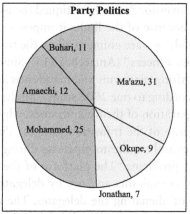

Party Politics

Buhari, 11

Ma'azu, 31

Amaechi, 12

Mohammed, 25

Okupe, 9

Jonathan, 7

Share of references to party politics, by party leader:
Ma'azu 33%, Okupe 9%, Jonathan 7%, Mohammed 26%,
Amaechi 13%, Buhari 12%

Figure 3.7 References to party politics, by party and party leaders.

faced a house more deeply divided than ever before, with a wave of defections contributing to the formation of the APC in 2014. To deter further defections, it resorted to the familiar tactics of threatening members and former members with anti-party behavior as well as embarking on costly (in terms of political capital) litigation in the courts (Fashagba 2014; LeVan 2018).

For voters, the APC primaries in December 2014 revealed a stark contrast between the two major parties. "The APC selected its presidential candidate Muhammadu Buhari in a credible, transparent, and competitive party primary between four candidates broadcast on television across the country," write Owen and Usman. "Simultaneously, President Goodluck Jonathan was unilaterally endorsed in a tightly controlled PDP convention flanked by outgoing state governors" (Owen and Usman 2015, 458). The APC also seemed to take advantage of frustration and blocked ambition within the PDP. Article 21(A) of the APC's constitution established punishments for "alteration of Delegate lists, falsification of nomination results, and or tampering with the processes of internal democracy of the party" – precisely the issues that stimulated the first round of defections from the PDP outlined in the previous chapters.

On these issues, the APC positioned itself to run on positives – almost the opposite of what you would expect from an opposition party. Not long after APC formed, but before he became Buhari's campaign director, Governor Amaechi critiqued the use of rotating power within the party because of the limits it imposes on competition. Unlike the PDP, he said, "we are going to allow the transparent process by which we elect our officers" (Amaechi 2014). Similarly, internal party affairs such as drafting platforms and manifestos arguably took a turn for the better. According to one 2002 study, "all the parties were generally lazy in the preparation of their manifestoes, which could also be due to the rushed nature of the transition process" (Simbine 2002, 45). A study of platform and manifesto processes during the 2011 elections flagged a different problem: "The platform of the political parties is usually written by consultants and not by delegates to the convention" with the effect of alienating the delegates. The author urged those efforts to be "more participatory and democratic," pointing the finger at the PDP in particular (Galadima 2014, 124–7). The old political games of closed primaries, sham caucuses, and godfathers manipulating ballots frustrated both ambitious elites and the large number of citizens demanding democracy in 2015. A PDP party official admitted as much in an interview, tracing the problem back to Obasanjo's efforts to consolidate power in the party after 2003, including his aborted third-term bid. "He was convinced that the only way to control the party was through the governors ... they became like mini-gods." The governor of Enugu State, Sullivan Chime, was selected without the consultation of the party, said the state official, which in retrospect had a tremendous negative impact on the electoral process overall (Olotolo 2017).

Next, I turn to terrorism and insecurity. Here, one might expect similar numbers of references by each party; the APC knew it ranked very high in voters' minds while the PDP had invested time, money, and political capital in demonstrating progress against Boko Haram through the military's six-week offensive that had delayed the elections. Figure 3.8 displays the number of references to the security situation, by party and then by each party leader. The APC mentioned insecurity and the insurgency 98 times, compared to the PDP's 74 references.

This difference between the parties emerged even though the PDP devised a proactive strategy to promote the view that it was making progress. It first got the security chiefs to urge INEC to delay the election so they would have time to roll back Boko Haram. In late 2014, Boko Haram had successfully taken over strategic towns in the northeast. Because of the focus on territory, international experts

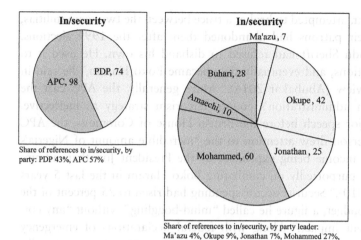

Figure 3.8 References to in/security, by party and party leaders.

quickly drew parallels with the Islamic State, while Nigerian analysts worried that the particular areas being seized were positioning Boko Haram to win the city of Maiduguri. It already controlled most of Sambisa Forest and much of the northeastern the border with Chad and Cameroon; now it sought a prized state capital (AllAfrica.com 2014; Adenusi et al. 2014; Marama 2014). After making some gains, with the help of foreign mercenaries from South Africa and elsewhere, the military could point to maps of reclaimed territories (Abubakar 2016; Nossiter 2015b). The Jonathan administration also went on a public relations offensive. It dispatched the country's two top intelligence officials to Washington, DC to proclaim progress against terrorism in public presentations in February 2015. At the same time, the PDP counter-narrative blamed the United States and other foreign powers for failing to provide them with military assistance (Agence France Press 2015). In a similar fashion, the party also tried to blame the opposition for the rise of Boko Haram by not sufficiently supporting the Jonathan administration's policies in the northeast. "They were against emergency rule in the north-eastern states and the proscription of the Boko Haram sect," a spokesperson said. "Without APC, there will be no Boko Haram and without Boko Haram there will be no APC" (Umoru 2015).

The APC had a clear response to the last allegation, pointing to evidence that Boko Haram originated in militias formed by PDP politicians in the early 2000s. The vice president at the time, Atiku

Abubakar, attempted to broker a truce between the two main militias, since their patrons had abandoned them after the 1999 elections. "Ali Modu Sheriff had refused to disband his own. He used it to win elections, and eventually they became Boko Haram," he said in an interview (Abubakar 2016).[6] More generally, the APC cast the Jonathan administration's counter-terrorism strategy as ineffective. In a major speech before the British House of Commons, the APC spokesperson drew attention to the "incredible amount of Nigeria's national income being expended, by the President Jonathan administration purportedly on combating Boko Haram in the last 5 years (since 2010)." Security-sector spending had risen to 25 percent of the annual budget, a figure he called "mind-boggling" without "any correspondent impact." Along with federal declarations of emergency rule in three northeastern states, Boko Haram "has become a political gimmick by the PDP now being counted as the GEJ [Jonathan] achievement in promoting peace and security" (Mohammed 2014b). He also noted that the states under emergency rule were all opposition-held states, enabling media crackdowns and restrictions on civil society. Further, the insurgency allegedly improved the PDP's electoral chances by suppressing turnout; not only were millions of internally displaced persons facing huge administrative barriers to voting, those who remained in the most violent northeast states might not vote at all out of fear of terrorism. He gave a similar speech to the Center for Strategic and International Studies in Washington, DC.

The APC also effectively seized on the Jonathan administration's missteps with the kidnapped Chibok girls. "With his utterances and actions or inaction, President Jonathan has deepened the pains of the parents and guardians of the girls, and indeed that of the whole nation, when he should have been the consoler-in-chief at such a difficult time for a nation he leads," said one APC statement. Referring to the president's canceled trip to Chibok, the APC further said, "A President and Commander-in-Chief, who is afraid to visit any part of his country, has betrayed the very people who voted him into office"

---

[6] To be clear, Abubakar was a member of the APC at the time of this interview. Sheriff has denied the allegations and some authors note that the evidence is circumstantial in nature (Smith 2015). But other sources, including the Borno Elders Forum and members of the Northern Elders Forum, point the finger at Sheriff (Abdullah 2016).

(Soriwei et al. 2014). Such critiques were even more pronounced at the state level. Recalling a Boko Haram attack on Gombe City, a party leader exclaimed, "There was each day a bomb blast. We had buried our people and so the insecurity issue ... the issue of Chibok girls too was a major concern for every one of us. These were the issues for me that were really very strong" (Ahaya 2016).

In addition, the APC made "comprehensive military reform" a talking point, calling for hiring 100,000 new police, along with pay increases and capacity improvements to the military services (Adeyemo et al. 2015). The party manifesto called for an audit of the security services to identify outdated equipment and large increases in military personnel levels, and promised to root out inefficiency (All Progressives Congress 2015b). Credible news reports, foreign intelligence, and other sources had begun to constitute a compelling body of evidence about large-scale corruption in the military (Page 2016), which helped make such language resonate with voters.

Both parties therefore offered ideas for defeating terrorism. The PDP advanced a military strategy to take back territory, hoping that it would psychologically destroy Boko Haram and deprive it of space it claimed to govern. The APC promised to hire more police, purge the military of corruption, and establish a new office to coordinate inter-agency efforts against terrorism (All Progressives Congress 2015b, 2015a).

Figure 3.9 provides a breakdown for references to social issues, the last of the five categories of the content analysis. Recall that the existing literature on the 2015 elections does not highlight performance on social policy among the explanations for President Jonathan's defeat (Lewis and Kew 2015; Siollun 2015), meaning that one function of this category within my research design is to see if a theme popular in African campaigns is missing from the existing research. The relatively modest number of overall references (69) suggests the literature on Nigeria's 2015 election is accurate in this regard. However, there is a notable difference between the two parties once again. The APC devoted much more attention to social issues such as health, education, and women's rights, mentioning them twice as often (39 times) as the PDP (20).

Despite the bad news about poverty rates and other social indicators from the National Bureau of Statistics widely discussed in the media, President Jonathan did have some basis for campaigning on a positive record of performance in the social sector. His administration bragged

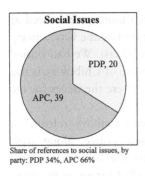

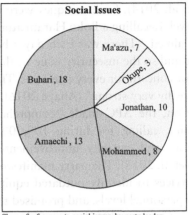

Figure 3.9 References to social issues, by party and party leaders.

about "life-saving initiatives, the dwindling figures in infant and maternal mortality, the eradication of guinea worm," and improvement in hospital infrastructure (Douglas 2014, 9). A report released in cooperation with the United Nations Development Programme assessing progress towards the Millennium Development Goals (MDG) for 2015 bore some good news for his administration, including declines in infant mortality and increases in immunization rates for diseases such as Polio and Diphtheria-Pertussis and Tetanus (DPT). Maternal mortality declined and the access to skilled birth attendants (such as midwives) increased. The gender disparity in education at the primary and secondary level virtually disappeared, prompting the report to conclude that Nigeria achieved the MDC target by enrolling one female for every male. The year 2014 also saw a slight increase in women's literacy and in secondary-school attendance rates (National Bureau of Statistics 2015).

There was room for improvement, since the MDG report noted that schools also saw declines in primary school attendance and completion rates. Significant regional disparities remained, Jonathan acknowledged in an interview with journalists, and this was why the role of the federal government remained so important. When he came into office, nine northern states had no federal university; within roughly three years, his administration had built one school in each state. "For you to liberate any group of human beings, whether they are from the Southern creeks or from the North, it is education," he said (Ohiomokhare 2013, 210).

Independent indicators of women's status also reported progress under the Jonathan administration. For example, one empirical study of women's participation begins with the caveat that "appointment into positions of authority is infinitesimal compared to their male counterpart of the same age" due to deeply rooted cultural practices extending back to colonialism. The authors then document important strides in offices held by women under Jonathan, compared to previous administrations. "This improvement is as a result of fulfilled promise of the president to implement the National Gender Policy of 2008 that supports the 35 percent affirmative action plan of women representation in government" (Gberevbie and Oviasogie 2013, 103). Given this scorecard, it is surprising that the PDP did not highlight it more frequently. This may be an important lesson for future elections.

The APC appears to have capitalized on this inattention to social issues, and advanced a compelling critique. "Only 3% of the population have health insurance and there are too many competing and ineffective agencies," declared the party platform. As for schools, it said the "education system is a scandal. There are now 10 million school age children out of school" and only 8.6 percent of government spending goes to education (All Progressives Congress 2015b). Empirics back this up. Simulated statistical models projected that the administration needed to invest much more on education in order to meet the MDGs and poverty reduction targets (Odior 2014). Another study found that by lagging far behind in capital spending, the Jonathan administration further undercut social investments necessary for poverty reduction. Only 51 percent of capital expenditures had been spent as of the end of 2012. The authors attribute the poor implementation to bad planning, slow bureaucratic release of funds, lack of budget monitoring, and delays in budget passage. The information also of course raises other profound questions about where the unspent 49 percent of the funds went. Overall, the authors conclude that this rate of spending is insufficient to foster rapid economic development and reduce poverty (Ogujiuba and Ehigiamusoe 2014).

In sum, the Jonathan administration made progress, but the APC's critique was fair. And while it is important to not overstate the findings here given the relatively small number of overall references to social issues, the APC's political leaders brought up social issues twice as often as the PDP. Voters heard critiques of health, education, gender,

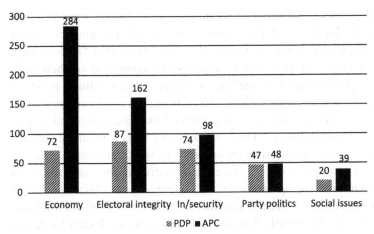

Figure 3.10 References to issue content of the APC and PDP campaigns.

and related policies twice as often as the "good" news from Jonathan and his team.

Conclusion

Existing literature often views African parties as devoid of meaningful differences, campaigning on ethnic appeals or staple issues such as anti-corruption, health care, and education. As Africa's experience with democracy deepens, the evidence from Nigeria's 2015 presidential election so far indicates that this somewhat cynical picture is changing. Across four out of the five issue areas examined, the APC referenced those themes in the campaign more frequently than the PDP. Figure 3.10 concisely summarizes these differences. This constitutes evidence of a pattern in campaign rhetoric of the winning party. "At the national level the APC decided to dwell around three areas," said a state party leader in an interview. "And that is what we did at the grassroots. The issue of insecurity. The issue of corruption. And the issue of the economy" (Ahaya 2016).

The APC built an electoral coalition on the basis of parties and interests from different parts of the country – from Governor Tinubu in the southwest to Governor Amaechi in the Niger Delta to the popular politician El-Rufai in Kadua in the north-central area. It offered a new logic of coalition-building based on issues and not just geography. Those issues provided a mixed-portfolio strategy. The "rational" counter-terrorist in the election was the politician who could align national insecurity with voter priorities. The APC correctly calculated that it could not win on counter-terrorism alone.

Five findings stand out from this figure and the preceding content analysis of over 2,390 articles in three of Nigeria's independent daily newspapers. First, with 356 total references, the parties campaigned on the economy (and corruption) more often than any other issue. "Going in to the 2015 election," says an APC party leader in Rivers State, "the corruption had become so high that he [Jonathan] lost the goodwill of the southwest," referring to the Yoruba region that threw its support behind Buhari and the APC (Finebone 2017). To some observers this might not be surprising, but recall I presented extensive survey evidence documenting that Nigerians were more worried about insecurity and terrorism. In this sense, the APC's decision to emphasize the economy constitutes a small but calculated risk that paid off. Counter-terrorism by itself was hardly rational; economic issues were the key to a winning strategy.

A second, also somewhat unexpected finding concerns the priority that both campaigns gave electoral integrity. This suggests that the APC saw a voting constituency concerned about the quality of elections and the party set out to capture it. This also implies that the massive international and domestic attention that Nigeria's elections regularly receive has educated party elites about democratic expectations. Since Jega noted that the Jonathan administration deserves credit for leaving INEC alone, one could say that the PDP did not sufficiently take credit for its progress regarding electoral integrity. However, respect for Jega is also only one dimension of electoral integrity, and on the matter of internal party democracy the PDP was the architect of its own defeat, according to a former party chair for Plateau State. By blocking candidates and routinely limiting political opposition, the "buildup for opposition was becoming stronger and stronger." The 2015 elections distinguished themselves from the old ways of doing business (Akun 2016).

A third, related finding concerns the significant *difference* between the parties on electoral integrity. The APC mentioned these issues 162 times while the PDP did so only 87 times. In fact, the parties made a similar number of references only with regard to party politics. President Jonathan said, "One thing that I want to leave behind is that elections in Nigeria are credible ... The world should know that our method of electing those who govern us either at the executive level, governors, chairmen of local governments or presidents or at the parliamentary level are duly elected by their people" (Clottey 2013). Though the elections fulfilled Jonathan's wish, the APC appears to have made more effective use of electoral integrity as a campaign issue. By doing so, this also helps to disaggregate Lindberg's findings about the learning effects of repeating the ritual of elections; by becoming a major part of the campaign itself, democratic expectations were "politicized" with positive connotations.

Fourth, the PDP made a visible effort to emphasize its proactive military strategy. In the face of lingering accusations about PDP elites' links to Boko Haram and ongoing embarrassment from the #BringBackOurGirls movement, the administration's national security team presented evidence of recaptured territory. However, the APC advanced a compelling critique of the administration's consistent mis-handling of the Chibok families, in addition to critiquing the national security team's approach. It offered military reform as a central plank in its platform, which had organically emerged from earlier victories against the PDP in debates over the Anti-Terrorism Law.

Finally, the relatively low priority given social issues is worth noting. Like campaigning on anti-corruption, promises to spend more in areas such as health and education had long been a staple of African polit-ical parties (Hyden 2013; Basedau et al. 2007). Sexual minority rights remain completely taboo. Women's rights came up only a handful of times, again, even though women's socio-economic condition and political standing had arguably improved slightly under President Jonathan's administration. The next chapter elaborates on this ana-lysis, emphasizing the PDP's error.

These findings add an empirical layer of nuance and detail to our understanding of what African political parties actually talk about. Since there were significant differences between the winning party and the losing party on the issues, this analysis also provides information about what wins; even in the face of the bloodiest violence since the civil war (or at least since the Maitatsine uprising in the early 1980s), the APC campaigned on the economy, corruption, and electoral integ-rity. As is visible in Figure 3.10, the APC had more total references overall, and some skeptical readers might flag this as biasing the results. It is therefore important to remember that this occurred after the elimination of the PDP's references to weddings and similar matters.

The APC's larger number of references could also be interpreted as important in a different way; the APC did a better job getting its policy positions covered, while the PDP perhaps spent too much time practising old patronage-based campaigning that failed to highlight its platform. In a sense, the PDP continued with the elitist modality of organizing rooted in the party's origins outlined in Chapter 2.

It is also important to clarify what this study does not do. A content analysis neither assesses whether a party lived up to its promises by evaluating implementation, nor does it evaluate the truthfulness of parties' claims.[7] Also, as a study of campaign rhetoric, it is explicitly a study of political elites. We have not yet examined how citizens actually decided to vote. In the next two chapters, I take on that task. Statistical evidence complements the findings here by identifying patterns of voting behavior and, separately, voting outcomes across states. The tests indicate that Nigerian citizens did indeed vote according to what Obasanjo above called the administration's "track records of achievement."

---

[7] For example, PDP campaign material stated that 9 percent of Nigerians had health care while the APC campaign pegged the figure at 3 percent.

4 | Voting against Violence? Economic Uncertainty and Physical Insecurity in 2015

In South Yola Local Government Area, in a bucolic village accessible only by foot, the village chief began his interview with me by complaining, "The governor himself came here to ask for the vote. But none of them have helped." On top of familiar challenges such as cattle thieves, access to potable water, and too few reservoirs where the estimated one million cattle roaming the region can drink, he worried about increasing tensions with farmers and caring for the hundreds of displaced persons fleeing Boko Haram whom he had welcomed into the community. Why weren't the ethnic Fulani, who had dominated politics for so long, helping their people? "It's a class issue," he said. "They don't see this as their problem" (Chief of a village near Girei 2016). The economic critique that formed the core of the opposition campaign's rhetoric not only distinguished the APC from its rival; it also appealed to people like the chief, whose village had been left out of the economic largesse during years of macroeconomic growth. In 2011, President Jonathan prevailed over Buhari in Adamawa State with 56 percent of all valid votes. In 2015, the tables turned against the PDP. The newly formed APC, with Buhari at its helm, swept the state with 59 percent of the vote. Since local Fulani (and various minorities) had voted for PDP in in the past, the APC needed something other than ethnic appeals to convert voters in the remote village outside Girei town. Was the average voter in any given state more inspired by the APC's economic alternative or by its critique of counter-terrorism?

The previous chapter demonstrated that the presidential campaigns of the two major parties significantly differed on four out of five issues. This chapter compliments that analysis of elite behavior by presenting empirical evidence that patterns of electoral outcomes across states strongly correlate with the economic issues emphasized by the APC. Perceptions of national economic performance, average levels of citizens' wealth, and expectations for whether Buhari or Jonathan was more likely to improve the economy all systematically correlate with presidential electoral outcomes. Further, control variables in these tests show that where states had healthy economies, voters were risk-averse and overwhelmingly voted to keep the PDP. Meanwhile, states struggling economically voted for Buhari's promises and the APC. Other tests suggest that the critique of counter-terrorism was less important. Neither proximity to violence nor the level of government security presence systematically shaped electoral outcomes at the state level. This is surprising given the scale and scope of Boko Haram's terrorism as well as numerous polls indicating nationwide frustration with insecurity. All of the tests hold across a range of variables controlling for economic and social contexts, including ethnicity.

The first section of this chapter reviews relevant literature on voting behavior, mostly in Africa, in order to inform my hypothesis formulation and to situate Nigeria's 2015 election within broader comparative discussions. For many years, African elections seemed dominated by clientelist relationships or ethnic appeals. Such motivations for voting were often rooted in colonial practices that favored some "tribes" over others, creating ethnic cleavages that remained salient long after the post-colonial era and into the democratization of the 1990s. Research increasingly suggests that ethnic voting is contingent upon context or institutions, and that programmatic appeals to voters are often effective. In addition, evidence from numerous countries with histories of clientelism points to a rise in "economic voting" based on evaluations of policy performance or subjective assessments of economic conditions. Other scholars explore topics such as vote buying and electoral violence (by political parties or candidates' thugs), with comparably little research about how terrorist violence shapes voter behavior in the developing world.

Second, I formulate two hypotheses and outline the variables I use to test each one. A "national in/security" hypothesis explores how violence and insecurity, and Boko Haram's terrorism in particular, shaped voting behavior. One version of this hypothesis considers proximity to violence, expecting higher levels of violence to correspond with support for the APC. Another considers the effects of state penetration, predicting that in states with more police, voters feel pressured into voting for the PDP. Next, I formulate an "economic voting" hypothesis. It predicts that citizens voted based on objective economic conditions as well as their subjective evaluations of the incumbent administration's national policy performance. I also test to see if optimism about each candidate's promises to improve the economy corresponded with electoral outcomes. This is an important question since opposition parties face significant challenges in making credible promises, especially if they have never held power before, as was the case with the APC.

In the third section, I test these two hypotheses under different statistical specifications. I start by describing extant data sets and operationalizing my dependent variable (the outcome I am seeking to explain) as the change in the ruling party's vote share between the 2011 and the 2015 presidential elections. I also outline variables that control for various economic, social, and political conditions that could interfere with the hypothesized relationships. Tests of the national in/security hypothesis are somewhat mixed. There is no systematic relationship between proximity to violence and support for the opposition party. Nor is there any statistically significant relationship between police presence and electoral outcomes. In some ways, this is unexpected since, as noted in the previous chapter, citizens repeatedly listed insecurity as their foremost concern. It also raises questions about some of the existing literature about electoral violence. However, using survey questions asking about whether "extremist attacks" would increase under Jonathan or Buhari, I find that PDP voters overwhelmingly feared that violence would *increase* under Buhari. Read alongside Chapter 3's findings, this suggests that the PDP played to its base, while the APC managed to build a larger political coalition by focusing on the economy and the issues that more voters found appealing.

Next, I find robust statistical support for the economic voting hypothesis. Across thirty-six states (plus the capital), voters with negative assessments of the national economy over the previous twelve months were more likely to support the APC. States with weaker economies were also more likely to cast their vote with the opposition. Most compellingly, the cross-sectional evidence suggests that Buhari's inspirational message for improving the economy appealed to a broad base of voters. In sum, all four models offer strong support for the economic performance hypothesis. The statistically significant values of a variable measuring state-level debt in all eight of the chapter's tests reinforces this conclusion, and has important implications for comparative fiscal federalism; internal revenue generation might help gauge fiscal ties to the center, but it is subnational debt that really endows the party controlling the center with tremendous political leverage at election time.

The conclusion interprets these results and draws out implications. Taken together with the previous chapter, one observation is that the APC's political strategy largely worked. "It is too late in the day for President Jonathan to engage in sophistry over the twin evil of corruption and insecurity," said the APC spokesperson just weeks before the election. "He has reached the limit of his capacity to tackle these challenges and it is time to allow those with necessary political will and capacity to take on the challenges before they crush the country" (Usman and Agande 2015). Despite overwhelming national concern about terrorism, party leaders calculated that the economy and corruption would resonate more deeply with voters. Nigerians in the 2015 election joined voters in other young African democracies who increasingly evaluate policy performance rather than merely gravitating toward ethnic loyalties or clientelist promises. In doing so, Nigerians also exercised a measure of power over elites who had managed or limited popular participation trough the transition's founding bargain.

Historical and Contemporary Contexts of Research on Voting Behavior

How do Africans decide who to vote for? Answers to this question generated unexpected complexities for the post-colonial generation. During decolonization in the 1950s and 1960s, social movements demanding independence or "self-rule" entered electoral politics as political parties with mass bases rooted in unions, women's groups, student organizations, and other groups (Hyden 2013). Nationalist leaders' demands for the pace and scope of change varied. In Kenya, for example, clear ideological and tactical divergences emerged between "constitutionalist" moderates and more radical activists who went underground to fight (Throup 1985). Broad social movements held together by an overarching opposition to colonialism saw their bonding glue weaken in the face of the electoral politics that replaced imperial rule. Independence-era regimes proffered competing legacies of freedom and unity in the anti-colonial struggles (Cheeseman 2015). Where African colonies such as Angola or Mozambique waged violent liberation struggles for independence, or where "majority-rule rebels" fought for democracy in white settler colonies such as Rhodesia, political cleavages tacked closely with competing Cold War ideologies (Reno 2011).

Among ordinary voters and intellectuals today, it is not hard to find nostalgia for coherent and competing ideologies. "One is struck by the ideological homogeneity of Nigerian political parties, names and slogans apart," writes an author in the journal of one of Nigeria's leading think tanks (Tyoden 2013, 5). Nigeria's Obafemi Awolowo, the premier of the Western Region in the First Republic (1960–1966), remains widely admired for his willingness to stay in the opposition in order to defend his democratic socialist vision as an alternative post-colonial path (Adebanwi 2014). "Our politics do not really have an ideological ethos," lamented an APC party leader from Rivers State (Finebone 2017). One study concludes that African parties generally offer some "descriptive representation" for various social groups and civil society interests, but "evidence of more substantive, responsive representation" is "much harder to find" (Randall 2007, 101). A recent study mentions Kenya as an example where ideological differences "are generally not salient in politics" (Kramon 2016, 455). Sharp ideological distinctions historically presented voters with relatively clear choices and placed African political parties within a broader world of politics or, in the case of Kwame Nkrumah's Ghana, into a coherent and compelling defiance of Cold War global alignments via Pan-Africanism. In all cases, though, politicians seeking national power had to contend with the lasting effects of colonialism's "reifi-cation of tribe" (Cheeseman 2015, 23). Ethnicity (the term now typic-ally preferred over "tribes") offered a convenient cleavage for electoral mobilization. With the disappearance of Cold War ideological rival-ries, ethnicity remained an appealing alternative mobilizational tool for politicians.

The swift rise of electoral democracy, or "re-democratization" in the early 1990s, captivated global audiences with images of opposition organizing as dictators and dominant parties fell one after another at the polls. As scholars turned to understand trends such as civil society resistance (Harbeson et al. 1994; Bratton and Van de Walle 1997) or the return to multi-party politics (Widner 1994; Diamond and Plattner 1999), the study of parties in and of themselves suffered. Until fairly recently, this left a gap in our understanding of party systems in the so-called Third Wave of democracy. This literature review discusses some of this important new scholarship on parties and voting in Africa. Major themes include electoral violence, ethnic loyalties, and debates over whether parties campaign on programmatic appeals or clientelistic promises. This summary of existing research situates my own study of Nigeria's 2015 election within broader debates.

Votes and Violence

Violence has been an important theme in research on democratic transitions. Mansfield and Snyder) identify violence (and inter-state "aggression") as a major risk in transitioning countries, worrying in particular that nationalism can be awakened during transitions. By the late 1990s, it also became clear that a huge portion of the countries undergoing democratic transitions would hold elections without actually meeting other democratic standards. These "hybrid," semi-authoritarian, or "electoral authoritarian" regimes (Schedler 2006) lacked rule of law, freedom of the press, or adequate civil liberties (Levitsky and Way 2010). In a well-known book, Collier (2009) argues that holding elections at all in such countries actually increases the risk of political violence. Scholars such as Huntington were quick to blame electoral violence on old assumptions about ethnicity. "In many situations the easiest way to win votes is to appeal to tribal, ethnic, and religious constituencies. Democratization thus promotes communalism and ethnic conflict" (Huntington 1997, 6). The literature has since become careful about lumping ethnicity and electoral violence together so loosely (Mehler 2007; Varshney 2007). The headline-grabbing large-scale violence of the sort seen in Kenya in 2007 or Zimbabwe in 2008 is relatively rare (LeVan 2011a). Nevertheless, electoral violence does occur with unfortunate frequency – in 58 percent of all African elections compared to only about 19 percent globally. "Even more alarming," writes Burchard, "is the fact that since the proliferation of multiparty elections in the early 1990s the vast majority of African countries – 86 percent – have experienced electoral violence" (Burchard 2015, 11).[1]

This chapter builds on this research but differs in at least three ways. First, even though electoral violence is common, "elections per se are

---

[1] This is a slight increase from an earlier study of over 200 elections in Africa that found electoral violence occurred 80 percent of the time (Lindberg 2004).

not the main drivers of violence in sub-Saharan Africa"; in fact, non-election years are typically more violent than election years (Strauss and Taylor 2012, 33). I seek to understand how more generalized violence shapes the electoral context and party competition. Second, much of the research as well as the work of donors focuses on finding the causes of election violence (Sisk and Reynolds 1998; Bekoe 2012). For example, one survey of the literature lists both economic stress and the uncertainty generated by democratic transitions as common causes of electoral violence in Africa. "Even after third and fourth round rounds of competitive elections, Africa is still in a difficult process of transition" (Laakso 2007, 226). By contrast, this study is more interested in the *consequences* of violence. In this less-explored area of research, Burchard finds that fear of violence suppresses voter turnout, and those who fall into this category are also less likely to believe their country is democratic or to express satisfaction with democracy (Burchard 2015). For Nigeria, the context of possible violence shapes post-transition political processes in subtle but important ways.

Third, we have a comparatively weak basis for understanding how terrorism influences elections in the developing world, as noted in the book's Introduction. For example, one study of Israel finds that the incumbent party alters its counter-terrorism strategy during election time in order to appeal to core voters – even if that strategy potentially provides less security (Nanes 2016). That study is premised on a continuum of political positions that does not really exist in Nigeria or most of Africa, with "hawks" on the right and "doves" on the left. Also, without a history of party turnover, as in Nigeria, it is difficult to reliably identify and target "swing" voters who can be persuaded. The ways that terrorism in particular shapes party systems, campaign platforms, or voting behavior is less well understood. Thus, unlike numerous studies examining the causes of Boko Haram (Thurston 2018; Smith 2015; Comolli 2015), here, I am more interested in its broad effects.

Patrons versus Programs in African Elections

Another major research agenda in the study of African politics concerns whether elections are decided based on promises of ethnic patronage or if programs and policy platforms are becoming more important. On one level, objective economic conditions could drive variation in voting behavior. For example, Arriola's study of Ethiopia's 2005 elections finds that local economic conditions influenced voting patterns much more than ethnoregional politics (Arriola 2008). On another level, subjective perceptions of economic performance could shape voter preferences. Norris and Mattes (2013) rely on Afrobarometer survey data to document the declining political salience of ethnicity. Elischer agrees, but he also offers the thoughtful critique that research on party systems has relied too much on survey data. Moreover, foreign aid donors' push for democratizing countries to develop programmatic parties has generally clouded our understanding of party development. Donors tend to imagine stable, mass-based parties as indicators of an institutionalized party system. To understand the relationship between voters and parties, research needs to consider the historical conditions of party formation, organizational structure, and other factors (Elischer 2013).

Another large body of literature on the economic logic of voting explores the extent to which voters are motivated by direct benefits to their private welfare, or if they assess the economy in terms of broader, non-excludable public goods. In the case of the former, voters receive some concrete and excludable benefit, whether it is a bribe, another type of private compensation (monetary or otherwise), or a clientelist relationship. Clientelism refers to "the giving of material resources as a quid pro quo for political support," which Stokes says "is best understood as part of an ongoing exchange between patron and clients, with threats of defection, instead of, or perhaps in addition to, norms of reciprocity sustaining it" (Stokes 2007, 623).

Across the developing world, a central question of this literature on the electoral politics of economic distribution is whether parties run on broad programmatic appeals to change policy, or if their winning strategies depend upon the provision of excludable benefits such as those generated by patron–client relationships. Research from Indonesia, for example, finds that when both patronage and national policy changes are on the table, poor or less-educated voters prefer payoffs such as money or jobs (Shin 2015). In Egypt, voters value candidates who can offer them patronage in the form of jobs even more than those who share their ideology, but interestingly are willing to discount this for candidates who articulate a "pro-change ideology" for the political leadership (Al-Ississ and Atallah 2014). In Africa, clientelism undoubtedly still exists, both on the supply side from politicians and in the form of voter demands (Posner 2005). But electoral democracy increases the political risks of non-inclusive distribution (Acemoglu and Robinson 2012). One study of voting behavior in eighteen countries finds that "outsiders" who lack access to government patrons, and are therefore excluded from the benefits of clientelism, are much more likely to support opposition candidates (Chang and Kerr 2016). There is also evidence of more direct inducements. For example, Bratton's (2013a) study of Nigeria's 2007 elections found widespread evidence of vote buying. Although efforts to buy the vote clearly occurred in 2015, they largely failed.[2] In one well-publicized blunder, Jonathan's campaign allegedly offered traditional Yoruba leaders large bribes in order to win the southwest (*The Punch* 2015). The effort failed, and the southwest states voted overwhelmingly for Buhari and the APC. "This was the first time Nigerians were saying no to money," said a state PDP leader reflecting on the positive changes in national elections (Akun 2016).

A decline of bribery and clientelism also seems compatible with the mounting evidence cited by Basedau (2011; Basedau et al. 2007), Elischer (2013) and others that African parties see the electoral benefits of programmatic appeals. In a surprising range of cases, parties effectively mobilize voters with policy-based platforms because they generate a broader voter base. Lindberg and Morrison's (2008) study of two rounds of elections in Ghana, for example, found that rational evaluation of politics and policy outweighed "non-evaluative" considerations, such as patronage or ethnic ties. One study of Uganda found vote buying to be ineffective in 2010–2011, suggesting that national economic performance and increased public safety enhanced the incumbents' prospects, in the eyes of surveyed citizens (Conroy-Krutz and Logan 2013). Winning elections requires the construction of broad elite coalitions, and providing a non-excludable public good to your partners is often more efficient that trying to pay each one off through clientelist exchanges (Bueno de Mesquita et al. 2003; LeVan et al. 2018).

---

[2] In a survey a few weeks before the election, 57 percent of respondents said that politicians offered them money – though tellingly only 28 percent of the 3,953 respondents in the sample were willing to answer the question at all (US State Department – sponsored poll 2015).

Information Cues for Economic Voting

Another area of research focuses on how parties prompt voters to shift their preferences by lowering information costs through "signaling." Kramon, for example, argues that Stokes' model of clientelism mischaracterizes vote buying in Africa. Patronage is relevant, he argues, but the problem for opposition candidates is their inability to make credible promises. His study of "electoral handouts" in Kenya demonstrates that they are not about "direct exchange for the subsequent political behavior of recipients but instead as an instrument through which politicians convey information to voters" (Kramon 2016, 490). Thus, the problem for opposition parties in Africa is whether voters believe the candidate can deliver on promises, not necessarily their access to resources. On the other side of the debate, among the research assessing the utility of programmatic appeals, is evidence of "economic voting." For example, Hart (2013) argues that parties can (or need to) "prime" voters by signaling the importance of the economy before citizens will actually vote on economic performance.

In either case, whether parties are running on patronage or on programmatic appeals, their ability to create a market for their ideas and lower the costs of information conditions voting behavior. To win, opposition parties do not only need to offer a thoughtful and viable alternative, they need messaging that effectively shapes the content of presidential campaigns by recalibrating voters' priorities. (This does not mean that all messaging is effective.) Kenya's 2013 election provides an example: incumbent Raila Odinga built a coalition based on implementation of the 2010 constitution, anti-corruption, and a critical posture toward the International Criminal Court. However, Uhuru Kenyatta pivoted to other issues, constructing an inter-ethnic coalition on security, employment, and the economy, prevailing over the incumbent in the election (Ferree et al. 2014). If the evidence in this chapter shows that Nigerian voters voted on the priorities set by political parties as defined by the previous chapter, rather than the issues voters identified as most important, this will suggest that APC successfully "primed" voters on economic issues, voting out Africa's largest political party, the PDP.

Some skeptical readers might wonder, don't voters always vote on economic interests? Perhaps, but if so, then it should be harder for incumbent parties to win elections during economic downturns. Moreover, as documented in the previous chapter, both parties had a good case to make to voters on the economy; the APC could campaign on anti-corruption, slowing growth, or rising inequalities, while the PDP could credibly run on economic diversification and overall economic expansion over President Jonathan's five years in office. Thus, what matters is both economic conditions *and* how voters see those conditions. The evidence in Chapter 3 strongly suggests that the APC articulated a compelling and credible economic critique.

Three observations emerge from this literature review and inform my hypothesis formulation in this chapter and in Chapter 5. First, there are good reasons to expect that if Nigerians did indeed vote on assessments of economic performance in 2015, they are in good company on the continent. Where programmatic party appeals have been effective, it has been an encouraging sign for African democracy by reinforcing the strategic electoral benefits (and not just the normative value) of mutli-ethnic coalitions. Second, it is difficult for voters to engage in "economic voting" on their own, meaning that parties or some other intermediate institution needs to lower the information costs of evaluating status quo policies. In some countries, civil society might be able to perform that role. But political parties have an underlying self-interest in undertaking this task, and doing so theoretically increases electoral competitiveness. Third, research on electoral violence is relatively narrow. It tends to focus on finding micro and macro "triggers" of violence, identifying party thugs, or making programmatic recommendations to reduce the likelihood of violence. I do not want to discount the importance of these topics. Instead, I seek to expand the literature by considering the *effects* of violence and terrorism – such as Boko Haram's – on voting patterns.

Hypotheses and Predictions

In the previous chapter, I mentioned how President Obasanjo, who won the 1999 transition's founding elections and served until 2007, urged voters in 2015 to vote on the Jonathan administration's record. I also documented how leaders of the two major political parties, the APC and the incumbent PDP, discussed the economy far more than any other issue during the presidential campaign. This was somewhat surprising given the priority citizens accorded security, the wave of violence that preceded the election, and the potential strategic benefits of campaigning on counter-terrorism.

In this section, I formulate two hypotheses to see if electoral outcomes across states correspond with the same issues that the parties campaigned on. A "national in/security" hypothesis predicts that proximity to violence or police presence corresponds with an increase in support for the ruling party. The logic here is that even though voters might be critical of the Jonathan administration's handling of Boko Haram, they do not want to take a chance on an untested opposition party. I test this in multiple ways: with observed levels of violence, with police presence per capita, and finally with public attitudes about each candidate's competence in handling violent extremism.

Next, an "economic voting" hypothesis anticipates that economic conditions shaped electoral outcomes. Specifically, I predict that positive evaluations of the national economy, higher disposable income levels, and high confidence in President Jonathan's ability to improve the economy will all correspond with greater support for the ruling PDP. Since I control for the subjective and objective economic conditions, I expect states with healthy economies to be more risk-averse and therefore more likely to vote for the PDP. Support for this hypothesis would indicate that Nigerians voted with their wallets as well as their evaluations of economic policy. Additionally, if the results point to a difference between voters' stated priorities outlined in Chapter 3 and their voting behavior, this would provide evidence that the parties "primed" voters on the economy. I focus on these two out of the five issue areas examined in that chapter because they are the strongest representation of the conventional wisdom about why Buhari won, and, combined, they also constitute a majority of the messaging of the two presidential campaigns. The next chapter will test the impact of electoral integrity, a third theme in the campaign.

National In/security Hypothesis

My national in/security hypothesis tests the notion that the 2015 election was effectively a referendum on the Jonathan administration's public safety record in general and its counter-terrorism strategy in particular. There are practical reasons why we might expect insecurity or concerns about safety to shape voting outcomes. As documented with survey data and other evidence in Chapter 3, citizens were deeply concerned about Boko Haram as the nation prepared for the elections. Citizens listed insecurity as their top priority, ahead of corruption and the economy combined. But they were evenly divided over whether the "frequency of extremist attacks" would increase (40.2 percent) or decrease (40.7 percent) if Jonathan was re-elected (US State Department – sponsored poll 2015). In addition, it is important to note that Nigeria does not have state or local police. Citizens, therefore, point the finger at the federal government when local insecurity increases because control over the instruments of public safety are so centralized. It therefore makes sense for voters to connect security with presidential performance and national public policies (Hills 2012).

My statistical estimates explore the potential effects of insecurity on state-level voting outcomes in four different ways. First, I predict lower levels of observed violence will correspond with support for the PDP. Conversely, if communities feel like the government has failed to provide security, which we could associate with the Hausa term *jingina*, then they are more likely to vote for the APC. Even though most violence was concentrated in three northeastern states (Borno, Adamawa, and Yobe) there are sound theoretical reasons why we would expect insecurity to have broader national-level effects. Terrorism seeks to instill a generalized sense of fear that far exceeds any tactical benefits of its targets. Research from both social psychology and political science bear this out. For example, following the September 2001 attacks, Americans reduced their air travel and increased their use of interstate highways in proportions that suggested a deliberate choice not to fly (Gigerenzer 2006). Psychiatry research highlighted a rise in post-traumatic stress disorder, stress, and anxiety attributed to terrorism, with the effects usually dispersed beyond the particular attack location (Hunter et al. 2016). Emotions triggered by terrorism have explicitly linked to broader social anxieties and political behavior through affective intelligence theory, which posits that citizens become more interested in politics and more vigilant about evaluating policies after a traumatic event (Marcus et al. 2000). Several studies, for example, point to an increase in voter turnout or other forms of political participation after violent events (Robbins et al. 2013; Blattman 2009). In a large-N analysis of countries that experienced terrorist attacks,

Hunter et al. (2016) find that affective intelligence threatens incumbent parties. This effect is especially pronounced in unconsolidated democracies due to weakly institutionalized party systems, where parties cannot withstand such shocks. In short, terrorism stimulates a generalized sense of fear in excess of the physical proximity to its victims. These emotions condition political behavior by heightening citizen scrutiny of policies and motivating voters. In Nigeria, I would expect support for the PDP to suffer, possibly in connection with an increase in voter turnout.

Second, I test to see how state penetration, by which I mean the capacity of the state to project power over territory (Herbst 2000), shapes electoral outcomes. A large security force is a sign that consent is more coerced than socially or culturally grounded. This approach to state penetration is well-suited to Nigeria specifically because the state, even under civilian rule, does not shy away from coercion to reassert control over space and populations (Serrano and Pieri 2014; Abidde 2017). Here the relevant Hausa idea is *tsoro*, referring to fear or generalized apprehensiveness. This idea is consistent with the steady decline in confidence in the police during President Jonathan's tenure, dropping from 49 percent in 2011 to 33 percent in 2014 (Loschky and Sanders 2015). Afrobarometer surveys also consistently report low levels of institutional confidence in the police. For example, in a 2009 survey, 43 percent of respondents said they trust the police "not at all" and only 8 percent said they trust the police "a lot" (Afrobarometer 2009b).

Much of the police's negative attention centers on corruption and brutality, but perceptions of police partisanship also fueled this mistrust. "Leaders are often appointed based on their political allegiances rather than on their experience or capabilities in law enforcement," reports a study commissioned by the Washington-based Africa Center for Strategic Studies. "Appointees under such circumstances feel loyalty to their political patron rather than to their institutions or citizens" (Okenyodo 2016, 2). The police also arguably displayed overt partisanship towards the PDP in 2015. A few weeks before the election, a leading human rights organization worried that partisan control of security institutions "could be a major threat to security" (CLEEN Foundation 2015). The National Human Rights Commission also reminded Nigerians that the previous elections in 2011 suffered from security lapses in part due to perceived partisanship of the security agencies. It went on to attribute political violence to the seventy-four executive-branch officials who hold legal immunity under the constitution.[3] "These are also the persons most likely to mobilize deadly violence, finance, procure or benefit from it" (National Human Rights Commission of Nigeria 2015, 35).[4] This is not to say that the army was above such partisanship. The executive director of the Centre for Human Rights, Development and Environmental Foundation, for example, concluded "the military is totally politicized" (Ijeohmah 2017). But data on the military are scarce, the police force is quite large, and the partisan bias of the police is better documented (LeVan 2018). Moreover, since approval ratings of the services have started to move together, the use of the *police* on its own is sufficiently valid. I expect to see a large police presence correspond with support for the PDP.

Third, I use a survey question about whether citizens believe the level of "violent extremism" will increase, decrease, or stay the same under Jonathan, and the fourth statistical test uses the same question with regard to Buhari. Since Chapter 3 demonstrated that the Buhari campaign deemphasized counter-terrorism compared to other issues, I do not expect the relationship to be statistically significant. The PDP may have failed to provide *jingina,* but did Buhari win on the rhetoric of *tsoro?*

---

[3] Section 308 (1) states: "Notwithstanding anything to the contrary in this Constitution, but subject to the conditions of subsection (2) of this section – (a) no civil or criminal proceedings shall be instituted or continued against a person to whom this section applies during his period in office; (b) a person to whom this section applies shall not be arrested or imprisoned during that period either on pursuance of the process of any court or otherwise; (c) no process of any court requiring or compelling appearance of a person to whom this section applies, shall be applied or issued; provided that in ascertaining whether any period of limitation has expired for the purposes of any proceedings against a person to whom this section applies, no account shall be taken of his period in office."

[4] Though my test focuses on the police, the military's role in 2015 contributed to concern about the politicization of the security services. For example, shortly after President Jonathan's director of publicity for the presidential campaign, Femi Fani-Kayode, defended an increased army role in providing security, the military surrounded the home of his APC counterpart (Stakeholder Democracy Network 2015).

Economic Voting Hypothesis

The "economic voting" hypothesis tests the basic insights from research offering evidence that Africans are increasingly voting on evaluations of policy performance rather than more parochial concerns (Bratton 2013b; Gibson and Long 2009). It predicts that in states where economies were strong, or where people viewed the Jonathan administration's economic performance favorably, citizens were more likely to cast their vote for the PDP. I test this first with an independent variable measuring subjective evaluations of national economic performance over the previous year. I predict that in states where citizens held the federal government's record of economic performance in high esteem, they were more likely to vote for the incumbent PDP. Next, I test the relationship between disposable income and support for the PDP. In states with more families who are economically better off, I expect higher income levels to correspond with support for the PDP, again, because those voters are more risk-averse. In all the tests, I also control for economic conditions in the states with objective economic measures, since perceived economic conditions and the actual economic conditions could differ, offering additional support for the notion that party messaging about the economy influenced voters. Finally, using a survey question, I test to see if voters really had more faith in Buhari than in Jonathan to improve the economy.

Empirical support for this hypothesis would suggest that Nigerians voted on evaluations of national economic performance. It could also support research pointing to the importance of subnational economic conditions in shaping electoral outcomes (Arriola 2008). Even more interestingly, such evidence would indicate that voters were effectively "primed" on the economy (Hart 2016). In the months leading up to the election, insecurity consistently topped citizens' concerns in national surveys. But, as indicated in the previous chapter, APC leaders campaigned more heavily on economic issues. So if Nigeria did indeed have economic voters in 2015, this would further support the findings from the previous chapter emphasizing the differences between the two presidential campaigns on economic appeals.

I do not test for the role of patronage in the election here because in other research, co-authored with Page and Ha, I find that patronage payments do not systematically explain voting patterns in the 2015 election (LeVan et al. 2018). That study uses the same dependent variable here, the change in the PDP's vote share in the 2011 and 2015 presidential elections.

Control Variables

All of the models include variables controlling for economic conditions, political context, and social demographics that could interfere with the hypothesized relationship. To control for economic conditions in each state, I opted not to use available data for gross domestic product (GDP) per capita due to reliability concerns; for example, some states have exactly the same GDP.[5] Instead, I control for each states' economic performance via an original instrumental variable measuring the change in internally generated revenue (IGR). The data are from the Central Bank of Nigeria's (CBN) Annual Reports for 2010–2013. The variable ΔIGR is a difference of ratio calculated by subtracting the mean IGR as a share of state revenue overall between 2010 and 2012 from IGR as a share of total revenue in 2013. This is expressed in Equation 1 as:

Equation 1:

$$\Delta IGR = \left[IGR2013 - \left(\frac{IGR2010_i + IGR2011_i + IGR2012_i}{3} \right) \right] \times 100$$

Until fairly recently, studies of fiscal federalism equated low levels of internally generated revenue with strong central control or weak federalism (Lijphart 2012). However, this overlooks programmatic autonomy of subnational units and authorities they may have for generating income through tax rates or other means (Rodden 2004). Thus, ΔIGR provides a good measure of subnational economic performance because it captures the ability of states to monetize their economic productivity. Increasing state revenue is difficult without economic growth and commerce that states can tax (Oseni 2013).

I also control for economic conditions with data from the government's Debt Management Office.[6] The variable, *StateDebt*, measures subnational fiscal discipline. Based on a variable used by

---

[5] http://services.gov.ng/states (accessed March 20, 2016).
[6] www.dmo.gov.ng/ (accessed January 10, 2016).

LeVan et al. (2018), it is calculated as logged ratio of each state's debt (foreign and domestic) between 2011 and 2014 in real terms, using the World Bank's GDP deflator. In broad political economy terms, fiscal discipline proxies for the willingness of politicians to borrow from the future in order to finance the present. Such "intertemporal transfers" have undermined African economic performance across a broad range of countries since the 1960s (Collier and Gunning 2008). The willingness to borrow is especially important in monocultural economies such as Nigeria's that are ill-prepared for exogenous shocks. States began borrowing during Jonathan's tenure not only because federal grants began to decline with the global fall in oil prices, but because the federal government under the ruling PDP's control denied politically troublesome states their share of revenue allocations (LeVan 2018). In this sense, debt levels are not merely an indicator of governors' time horizons, they also instrument for states' desperation vis-à-vis the federal government. Borrowing money generates political dependence on the center. In indebted states, governors have less leverage when bargaining with national party leaders or federal government officials. Debt also changes politics within states themselves by potentially increasing the ability of "godfathers" – informal power brokers with independent sources of wealth – to interfere in elections. At some point during the Fourth Republic, politicians in nearly every state have had to contend with godfathers exercising control over local party structures, influencing candidate selection, or paying voters (Obianyo 2013; Obafemi et al. 2014; Fashagba 2015).

To explicitly control for conditions reflecting the political status quo in each state heading into the March 2015 presidential election, I use a dummy variable *Governor* to capture the incumbent governor's party.[7] A value of 1 indicates a governor in the ruling PDP and 0 signals APC.[8] The PDP held 23 states after the 2011 elections, so the defection of 5 PDP governors to APC in 2013, along with 57 members of

[7] The Federal Capital Territory of Abuja does not have a governor. But since its citizens do vote in presidential elections, it is included in our dependent variable *APDPvote*.

[8] I coded Anambra State as 1 also, since the All Progressives Grand Alliance (APGA) had adopted Goodluck Jonathan as its candidate. Subsequent field research in the state validated this judgment, as party activists explained that APGA was formed for popular politicians in the PDP whose ambitions were blocked by godfathers.

the 360-seat House of Representatives and 22 of 109 senators, deeply damaged the ruling party party's credibility. The variable is coded after all of these defections. After the 2015 election, the PDP held only thirteen states. In addition, $\Delta Turnout$ controls for voter turnout, measured as percent change in turnout between the 2011 and 2015 presidential elections. As noted above, affective intelligence theory suggests that traumatic effects such as terrorism tend to increase interest in politics and voter turnout (Robbins et al. 2013). This means that an increase in political participation, rather than evaluation of policies or concerns about insecurity, could be driving electoral outcomes. Statistically, this could manifest itself in a decline in turnout in states that the PDP lost and an increase in turnout in the states that the APC won. Turnout is also an important control because millions of internally displaced persons (IDPs) presented a major logistical challenge for INEC, and fear of Boko Haram attacks could suppress turnout. For example, an APC official in Gombe State claimed in an interview that registered and resettled IDPs in the north overwhelmingly voted for the APC because they saw their plight linked in general to the government's handling of terrorism and insecurity. However most of the IDPs in Gombe were in informal "host communities" and therefore disenfranchised since they were supposed to vote in their home state (Ahaya 2016). During a visit to one such community in Gombe in 2016, IDPs repeatedly described such obstacles to voting.

Several variables also control for social and demographic variations across states. For example, the variable *Literacy* measures the literacy rate in English or the respective state's local language, expressed as a percent (National Bureau of Statistics 2010). It is statistically normal. This controls for the possibility that lesser-educated voters rallied behind Buhari. I also use a direct measure of the average level of state wealth, to control for the possibility that it is not less-educated people who voted for Buhari, but poorer people. The variable *Income* is based on a survey respondent's subjective evaluation of his or her own economic situation. The survey question asks, "With regards to your monthly household income, please tell me which of the following phrases best suits your household situation?" The choice of responses are: 1 = unable to meet basic needs without charity; 2 = able to meet basic needs; 3 = able to meet basic needs with some non-essential goods; 4 = able to purchase most non-essential goods; 5 = plenty of disposable money. A total of 3,953 respondents answered the question, with another 167 dropped from the variable for either not responding or answering "don't know" (US State Department – sponsored poll 2015). By separately controlling for both literacy and income, I am able to distinguish between any potential effects of wealth and education, and avoid using literacy as a proxy – instead measuring economic conditions more directly.

The tests also include a *Gender* variable, where 1 = male and 0 = other. Its values range from .48, indicating a state with more women, to .53, a state with more men; the standard deviation is .017. Citing a broad range of existing literature, Isaksson et al. (2014) note that gender gaps in political participation influence the types of issues that make it onto the political agenda. If women are disproportionately affected by a particular policy compared to men, but they participate in politics less, the problem reinforces existing social and economic inequalities. This makes the reason for differential rates of gender participation an important research question. Their cross-national study of twenty countries finds that "clientelism, restricted civil liberties, economic development and gender norms are potentially important determinants of the participatory gender gap in Africa" (Isaksson et al. 2014, 303).

Including a control for gender is important in Nigeria, and for the 2015 election in particular, for several other reasons. Women are woefully underrepresented in elected offices and the cabinet; women's formal role in politics has improved little during the Fourth Republic (LeVan and Baba 2017; Osori 2017). But as noted in the previous chapter, women also made notable gains in school enrollment, health, and other social indicators under President Jonathan's administration. If voters gave him credit for these gains, one might expect to see a positive coefficient. Even more importantly, Buhari made gender an issue in the campaign when he announced that he planned to abolish the office of the First Lady – a proposal that was generally condemned in the media as an effort to limit women's role in politics (Dori 2015). Analyzing the election in retrospect, gender seems even more relevant and the fears of chauvinism proved warranted. Buhari did indeed abolish the Office in August 2015. "President Buhari promised that there would be a clear difference between the role played by his wife during his tenure and that played by many previous First Ladies," said a statement from Aso Rock. "All that ostentation, ubiquitousness and arrogance we have come to expect from the office are over and done with. Change has come" (Nwabughiogu 2015). Then underscoring his views of women, he scolded his wife for expressing her political views. In a remark that exploded in social media, he said, "I don't know which party my wife belongs to, but she belongs to my kitchen and my living room and the other room" (Ukpong 2016).

Finally, controlling for the possibility of co-ethnic voting is important given how the comparative research cited in the literature review expects ethnicity to drive electoral outcomes (Huntington 1991; Horowitz 1985). This is also true in Nigeria, where political parties have long struggled to build inter-ethnic coalitions. For example, in the First Republic (1960–1966), the Northern People's Congress refused to change its name in part because the Hausa-Fulani elites thought they had the numerical superiority to win without southern support. Even after redesigning the electoral system in 1979, regional, ethnic-based parties retained their draw (Obafemi et al. 2014; Falola and Ihonvbere 1985). The data I utilize are from a national survey in which respondents were asked, "Would you mind telling me which ethnic group you belong?" and 99.1 percent of 3,953 respondents voluntarily identified themselves as belonging to a specific ethnic group (US State Department – sponsored poll 2015). Studies of Nigeria's ethnic composition have long estimated that the three largest ethnic groups – the Hausa-Fulani, Igbo, and Yoruba – constitute about two-thirds of the population (Osaghae et al. 2001; Nnoli 1995). Notably, in the survey, they collectively account for 64.8 percent of all respondents, suggesting that the sampling technique conforms to standard ethnographic estimations. To create *HausaFulani*, I recode the variable so that respondents who self-identified as either Hausa or Fulani are coded as 1, with all others coded as 0. Aggregating the variable to the state level generates a continuous variable with values ranging from 0 to 1. The values on the variable represent the relative frequency of people who self-identify as either Hausa or Fulani.[9] A check on the variable's values are consistent with ethnographic expectations for various states. For example, Katsina, a core northern state and the

---

[9] In his biography, Buhari identifies himself as part-Kanuri. However, only 0.2 percent of the respondents in the survey identified as Kanuri, so I did not include it in the variable. Moreover, combining Hausa and Fulani follows convention with the historical similarities between these two groups.

home of opposition candidate Buhari is 1, while Abia, a core Igbo state in the southeast, scores 0, while Gombe is .47.

There are some obvious limitations testing for co-ethnic voting in this way. Notably, the country has so many ethnic groups and languages that there is no theoretically obvious prediction for how many of these groups would vote. For example, in the survey used to generate the *HausaFulani* variable, respondents actually self-identified with 97 different ethnic groups. Only a single respondent self-identified as Laru, Ibusa, or Omuma, while 764 people described themselves as Yoruba and 956 people identify as Hausa. This also means that in any given state, the *HausaFulani* variable is making a strong assumption about homogeneity. (For this reason, I will conduct separate tests for my ethnic affinity hypothesis using individual-level data in the following chapter.) Yet, for purposes of a control variable, the simplified approach with the *HausaFulani* variable can still test widespread cultural tropes about the political dominance of the *HausaFulani* dating back to Britain's cultivation of northern elites for indirect rule. For example, a leading Christian intellectual who went on to become chair of the Christian Association of Nigeria (CAN), complained in the 1990s that "the ascendancy of Hausa-Fulani hegemony has coincided with the alienation and marginalization of the non-Muslims, Christians and adherents of traditional religions" (Kukah 2003, x). Such views remain widespread today, and have helped fuel the secessionist movement, discussed in greater detail in Chapter 6.

Statistical Tests and Estimates

In this section, I submit each hypothesis to empirical tests, using ordinary least squares (OLS) statistical models. Tests of the "national in/security" hypothesis find that neither observed levels of violence across states nor state penetration systematically explains electoral outcomes. Moreover, where voters worried that "extremist attacks" would increase if Buhari was elected, there is a strong correlation with support for the PDP. Next, and most importantly for my overall argument, statistical tests generate robust support for the "economic voting" hypothesis. Specifically, where voters believed the national economy had declined over the previous year, or where families had little disposable income, states were much more likely to vote for Buhari.

The dependent variable in the tests for both of these hypotheses is the change in the PDP's vote share, expressed as a percent based on the total number of valid votes in the presidential elections of 2011 and 2015. This means that a positive value indicates a rise in support for the PDP and a negative value signals a rise in the opposition vote share.[10] The variable $\Delta PDPvote$ is calculated with electoral results for each of Nigeria's thirty-six states as officially reported by INEC. The difference of PDP's vote share between 2015 and 2011 is then multiplied by 100. This is expressed in Equation 2 as follows:

Equation 2:

$$\Delta PDPvote = \left(\frac{PDP\ votes\ in\ 2015}{All\ Valid\ Votes\ in\ 2015} - \frac{PDP\ votes\ in\ 2011}{All\ Valid\ Votes\ in\ 2011} \right) \times 100$$

The mean value on the variable is –13.28, meaning that the PDP on average lost over 13 percentage points per state. More strikingly, the PDP lost votes in every state except two. The standard deviation is 10.6, with a minimum value of –35.57 and maximum value of 7.13. Where $\Delta PDPvote$ is the dependent variable, the base model for all of my tests is expressed in Equation 3 as:

Equation 3:

$$\Delta PDPvote = \beta_0 + \beta_1 (each\ IV) + \beta_2 (StateDebt) + \beta_3 (IGR) + \\ \beta_4 (Income) + \beta_5 (Governor) + \beta_6 (\Delta Turnout) + \\ \beta_7 (Literacy) + \beta_8 (Gender) + \beta_9 (HausaFulani) + \varepsilon$$

African elections are difficult to study due to missing data or insufficient confidence in the results. Most studies of Nigerian elections are qualitative, perhaps providing only lists or tables with information.[11]

---

[10] In 2011, the opposition was split: The Congress for Progressive Change (Buhari's party) won 12.2 million votes, Action Congress Nigeria won two million votes, and the All Nigeria Peoples' Party won 0.9 million votes. Other minor parties' candidates won less than 60,000 votes. By contrast, in 2015, the opposition was more united. The eleven minor parties received a total of 309,481 valid votes combined, representing a mere 1.08 percent of the vote.

[11] See, for example, Ujo (2000), LeVan et al. (2003), Kew (2004), Egwu (2007), Akhaine (2011), Obi (2011), Paden (2012), Ayoade and Akinsanya (2013), Owen and Usman (2015), and Lewis and Kew (2015).

Statistical tests, however, enable me to generalize about voting patterns, while holding constant a variety of factors or conditions that could interfere with the hypothesized relationship. Statistical confidence levels and data about any correlations enable readers to assess the validity of inferences drawn from the results by quantifying the likelihood that complex relationships are non-random.

Tests of the National In/security Hypothesis

The national in/security hypothesis predicts that higher observed levels of violence, or the anticipation of such violence in different ways, will correspond with increased support for the APC. I test this under multiple specifications, operationalizing insecurity a different way in each statistical model. The first model uses observed levels of violence as the independent variable. The variable *violence* is constructed with data from the Nigeria Watch database, maintained by the Institute on Francophone Research in Africa (IFRA) at the University of Ibadan.[12] This database has some advantages over other sources such as the Council on Foreign Relations' Security Tracker because it extends back to the beginning of Goodluck Jonathan's presidency in 2010. This allows for a baseline prior to the 2011 election and the dramatic increase in violence later in his term. Only violent deaths are recorded, and the database is also specifically constructed to maintain high reliability even at disaggregated levels (Chouin et al. 2014). The variable *deaths* is the number of deaths in each state relative to the population. *Deaths* is then averaged over the five years prior to the election and divided by five to create the variable *Violence* as follows:

Equation 4:

$$Violence = \frac{(deaths2010 + deaths2011 + deaths2012 + deaths2013 + deaths2014)}{5}$$

Its distribution is positively skewed so I log the variable creating *LogViolence*. It is important to remember that this variable includes all types of publicly reported violent deaths, and is not limited to electoral violence or terrorism. Boko Haram-related incidents are by far the largest share of deaths, especially after including deaths attributable

---

[12] I am grateful to Manuel Reinert for his assistance navigating this dataset.

to state security services while fighting terrorism. This broad measure of violence also includes other categories of violence, such as farmer–pastoralist conflicts. Confirmation of the national in/security hypothesis would appear as a negative coefficient on *LogViolence*, the main independent variable of interest in the model.

Model 2 tests for the impact of state penetration on electoral outcomes. I operationalize this in terms of the number of police per state in per-capita terms. This follows Lange (2009), who finds that the number of police is highly correlated with other measures of state capacity across forty-nine former British colonies. The variable *police* is constructed with data from the Nigeria Police Force[13] and the federal government's *Annual Abstract of Statistics* (Nigerian Bureau of Statistics 2012). It is not normal, so I create *Log.Police*. For all the reasons outlined above, I predict that a large, regular police presence will correlate with support for the PDP. The public's confidence in the huge federally controlled police force dipped to new lows prior to the election, and concerns about police partisanship were widespread. In this climate one would expect voters to side with the ruling party out of fear. Support for the hypothesis would appear as a positive coefficient.

The third and fourth models focus more explicitly on counter-terrorism. I seek to determine how attitudes about each presidential candidate's likelihood of reducing the level of "extremist attacks" – a term that implicates Boko Haram – influenced voting patterns. A survey question asks, "And do you think the frequency of extremist attacks will increase, decrease or stay the same if Jonathan is re-elected in 2015?" (US State Department – sponsored poll 2015). To create the variable *Attacks.GJ*, I recoded the respondents' three answers so that 1 means that attacks would "decrease," 2 means the frequency would "stay the same," and 3 means that attacks would "increase." The variable *Attacks.MB* asks the same question, substituting Buhari for Jonathan. Two states, Yobe and Borno, are not included because the high level of insecurity there in early 2015 made the survey too risky.[14] Support for the hypothesis would appear as a positive coefficient on *Attacks.GJ*, indicating that most voters worried that

---

[13] http://npf.gov.ng/zone8.php (accessed August 1, 2017).
[14] The PDP lost both states by large margins in 2011.

extremist attacks would increase if Jonathan was re-elected, and a negative coefficient on *Attacks.MB,* indicating that voters cast their lot with Buhari because they hopefully believed it was he who could reduce terrorism.

This approach means that I am testing how observed levels of violence, state penetration (in terms of a regular police presence), and citizens' predictions for each candidate's ability to provide security influenced election outcomes across states. Table 4.1 displays the results of these four models.

The variable *Log.Violence* has a negative coefficient, as predicted, but it is not statistically significant. The tests of proximity to violence therefore suggest that there is no systematic correlation between the average level of violence in the years prior to elections and how people in those states voted in 2015.[15] *StateDebt,* ΔIGR, and *Income* are all statistically significant, indicating that states with high debt, healthy economies, and more denizens with disposable income were more likely to vote for the PDP. The positive coefficient on the *Governor* variable indicates that states with PDP governors were more likely to vote for the President Jonathan though it is significant only at the .1 level. The model explains over 22 percent of the predicted variation (adjusted R^2 of .222), but does not offer support for the national in/security hypothesis. The coefficient on *Log.Police* in Model 2 is negative, contrary to my prediction. This could indicate that a police presence increased citizens' confidence that they could vote freely; however, it is insignificant. In fact, only *StateDebt,* ΔIGR, and *Literacy* are statistically significant. The adjusted R^2 of .246 indicates that the model explains nearly 25 percent of the predicted variation.[16]

---

[15] There was no violence data for Cross Rivers State and the federal capital of Abuja.

[16] I also ran a test, not shown here, with a variable instrumenting for fear of electoral violence. A statistically significant relationship could indicate that the *type* of violence needs to be specified or that voters feared intimidation from the PDP – a party that had never lost an election and had demonstrated a willingness to engage in desperate measures to hold on to power. I created an independent variable using a survey question which asks, "During election campaigns in this country, how much do you personally fear becoming a victim of political intimidation or violence?" Respondents could answer on a scale where zero indicates "a lot," 1 means "somewhat," 2 means "a little," and 3 indicates "not at all" (Afrobarometer 2016). The coefficient was –.143

Table 4.1 *Test Results for National In/security Hypothesis.*

	Model 1 (Violence Proximity)	Model 2 (State Penetration)	Model 3 (Attacks if Jonathan)	Model 4 (Attacks if Buhari)
Constant	22.289	71.176	4.414	−18.090
	(.238)	(.670)	(.047)	(−.236)
LogViolence	−1.592			
	(−.589)			
Log.Police		−4.738		
		(−1.054)		
Attacks.GJ			4.896	
			(.475)	
Attacks.MB				20.243***
				(3.330)
StateDebt	6.060**	6.153**	5.597**	5.092**
	(2.645)	(2.726)	(2.269)	(2.657)
ΔIGR	.795*	.816*	.740	.142
	(1.717)	(1.799)	(1.504)	(.327)
Income	11.937*	11.638	11.124	6.118
	(1.816)	(1.809)	(1.542)	(1.074)
Governor	8.413*	7.324	8.378*	4.241
	(1.910)	(1.634)	(1.893)	(1.098)
ΔTurnout	−.174	−.178	−.120	.077
	(1.115)	(-1.163)	(-.664)	(.522)
Literacy	.251	.314*	.248	.159
	(1.449)	(1.787)	(1.413)	(1.089)
Gender	−161.873	−187.287	−143.372	−109.683
	(−.942)	(−1.091)	(−.831)	(−.771)
HausaFulani	−5.432	−5.860	−3.214	7.214
	(−1.007)	(−1.116)	(−.544)	(1.298)
Adjusted R^2	.222	.246	.218	.467
N	32	32	32	32

T-statistic in parentheses; *** $p < .01$, **$p < .05$, *$p < .1$

(T-statistic of .028) but it was not significant. Similar to my other tests in this chapter, *StateDebt* was statistically significant (at the 95-percent confidence interval), while *Income* and *Governor* are weakly significant (at the 90-percent confidence level). The adjusted R^2 was .200.

The two remaining estimates are more direct tests of how Boko Haram's terrorism shaped the election. In model 3, the coefficient on *Attacks.GJ* is positive but insignificant. Among the control variables, *StateDebt* is significant at the .05 level and *Governor* is significant at the .1 level, indicating, respectively, that states with higher debt levels and with an incumbent PDP governor were more likely to vote to re-elect President Jonathan. The adjusted R^2 is .218. It is useful to interpret these results alongside model 4 before interpreting any support for the national in/security hypothesis. *Attacks.MB* is highly significant but it tells a surprising story: each unit of change on the primary independent variable (whether extremist attacks would decrease, stay the same, or increase) correlates with a twenty-percentage-point increase in support for the PDP. The only other statistically significant variable is *StateDebt* (at the .05 level). The adjusted R^2 indicates that the model explains nearly 47 percent of the variation in the dependent variable, the change in PDP's vote share compared to 2011. The combined results of models 3 and 4 suggest that the ruling party's scaremongering about extremist attacks increasing under a president Buhari mobilized its base, while for APC voters the topic was less important. Though I did not fully test for the impact of insecurity on political participation in order to test affective intelligence theory, the insignificance of $\Delta Turnout$ in all four models suggests that an increase in voter turnout did not systematically affect electoral outcomes.

In the end, the PDP played to whatever implicit fears its core supporters had about putting a Muslim northerner in charge of the fight against Boko Haram. However, this produced a narrow electoral coalition. The PDP failed to provide *jingina,* and these tests show that Buhari won less on the rhetoric of *tsoro* than on the portfolio of policies identified in Chapter 3's content analysis of the campaign. The Buhari campaign deemphasized counter-terrorism, with good electoral results.

Tests of the Economic Voting Hypothesis

The economic voting hypothesis examines how economic conditions and people's perceptions of them shape state-level voting outcomes. I test this in three different ways. First, model 5 tests for a systematic correlation between negative opinions of recent economic performance and support for the APC. I measure evaluations of the economy with the variable *EconOpinion,* which uses Afrobarometer Round 6 survey data.[17] The survey question asks how the respondent would rate the economic condition of Nigeria compared to twelve months ago, on a scale of 1 to 5, where 1 = much worse, 2 = worse, 3 = same, 4 = better, and 5 = much better (Afrobarometer 2016). Aggregating this variable to the state level transformed it from a categorical to continuous variable, increasing the overall number of values the variable can take on. I expect the PDP vote share to increase in states where citizens have positive views of the economy. This would appear as a positive coefficient on the independent variable.

Next, I test to see how the average income level influenced voting patterns. Here, the test uses *Income* as the primary independent variable of interest. Consistent with the theory of economic voting, I predict that states where more people indicated they have disposable income were more likely to vote for the ruling PDP. This would appear as a positive coefficient on the variable *income* in model 6.

Finally, a pair of tests examine whether people on average have a more optimistic vision of the country's economic future under either Jonathan or Buhari. For model 7, I used a survey question that asked, "And please tell me whether the following statement applies to President Jonathan or not. He can improve Nigeria's economy" (US State Department – sponsored poll 2015). The variable *Jonathan. Econ* was recoded so that a value of 1 = yes, and 0 = other. "Other" includes 2,015 respondents (51 percent) who answered "no," plus 71 who said "don't know" and 20 who gave no response. In model 8, the variable *Buhari.Econ* asks the same question of Buhari. In that instance, "other" includes 1,520 "no" responses, plus 202 respondents who said "don't know" and 23 people who did not reply. Support for the economic voting hypothesis would appear as a positive coefficient on *Jonathan.Econ* and a negative coefficient on *Buhari.Econ.* The results of these statistical estimates are displayed in Table 4.2.

All four tests in Table 4.2 offer strong statistical support for the economic voting hypothesis. In model 5, the positive coefficient on *EconOpinion* means that an increase in one unit of favorable views

---

[17] This survey omitted three states due to security concerns: Adamawa, Borno, and Yobe, meaning $N = 34$. Notably, all of the omitted states are poor states that have been dominated by the opposition during the Fourth Republic, suggesting that, if anything, respondents in these states would be critical of the country's recent economic performance and would characterize themselves as fairly poor.

Table 4.2 *Test Results for Economic Voting Hypothesis.*

	Model 5 (National Economy, last 12 Months)	Model 6 (Income Level)	Model 7 (Jonathan Will Improve Economy)	Model 8 (Buhari Will Improve Economy)
Constant	41.531	12.729	12.516	54.035
	(.523)	(.140)	(.153)	(.699)
EconOpinion	14.908***			
	(2.835)			
Income		12.627*		
		(1.979)		
Jonathan.Econ			29.266**	
			(2.791)	
Buhari.Econ				−28.061***
				(−2.920)
StateDebt	4.634**	6.025**	4.789**	4.733**
	(2.235)	(2.667)	(2.326)	(2.325)
ΔIGR	.731	.819*	.347	.340
	(1.726)	(1.801)	(.793)	(.788)
Governor	4.838	8.551*	4.342	4.564
	(1.152)	(1.971)	(1.055)	(1.129)
ΔTurnout	.061	−.163	.201	.202
	(.369)	(−1.065)	(1.020)	(1.053)
Literacy	.026	.264	.109	.151
	(.145)	(1.556)	(.112)	(.960)
Gender	−196.496	−151.982	−104.336	−131.642
	(−1.275)	(−.901)	(−.652)	(−.848)
HausaFulani	−4.486	−4.553	10.594	9.083
	(−.931)	(−.890)	(1.460)	(1.363)
Adjusted R²	.349	.243	.335	.350
N	31	32	32	32

T-statistic in parentheses *** $p < .01$, **$p < .05$, *$p < .1$

of the economy over the previous year correlates with 14.9 more percentage points for the PDP. The variable is significant at the .01 level. The only other variables that are significant are the controls for observed state economic conditions: *StateDebt* ($p < .05$) and *ΔIGR* ($p < .1$). The adjusted R² of .349 indicates that the model explains nearly 35 percent of the variation across states. Model 6 also offers support for the hypothesis by showing that in states where families on average see themselves as economically better off and with more disposable income, they were more likely to support the PDP. The positive coefficient of 12.627 on the *Income* variable, significant at the .1 level, means that, on a scale of 1 to 5, each unit of additional disposal income indicates an increase of nearly 13 percentage points of additional support for the PDP in that state. Again, only *StateDebt* ($p < .05$) and *ΔIGR* ($p < .1$) are statistically significant. The adjusted R^2 .243 indicates that the model explains over 24 percent of the predicted relationship.

Finally, the pair of survey questions that assess citizens' hopefulness about the economy support the economic voting hypothesis. Model 7 shows that states where the average citizen believed that President Jonathan can improve the economy were very likely to vote for the PDP, and the positive coefficient on *Jonathan.Econ* is significant at the .05 level. In model 8, there is a strong, negative statistical correlation between *Buhari.Econ* (significant at the .01 level) and the share of the PDP's vote in any given state. Voters who believed Buhari would improve the economy were far more likely to vote for the APC. Also, voters in states with higher rates of literacy were also more likely to vote for the PDP ($p < .1$ on *Literacy*). The adjusted R^2 of .350 indicates that the model explains 35 percent of the predicted relationship. Across all four models *StateDebt* is statistically significant at the .05 level.

Analysis and Interpretation

Was the 2015 election indeed a referendum on President Jonathan's counter-terrorism strategy, as several surveys and much of the popular press would suggest? This is an important question not just for understanding why the PDP lost, but because it could offer evidence that citizens' evaluation of public safety influenced their voting choices. The election offers a good test of counter-terrorism as a national policy because even though a vast majority of the violence was concentrated in only three states (Adamawa, Borno, and Yobe), national surveys (noted earlier) identified Boko Haram's insurgency as a *national* problem – with few differences in this view between north and south. Moreover, as noted in formulating my hypotheses, comparative studies of terrorism show how it has generalizable effects measurable at the national level, not just in the regions where it takes place. Alternatively, did the APC's critiques of corruption and economic decline resonate? Though it is important to cautiously interpret tests based on aggregated state-level data, especially with the relatively few statistical degrees of freedom, the results here offer support of the economic voting hypothesis and very little support for the national in/security hypothesis. Confirming the predictions under different specifications and operationalizations of economic conditions further strengthens the evidence of economic voting.

The result that proximity to violence (the Hausa *jingina*) did not systematically impact electoral outcomes is surprising given the high priority that citizens gave insecurity and terrorism vis-à-vis other issues. It was reasonable to expect that citizens in states that experienced more violence would vote for more security out of self-interest, yet I did not find any systematic evidence of this. Nor did I find evidence that police presence, which could have influenced voting patterns in light of evidence of police partisanship, also did not correlate with voting outcomes at a statistically significant level.

These indeterminate results do not mean that violence did not play a role in shaping voting behavior, especially since we are only observing state-level patterns instead of more localized dynamics. Nigerian civil society observers reinforced this view shortly after the election, cautioning against overstating the peacefulness of the elections and understating the role of less-visible violence. "In spite of the outcome 2015 elections and the perceptions of its being generally peaceful, it is generally [agreed], there magnitude of violence before, during and after the elections cannot be ignored," said the organizations convened by the Civil Society Legislative Advocacy Centre. "While many parts of the country remained relatively peaceful during the elections, some states including Rivers, Akwa Ibom, Cross River, Ebonyi and Ondo states recorded a significant number of violent incidents, claiming lives and property" (Civil Society Legislative Advocacy Centre 2015). Notably, President Jonathan won Rivers, Akwa Ibom, Cross River, and Ebonyi by large margins (and the PDP went on win a contentious by-election in Ondo in 2017). This experience seems to affirm Strauss and Taylor's (2012) observation that the competitiveness of elections inspires desperate measures by African incumbents.

The combined results with the variables based on the survey questions asking whether respondents thought the "frequency of extremist acts" would increase under Jonathan or Buhari are important. These two models are more direct tests of candidates' policies pertaining to insecurity and Boko Haram in particular, and thus constitute an important element of this study's stated goal of exploring the impact of terrorism on parties and electoral behavior in the developing world. The coefficient on *Attacks.GJ* is neither in the predicted direction nor significant, while the positive coefficient on *Attacks.MB* is highly significant. I interpret this to mean there was no systematic pattern between the average feeling about how Jonathan's re-election would increase or decrease extremist violence and terrorism. In particular, if the election was a referendum on counter-terrorism strategy, we would have expected support for the APC to correlate with concern that attacks would increase under Jonathan. The lack of statistical significance here further implies that even in states that voted for Buhari, whether attacks would increase or not under his opponent was just not that important. By contrast, model 4 suggests a compelling story; PDP voters voted for Jonathan out of concern that extremist attacks would increase under Buhari, and the model explains over 46 percent of the variation.

Interpreting the models together, and reflecting on the literature from developed countries and referenced in the book's introduction, the results suggest that terrorism, such as Boko Haram's, does shape voting behavior. But it does so not necessarily by shifting voters' issue prioritization when the threat is national (and the primary concern related to insecurity stems from either state security services or thugs). As Oates (2006) proposes, the role of terrorism in an election is conditioned by context, including rhetoric explored in Chapter 3 and the expectation that power would "shift" from south to north, explored in Chapter 2. Terrorism promoted party polarization, reinforcing perceptions among Jonathan's base that putting a Muslim northerner in charge of the fight against terrorism would be a mistake. The PDP's voters were mobilized on the negatives: *fear* of how violent extremism would rise under a Muslim northerner. APC voters, on the other hand, were informed by economic considerations and the hopeful messages of anti-corruption and economic growth promised by Buhari. These sharp differences were not exactly ideological, as the existing literature reviewed in the book's introduction highlights (Nanes 2016), but they do suggest polarizing effects on the party system.

All four statistical specifications in Table 4.2 offer strong support for the economic voting hypothesis. First, I found that more favorable views of the economy over the previous twelve months correlate with a nearly 15-percentage-point increase in support for the PDP. Next, I found strong support for my prediction that in states where more families see themselves as economically better off, with more disposable income, they were somewhat more likely to support the PDP. Finally, and most compellingly, I demonstrated a strong and inverse correlation between the PDP's vote share and the mean citizen assessment for whether Buhari would improve the economy. States where voters did not believe Buhari would improve the economy were overwhelmingly more likely to support the PDP. In states where the average voter believed Buhari would improve the economy overwhelmingly cast their lot with him. This result is even more statistically significant (at the .01 level compared to .05) than the results for the PDP. Voters in both parties cared about the economy, but, as shown in Chapter 3, the APC hammered home the hopeful message of reform to voters, with the 284 references to the economy and corruption, compared to the PDP's 72. The APC primed voters. Had Nigeria's economy not declined in 2014, just as Jonathan informally launched his re-election campaign with a public relations effort centered on the recalibration of the country's massive GDP, Nigeria might have looked more like Uganda, where research cited earlier notes that economic performance enhanced incumbent advantage (Conroy-Krutz and Logan 2013). The PDP still had a chance to campaign on socio-economic positives (including improvements in women's welfare), as noted in Chapter 3. But with regard to the economy, on which much of the election pivoted, the PDP seems to have misread the possibilities for building a broad electoral coalition based on the salient issues of the day.

The statistical significance of *StateDebt* at the 95-percent confidence interval in all statistical models in Table 4.2 is important. By itself, it should prompt readers to wonder how subnational economies shaped patterns of electoral outcomes. More indebted states were far more likely to support the ruling PDP. This makes sense since this debt increases the states' dependence on the center. While state governments have broad latitude to borrow money, the positive relationship between borrowing and support for the PDP could also mean that PDP governors borrowed money expecting to be bailed out by their own party if necessary. When Buhari actually won, one of his first acts was in fact to bail out the states following a meeting with desperate governors. Barely a month after he took the oath of office, the bailout dubiously drew upon the excess crude oil account and borrowed large sums from the Central Bank (Anonymous 2015a).[18] This made perfect political sense; Buhari did not want his party's state lieutenants inheriting the fiscal mess of their predecessors. This represents an important finding for the literature on fiscal federalism, which has long presumed that low levels of internally generated revenue in subnational units (such as Nigeria's states) is a sign of weak federalism (Amuwo et al. 2000; Ekpo 1994; Ikein and Briggs-Anigboh 1998). I maintain that after four election cycles and sixteen years of electoral democracy, the weak and inconsistently significant values on ΔIGR mean that debt drives political dependence. Though I have found in other research that discretionary deviations from the statutorily based revenue allocation do occur, they are politically costly and cumbersome to conceal (LeVan 2018). The lack of statistical significance on the *HausaFulani* variable suggests that ethnic considerations, at least at the aggregated state level, had a smaller effect than economic considerations.

Two important caveats are in order regarding the results. First, states are not the ideal unit of analysis for tests of the in/security hypothesis. But read within the context of affective intelligence theory, and the literature outlined in the Introduction pointing to effects of violence that extend beyond localized proximity, the results are persuasive. Second, since each of Nigeria's thirty-six states is actually quite diverse internally in economic, social, and political terms, this means I have to make some fairly strong assumptions of homogeneity, i.e., that state X is more or less the same throughout its boundaries. The tests make sense in Nigeria for a variety of reasons, though. States are powerful in Nigeria's federal system; even in states with little indigenous capital and small private sectors, governors control huge budgets due to the federal revenue allocation system. Governors are powerful figures in their parties, acting as political "godfathers" who can undermine or advance aspiring politicians (Fashagba 2015; Ayoade and Akinsanya 2013). And through associations such as the Nigerian Governors' Forum (NGF), governors coordinate for states' rights vis-à-vis the center (Suberu 2008). An acrimonious dispute over sovereign wealth

---

[18] Since virtually all spending by the executive requires authorization by an act of the National Assembly, the bailout of the states took place under questionable constitutional authority.

funds between President Jonathan and Governor Rotimi Amaechi, chair of the NGF in 2014, played an important role in the formation of the APC (LeVan 2018).

Even so, the support for the economic voting hypothesis in this chapter is statistically robust and consistent with research cited in the literature review. For example, Norris and Mattes (2013) find that individual-level perceptions of the economy systematically correspond with voter preferences, and Arriola (2008), in his study of Ethiopia, reports that key objective and subjective measures of economic conditions also correspond with voting patterns. Even more explicitly, the test results here buttress recent findings by LeVan, Page, and Ha (LeVan et al. 2018). Using literacy as a proxy for wealth and an original variable measuring electoral results at the local government level, that study offers evidence of economic voting across 583 of Nigeria's 774 Local Government Areas. (Since INEC never released presidential results at the LGA level, those tests are especially important for scholars interested in African elections.) Those statistical tests show that local governments with lower levels of socio-economic development were more likely to vote for the APC in 2015. Conversely, better-off areas were more likely to vote for the PDP. Because the unit of analysis is much smaller than a state, that study provides a good basis for making inferences about voting behavior specifically, rather than patterns across states, as the tests show here. Overall, this means that across multiple tests, using both objective measures of economic performance and subjective perceptions of the economy, scholars have compelling empirical support that Nigerians in 2015 engaged in economic voting. As Basedau et al. (2011) put it, evaluations of economic performance do matter more and more in Africa.

As the economy declined in 2014, it was logical for the opposition to run on the economy. However if the salience of the economy trumps counter-terrorism as a politically useful issue, then democratic governments have few reasons to fear being held accountable for ineffective counter-terrorism. This heightens the paradox of democratic counter-terrorism identified in the book's Introduction. After a relative lull in attacks 2014, terrorism took a turn for the worse in Adamawa, home to the chief who introduced this chapter, and in Borno State (Thurston 2018). Then the Buhari government's new national security team faced horrific new tactics from the same stubborn threat that had bedeviled the PDP. In the five months starting in April 2017, Boko

Haram killed at least 381 civilians, more than doubling the civilian deaths compared to the previous five months. By another measure, between May and August, seven times more civilians were killed than in the preceding four months (Amnesty International 2017). The deaths were largely due to Boko Haram's increased use of suicide bombers (Matfess 2017). For the APC, the shoe was now on the other foot as its own national security strategies seemed in doubt. In the book's Conclusion, I will argue that due to the paradox of democratic counter-terrorism, electorally responsive government by itself is insufficient for generating public safety as a public good enjoyed by all. Good counter-insurgency will require horizontal accountability – the checks and balances increasingly absent in government and central to the hopes of new civil society campaigns.

Conclusion

A few weeks after Buhari took the oath of office, he wrote an opinion piece entitled "We Will Stop Boko Haram," highlighting the Jonathan administration's failure to defeat the terrorist group and the national embarrassment due to the kidnapping of the Chibok girls. "My administration will act differently," he wrote in the *New York Times*, "indeed it is the very reason we have been elected" (Buhari 2015). While insecurity played an important role in the campaign, the test results in this chapter indicate that when voters went into the polling booth, Buhari's supporters more often had the economy on their minds. To win, African opposition parties need an informed critique of the status quo alongside a thoughtful alternative such as the APC's platform for anti-corruption, economic growth, and electoral integrity in the previous chapter. The large number of PDP defectors in the APC, including five governors and dozens of National Assembly members, boosted the credibility of the APC's promises on the issues examined here. This helped an untested opposition party overcome a lack of experience at the federal level that otherwise impedes electoral competition in Africa. The first party turnover in Nigeria's history was not an accident of history. It resulted from a campaign that highlighted the PDP's vulnerabilities and lowered the costs of voting against the party that had ruled since the 1999 transition.

There were many reasons to expect citizens to "vote against violence," as this chapter's title proposes: surveys had repeatedly identified Boko Haram's terrorism as the nation's top priority, the Jonathan administration had suffered embarrassment from the #BringBackOurGirls social media campaign around the schoolgirls kidnapped from Chibok, and confidence in the police and the military had reached new lows. However, my statistical tests offered little support for the national in/security hypothesis. These tests constitute useful contributions to the literature. We generally know less about the effects of violence on voting behavior in the developing world, as noted by Burchard (2015) and explained in the book's introduction. Moreover, by testing the hypothesis in different ways, my empirical examination was able to compare the effects of violent deaths overall and evaluations of national security policy on electoral outcomes. These are suitable tests since, as noted in the literature review, most violence in Africa actually does not occur during election years (Strauss and Taylor 2012). Without these different measurements, we might have missed potential political effects of violence. In the end, insecurity was less of a priority in the states supporting APC, much as Chapter 3 would suggest. I also found that PDP voters were risk-averse when it came to security, and they were unwilling to put their faith in a former Muslim dictator from the north. Then, with the growing possibility of electoral defeat, the PDP engaged in "demonstration counter-terrorism" with a military surge through the northeast accompanied by a public relations campaign.

PDP voters were also risk-averse on economic issues, and the economic voting hypothesis convincingly demonstrated that APC supporters were willing to believe the promises of an opposition party less than two years old. Voters with more favorable opinions of the economy over the last year, with higher levels of disposable income, and with large doubts about Buhari's ability to improve the economy overwhelmingly voted to re-elect President Jonathan. The coefficients on my variables measuring state-level economic conditions reinforce this interpretation; economically indebted states voted to keep Jonathan, while states that were enjoying economic expansion (and therefore collecting additional internal revenue) wanted to keep the good times rolling. These separate control variables helpfully contribute to the literature on fiscal federalism, which has long asserted that low levels of IGR correspond with states' weak political autonomy (Lijphart 1999; Onwudiwe and Suberu 2005). As a result of these two variables, I am better able to specify debt as a mechanism of fiscal dependency that undermines political autonomy, and to consider IGR as a tool for estimating wealth generation.

The results of the economic voting hypothesis generally support the research by Basedau et al. (2011; 2007), Elischer (2013) and others who have documented the electoral benefits of programmatic appeals. Importantly, Nigerians in 2015 voted not just on their own economic situation but on evaluations of economic policy performance. This is also interesting because existing research notes that African voters often care about different issues than the ones that parties campaign on (Uddhammar et al. 2011). In Nigeria, the two major parties ran on different issues and the APC's efforts to give the economy primacy among its campaign themes paid off. As I found in my research with Page and Ha (2018), clientelism can be costly, making provision of public policy the more rational political decision because it caters to a broader base of voters. This also echoes Lindberg and Morrison's (2008) study of Ghana's elections, where evaluations of politics and policy outweighed "non-evaluative" considerations, such as patronage or ethnic ties. The next chapter explores such considerations including ethnic voting, a major theme in studies of African elections but a variable that played no significant role in the tests here. After examining the role of ethnicity and religion in shaping preferences among individual voters, the next chapter offers a more worrisome message than the conclusion here.

Appendix 4.1
Descriptive Statistics and Data Sources

Table 4.3 *Descriptive Statistics for State-Level Data.*

Variable	Number of Observations	Mean	Standard Deviation	Min.	Max.
ΔPDPvote	37	−13.282	10.663	−35.5707	7.128
Violence	35	1.429	.837	.185	3.893
Log.Police	37	733.297	314.215	172	1627
AttacksGJ	35	1.706	.246	1.029	2.040
AttacksMB	35	1.602	.414	1.07	2.477
EconOpinion	34	2.735	.420	1.940	3.591
Income	35	2.024	.288	1.509	2.688
Jonathan.Econ	35	.5274	.319	.01	.98
Buhari.Econ	35	.536	.317	.030	1
StateDebt	35	.096	.957	−1.947	2.391
ΔIGR	36	.279	4.348	−8.927	12.911
Governor	36	.611	.494	0	1
ΔTurnout	35	−10.920	12.817	−49.025	8.334
Literacy	37	68.550	11.729	40.879	88.346
GenderRatio	35	.503	.011	.480	.531
HausaFulani	35	.264	.375	0	1

ΔPDPvote, dependent variable

Data collected from the Independent National Electoral Commission (INEC). Measures the change in the PDP's vote share between 2011 and 2015. Calculated as the percent change vote share between the 2015 and 2011 election in each state. This variable and several others are available for download at carllevan.com/data/elections2015-levan-page-ha/.

Violence, independent variable

Data collected from the Institute on Francophone Research in Africa (IFRA) at the University of Ibadan's Nigeria Watch database. Measures average of publically reported deaths from 2010 to 2014.

Log.Police, independent variable

Measures the police per capita in each Nigerian state. Figures are for 2012, gathered from the Nigerian Police Force's website (http://npf.gov.ng/), except for the following states, where online figures were missing and the figures from the *Annual Abstract of Statistics 2012* were therefore used: Abuja, Kaduna, and Niger are for 2010, and Abia, Anambra, and Enugu are for 2011.

AttacksGJ, independent variable

Data collected from US State Department – sponsored 2015 pre-election survey question: "And do you think the frequency of extremist attacks will increase, decrease or stay the same if Jonathan is re-elected in 2015?" Measures self-reported perceptions of electoral voting. Coded as 1 represents that attacks would "decrease," 2 means attack frequency would "remain the same," and 3 indicates that attacks would "increase." Calculated as a state-level aggregate.

AttacksMB, independent variable

Data collected from US State Department-sponsored 2015 pre-election survey question "And do you think the frequency of extremist attacks will increase, decrease or stay the same if Buhari is elected in 2015?" Measures self-reported perceptions of electoral voting. Coded as 1 represents attacks would "decrease," 2 means attack frequency would "remain the same," and 3 indicates that attacks would "increase." Calculated as a state-level aggregate.

EconOpinion, independent variable

Data collected from the Nigerian responses in the Afrobarometer Round 6 survey asking how the respondent would rate the economic condition of Nigeria compared to twelve months ago on a scale of 1 to 5, where 1 = much worse, 2 = worse, 3 = same, 4 = better, and 5 = much better. Measures self-identified perceptions of recent national economic performance. It is aggregated at the state level, transforming it from a categorical to a continuous variable.

Income, independent variable

Data collected from US State Department-sponsored 2015 pre-election survey question asking, "With regards to your monthly household income, please tell me which of the following phrases best suits your household situation?" Measures self-reported perceptions of purchasing power. Calculated as an aggregate at the state level of the categorical values of 1 = unable to meet basic needs without charity, 2 = able to meet basic needs, 3 = able to meet basic needs with some non-essential goods, 4 = able to purchase most non-essential goods, 5 = plenty of disposable money.

Jonathan.Econ, independent variable

Data collected from US State Department-sponsored 2015 pre-election survey question asking, "And please tell me whether the following statement applies to President Jonathan or not. He can improve Nigeria's economy." Measures self-identified perceptions of the country's economic future with Jonathan. Calculated by recoding as a dichotomous dummy variable with 1 = yes and 0 = other, adding the individual-level (urban/rural respondent) weights, and aggregating the variable by using state as the breakout variable.

Buhari.Econ, independent variable

Data collected from US State Department-sponsored 2015 pre-election survey question asking "And please tell me whether the following statement applies to General Buhari or not. He can improve Nigeria's economy." Measures self-identified perceptions of the country's economic future with Buhari. Calculated by recoding as a dichotomous dummy variable with 1 = yes and 0 = other, adding the individual-level (urban/rural respondent) weights, and aggregating the variable by using state as the breakout variable.

StateDebt, control variable

Data collected from the Nigerian Government's Debt Management Office (http://services.gov.ng/states). Information cross-referenced and missing data gathered from newspapers including: *Premium Times, Daily Independent, Vanguard, Daily Times, Guardian, Leadership,* and *Punch.* Other sources consulted include: yourbudgit.com, Channelstv.com, Naijapolitica.com, and aitonline.tv. Measures subnational fiscal discipline. Calculated in real terms the logged ratio of each state's (foreign and domestic) debt between 2011 and 2014 using the World Bank's Gross Domestic Product GDP deflator.

ΔIGR, control variable

Data collected from the Central Bank of Nigeria's *Annual Reports* for years 2010 through 2013. Measures the change in subnational internally generated revenue (IGR). Calculated by subtracting the mean IGR as a share of state revenue between 2010 and 2012 from IGR as a share of total revenue in 2013.

Governor, control variable

Data from INEC. This dummy variable indicates the incumbent governor's party, with 1 indicating a governor in the ruling PDP and 0 signaling the APC. Imo State is coded as 1 because the All Progressives Grand Alliance adopted Goodluck Jonathan as its candidate. The PDP held twenty-three states after the 2011 elections, so the defection of five PDP governors to APC in 2013, along with 57 members of the 360-seat House of Representatives and 22 of 109 senators is important; the variable is coded after all of these defections.

Δ*Turnout*, control variable

Data collected from INEC. This measures the percent-change in voter turnout between the 2011 and 2015 presidential elections.

Literacy, control variable

Data collected from the *National Literacy Survey* (National Bureau of Statistics 2010). Measures the rate of literacy in English or the state's local language, expressed as a percent.

GenderRatio, control variable

Data collected from US State Department-sponsored 2015 pre-election survey, where questioners discerned the gender of the survey participant. Measures the gender ratio in each state. Calculated by weighting for urban/rural and recoding as a dichotomous dummy variable with 1 = male and 0 = other.

HausaFulani, control variable

Data collected from US State Department-sponsored 2015 pre-election survey question asking, "Would you mind telling me to which ethnic group you belong?" This represents self-identified ethnicity. Calculated as an aggregate at the state level of individual responses categorized as a dummy variable between self-identified Hausa or Fulani coded as 1, with all other ethnic groups represented with 0.

Appendix 4.2

Dependent Variable *ΔPDPVOTE*

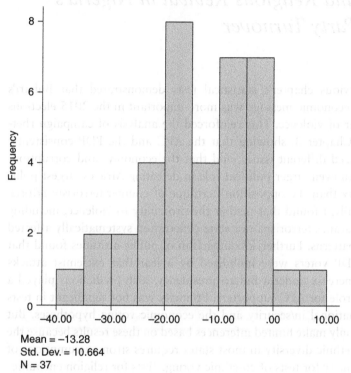

Mean = −13.28
Std. Dev. = 10.664
N = 37

Figure 4.1 Frequency of values on dependent variable.

5 | Electoral Integrity, Ethnic Affinity, and Religious Revival in Nigeria's Party Turnover

The previous chapter's statistical tests demonstrated that Buhari's hopeful economic message was more important in the 2015 elections than fear of violence. This reinforced the analysis of campaign rhetoric in Chapter 3, showing that the APC and the PDP consistently emphasized different issues, and that the economy (and corruption) played an even larger political role in defeating Africa's largest political party than the opposition's critique of counter-terrorism efforts. Specifically, I found that neither the proximity to violence, including Boko Haram's terrorism, nor state penetration systematically affected voting patterns. Further, a comparison of public attitudes found that while PDP voters were mobilized by a fear that extremist attacks would increase under a Buhari presidency, such predictions played a smaller role for APC supporters. Ethnicity was not significant in tests of the national in/security and the economic voting hypotheses. But we can only make limited inferences based on these results because the level of ethnic diversity in most states requires strong assumptions of homogeneity for tests of co-ethnic voting. Tests for religion encounter a similar problem, especially in areas such as the Middle Belt (I omitted religion as a control variable due to statistical collinearity with ethnicity).[1] In addition, just because politicians did not campaign using overt religious and ethnic appeals, at least in the operational terms used in Chapter 3's content analysis, that does not mean that they were not shaping voter choice. Such appeals could appear indirectly through socialization or messaging by ethnic and religious leaders.

This chapter tests for the influence of religious and ethnic identity on voting with finer granularity by utilizing individual-level data from

---

[1] Religious diversity also appears to be understated in conventional characterizations of the north. The kidnapping of the Chibok girls in 2014 served as a reminder to pay attention to pockets of Christianity, even in "core" northern states such as Borno and Adamawa that are generally associated with Islam.

surveys. First, I outline reasons why we would expect religious affiliation to influence voting behavior, notably by reminding the reader that
the incumbent president was an Ijaw Christian from the south, while
the opposition candidate, Buhari, was a northern Muslim with Fulani
heritage. A "religious referendum" hypothesis predicts that Muslim
voters were far more likely to vote for Buhari. Second, to supplement
the previous chapters' discussion about the role of ethnicity in politics, I explain Nigeria's "connected plurality" electoral threshold for
winning presidential elections, which was explicitly designed to promote ethnoregional coalition-building. One map illustrates the states
that each candidate won, with Buhari unsurprisingly winning across
the north. Another map then shows that while the north–south divide
remains vivid, Jonathan made some inroads into the north-central
region as well as the Middle Belt. It is also encouraging that Buhari had
some appeal in sectors of the south. To statistically test the extent to
which Nigerians voted along ethnic lines, an "ethnic affinity" hypothesis predicts that voters who self-identify as either Hausa or Fulani
are more likely to vote for Buhari. Next, because Chapter 3 found
that the issue of electoral integrity played a larger role in the parties'
campaigns than expected, I conduct a test for how voters' perceptions
of the Independent National Electoral Commission (INEC) influenced
choice of presidential candidate.

Fourth, tests confirm each hypothesis, first at the bivariate level and
then with multivariate probit tests that control for potentially intervening conditions. Unlike the statistical tests in the previous chapter,
here I use citizens' voting intentions as the dependent variable. The
tests show that citizens with more negative evaluations of INEC were
more likely to support Buhari. They also show that ethnic identity
proved a reliable predictor of voter preferences – and religion even
more so. My analysis of the results notes that these findings on ethnicity are generally consistent with the research discussed in the literature review; even as citizens increasingly vote on policy evaluations,
ethnicity still has a strong appeal. The strong correlation between religion and voting, in light of the politicization of religious institutions as
well as Boko Haram's terror, is more worrisome.

The previous two chapters amounted to a hopeful message by
implying that Nigerians share with other Africans a growing interest
in evaluating policy performance rather than relying on ethnic loyalties or clientelist promises. This chapter offers a warning of sorts. To a

significant degree – and one might say to an alarming extent – Buhari was "the Muslim candidate." The 2015 election amounted to a religious referendum more than the analysis of rhetoric in Chapter 3 by itself indicates. Religion's powerful allure means that new peacebuilding leadership and possibly urgent new electoral reforms may be necessary to weaken the political salience of faith in the future.

The Religious Referendum Hypothesis

A Plateau State politician, Zaka Akos, summed up the powerful effects of religion on elections: "they take religion first, before the political parties. For example, if you bring a good politician for governor and you are touching on a religion other than Christianity, you will find it difficult to sell, no matter how good he is" (Akos 2016). This is actually a relatively new problem in Plateau State. According to a recent study, inter-religious violence was almost unheard of before 1986. But, since the 1999 transition, it has been the site of major inter-religious clashes in 2001, 2004, 2006, 2008, and 2010, plus numerous recurring, minor incidents (Vinson 2017). Does religion really impact politics, as local politicians like Akos fear?

There are many ways that religion could influence the social and political context of voting. One obvious influence could be visible in the twelve of the thirty-six states that have some version of Islamic law on the books, a result of state legislatures passing such laws immediately after the 1999 transition to democracy (Paden 2005). Those states constitute a large plurality, and possibly a majority of the population overall. Given the popular demand for Sharia, when understood as a social justice framework (Afrobarometer 2009a), it is reasonable to expect that Muslim voters would strongly prefer Buhari, the Muslim candidate. However, a large share of Yorubas in the southwest – perhaps half of them – are Muslim. Historically their faith did not fall under the suzerainty of the nineteenth-century Caliphate, and in the twentieth century they have clashed along communal lines rather than on religious terms (Laitin 1986). This is reflected in their voting patterns too, with the southwest sometimes voting for a Muslim candidate (for example, in 1993 and 1999) and other times supporting the Christian candidate (as in 2003 and 2011).

Religion has also taken on new politicized forms since the 1999 transition, detailed in Chapter 2. "The return of democratic rule created an enlarged public space for the free pursuit of religious and political programs without fear of secret service harassment," writes Kalu in *African Pentecostalism* (Kalu 2008, 231). The rise of Boko Haram since 2009 increased hostile feelings about Islam in much of the south, to put it politely. Talk about "the mistake of 1914" – referring to the year that the British amalgamated the northern and southern regions – became especially pronounced (LeVan 2015b). In the Niger Delta, ethnic Ijaws were united behind the incumbent president, one of their own, while elsewhere in the south some Christians saw the election as a kind of referendum on religion. Christian Pentecostals use the Old Testament parable of "the bondswoman," in which servants ride horses and princes walk as servants, to assert that, "years of Muslim control of governance must be unnatural; it was time for Christians to regain their lost saddle" (Kalu 2008, 243). According to Kalu, Sunday sermons often legitimize Christian complaints passed down since independence; northerners have dominated politics – a perception seemingly validated by long stretches of military rule by northern dictators prior to 1999. For such reasons, we might expect to see a positive correlation between Christian voters and support for the PDP. We would conversely expect to see a correlation between Muslim identification and support for Buhari. Seemingly anticipating the rise of Buhari, Kalu says of the post-transition years, "It was now possible for populist politicians to mobilize against wealthy Muslims and tap into the radicalism of either students or *almajiris*" (Kalu 2008, 231). Almajiris are poor youth sent by their families to religious schools or to study under imams; later on, I mention how they also relate to analyses of Boko Haram. Religion has always been important in Nigerian politics, but, for all these reasons, it is especially important for understanding the climate in 2015.

The "religious referendum" hypothesis, therefore, predicts that Muslim voters were more likely to support the Muslim candidate. Here, I create the variable *Muslim*, where 1 = Muslim and 0 takes on all other values. In the survey, 37.9 percent of the respondents described themselves as Muslim, 60.8 percent called themselves Christian, and only 18 people out of 3,953 said they were not religious, did not know, or did not respond. If Nigeria had a different sociocultural composition, I might have simply been able to include this variable in Chapter 4's state-level regression analysis. However, I opted to drop it due to high collinearity with *HausaFulani*, meaning there is a very close statistical association between religion and ethnicity.[2] Unlike the previous tests, these statistical specifications utilize survey data at the individual level, obviating the need to make assumptions about unit homogeneity.

The Ethnic Affinity Hypothesis

In ethnolinguistic terms, Nigeria stands out as the most diverse country in Africa. The Secretary to the State Government in Adamawa, one of the states hardest hit by Boko Haram, described how such diversity impacts politics this way: "Adamawa also happens to be one of the states where you have nearly one hundred different tribal entities that do not necessarily like each other. And therefore communal clashes are one of the things we also have been experiencing over the years. If you latch political system onto these differences, then you find that people are fighting for the same thing over and over again" (Bindir 2016).

In this section, I formulate an "ethnic affinity" hypothesis to see if citizens who identified themselves as Hausa or Fulani simply engaged in co-ethnic voting by supporting Buhari. I expect to find that the ethnic identity of the candidate remains important for Nigerian voters. But if politicians know that ethnicity alone offers an inadequate basis for forming a winning electoral coalition, rational politicians prime voters to vote on other interests, too. As noted in Chapter 4's literature review and analysis of the findings, ethnic voting often operates alongside issue-based politics, similar to Norris and Mattes' (2013) findings. As Basedau (2011) puts it, ethnic campaigning is increasingly a losing strategy for political parties; evaluations of government performance matter more and more. Thus, even if voters continue to self-identify with their ethnic group, and such cultural saliencies increase around election time, political parties need to campaign on broader appeals to win at the national level. In Ghana's 2008 election, for example, exit polls show that support for political parties cut across ethnic groups, and the incumbent's performance and economic conditions affected voter choice more than their ethnic group (Hoffman and Long 2013). Bratton et al.'s (2013) study of sixteen countries finds that "without denying that ethnic sentiments play a role in shaping vote choice, we

---

[2] The estimated value for the variance inflation factor tests for each of these two variables, ranged between 7 and 10.

note that rational calculations about material welfare are apparently at the forefront of voters' minds" (Bratton et al. 2011, 96).

Managing diversity has been one of Nigeria's great post-colonial projects of nation-building though civic education (Agbaje 1997), federalism and state creation (Suberu 1991), the use of ethnic quotas known as "federal character" (Ekeh and Osaghae 1989), and the rotation of political offices at every level of government (Olaitan 2000). Various policies and laws assume strong links between ethnicity and geography. Federal character in fact operationalizes this idea by mandating the federal cabinet to be representative of the country's diversity, which by convention means at least one minister from each of the thirty-six states. Federal character may help represents states, but less and less so the ethnic communities who actually live in them. This is increasingly the case with a rise in involuntary migration due to the sprawling conflict with Boko Haram, in addition to natural disasters and climate-induced migration such as the receding Lake Chad (LeVan 2015b).

Rotation effectively renders certain groups or individuals ineligible for office when it is not their "turn." Politically, though not constitutionally, the country is divided into six ethnoregional "zones," making it possible for political party rules and the National Assembly's internal rules to allocate and rotate offices by zone. These various political units mean that Nigerians assess inclusiveness based on different units of scale: states, zones, or, at the broadest level, north/south. Another tool for managing diversity is what political scientists refer to as a "connected plurality" (Shugart and Carey 1992). The constitution stipulates that winning a presidential election requires meeting complex criteria. Section 134 (2) states that the winning candidate needs both the highest number of votes *and* "not less than one-quarter of the votes cast at the election in each of at least two-thirds of all the States in the Federation and the Federal Capital Territory, Abuja." By mandating a geographical distribution of support, candidates must make broad national appeals across ethnic groups and regions in order to win.[3] Incredibly, in 1979 no candidate obtained 25 percent of the vote in two-thirds of the states, so the Supreme Court decided the election by declaring that 12-and-2/3 was close enough to 13 out of the

---

[3] Kenya's 2010 constitution adopted similar provisions.

then-19 states. As a result, the 1999 constitution in effect today contains elaborate provisions for runoff elections.[4]

For these and other reasons, formulating a good test of the ethnic affinity hypothesis is more complicated than simply predicting that citizens will vote for the candidate from their ethnic group. For example, in 2011, a highly suspicious 97.3 percent of voters in the South-South zone, encompassing the Niger Delta, voted for Goodluck Jonathan, an ethnic Ijaw from the area (Paden 2016, 53). This suggests that Ijaws voted overwhelmingly for their ethnic kin, but that leaves the voting behavior of people in the other thirty states (plus Abuja) unexplained. The confusing results of the 1999 election offer another sort of complexity; in 1999 the six Yoruba-dominated states in the Southwest zone voted 3:1 *against* Olusegun Obasanjo, a Yoruba Christian, mainly due to historical resentment over his handling of the 1979 election debacle (LeVan et al. 2003).[5] In addition, the 2015 election arguably did not provide an ideal test of ethnic voting since Buhari came from the largest ethnic group, the Hausa-Fulani, while the Ijaws are a minority group (albeit a large one).

In light of these characteristics of the main candidates in the 2015 election, it is useful to examine patterns of ethnic voting in different ways. Before statistically testing the ethnic affinity hypothesis, I therefore produce two maps of the election results. The first one shows who won each state, while the second one illustrates the states where Buhari secured at least 25 percent in order to satisfy the electoral system's connected plurality requirements. The electoral system alters the geographical logic of campaign strategy. A party can make inroads into its rival's stronghold without necessarily seeking to win the state outright; this requires the other party to defend itself on its home turf. In 2015, we would expect to observe the APC clearing the connected plurality

---

[4] In the first runoff, the candidate who scores the highest number of votes competes against the candidate who received a majority of votes in the highest number of states. If neither candidate meets the connected plurality requirement plus a *majority* of votes nationally at that point, then INEC schedules a second runoff election, seven days later. That second runoff pits those two candidates against each other a second time, with the winner determined by simple majority.

[5] When they voted overwhelmingly *for* him in 2003, evidence points to a deal for the Alliance for Democracy, the dominant party in the southwest, to not run a presidential candidate in return for Obasanjo's help securing gubernatorial seats (Momoh 2014). It was thus party strategy and not necessarily ethnic loyalty.

threshold in a few states in the Niger Delta, where Jonathan is from, and/or the southeast, which has cultural and historical connections (discussed further in Chapter 6) with the core Delta states, and which has been a reliable base for the PDP since 1999.

If we take the historical and cultural differences between north and south, rooted in their different histories divergent colonial experiences (Falola 2009), we can think of these maps as a preliminary – or simplified – test of ethnic voting. Here we would predict that voters in the nineteen northern states would vote for Buhari (including Abuja, the Federal Capital Territory), the "northern" candidate, while voters from the eighteen southern states will vote for Jonathan, the "southern" candidate. The "core" north is typically limited to the twelve states whose legislatures passed some form of Sharia law in 1999–2000 (Paden 2012). I count as a northern state all members of the Northern Governors' Forum, an organization that defends states' rights. Figure 5.1 illustrates each candidates' victory by state.

It is clear from the map of election results that the APC drew most of its support from the northern states, while the PDP received the strongest levels of support from the Niger Delta states of the South-South zone and from Igbos in the southeast. However, it is important to note the distribution of electoral support not apparent in this map; the APC received over 4.3 million votes in the south, while the PDP received over 3.8 million votes in the north. Such a distribution of support is necessary to meet the connected plurality threshold, which requires obtaining at least 25 percent of the vote in at least nineteen of the thirty-six states (plus Abuja). It is therefore some evidence of voting beyond coethnicity. Figure 5.2 re-codes the map to illustrate the states where Jonathan won at least 25 percent of the vote. Doing so in effect sets the bar lower for assessing citizens' willingness to cross ethnic lines to support a candidate; the candidate does not need to "win" the state in the sense of getting the most votes. This resembles the actual constitutional requirements for being elected president, and it enables an assessment of voting behavior that better mirrors political parties' campaign strategies. States such as Ekiti and Edo were "battleground states" for the PDP, where the party spent millions of naira in efforts to buy off traditional rulers, priests, and influential pastors. The APC did not win the states, but it did challenge Jonathan's base, requiring him to divert time and resources to states that should have been easy electoral victories (Emeana et al. 2017).

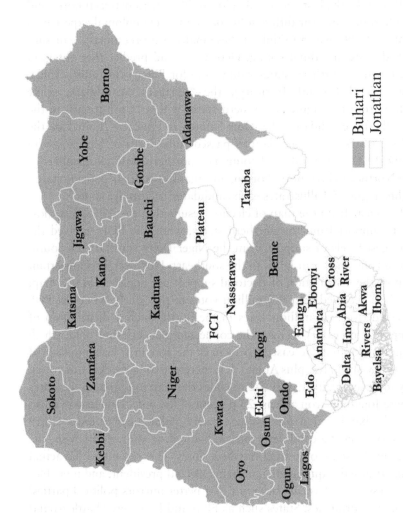

Figure 5.1 Presidential election results by state, showing candidate with most votes.
Source: Official INEC results

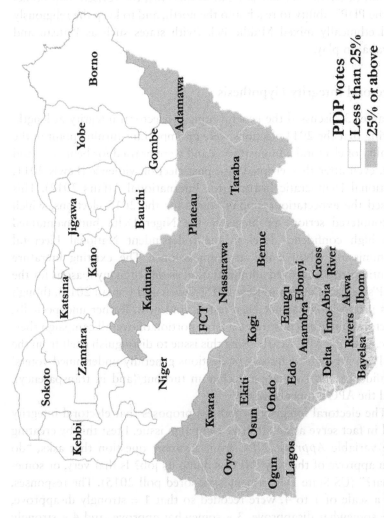

Figure 5.2 Presidential election, showing states where Jonathan won at least 25 percent.

Source: Independent National Election Commission

Thinking about the 2015 election this way generates a different visual, providing some evidence of inter-ethnic voting. Figure 5.1 shows that Buhari got more votes than Jonathan in twenty-one states. But Figure 5.2 shows that Jonathan secured more than 25 percent in a total of twenty-six states. Read in this way, the revised map points to the PDP's ability to reach into the north, and to keep the religiously and ethnically mixed Middle Belt (with states such as Plateau and Taraba) in play.

Electoral Integrity Hypothesis

Chapter 3 discussed the general topic of electoral integrity at length, noting that the 2011 elections were an important turning point in the quality of electoral administration and were praised for being free and fair, even after they erupted into post-election violence (Lewis 2011; National Democratic Institute for International Affairs 2012). This raised the expectations among voters for the 2015 elections, which encountered serious problems in the Niger Delta but maintained the high confidence level in the Independent National Electoral Commission (INEC) and its commissioner. The existing literature mentions this improved administration as one of many reasons for the PDP's defeat (Lewis and Kew 2015; Owen and Usman 2015), though this proposition has not been tested until now. Rather unexpectedly, electoral integrity constituted a large portion of overall campaign rhetoric, with the APC clearly using this issue to distinguish itself from the PDP, a party whose history of elections generally undermined voters' confidence and oversaw a decline in turnout (and in transparency). Did the APC's appeals work?

The electoral integrity hypothesis proposes that electoral integrity did in fact serve as an effective campaign issue. I test this by creating the variable *Approve.INEC* from a survey question that asks, "do you approve of the way INEC is doing its job? Is that very, or somewhat?" (US State Department–sponsored poll 2015). The responses, on a scale of 1 to 4, were recoded so that 1 = strongly disapprove, 2 = somewhat disapprove, 3 = somewhat approve, and 4 = strongly approve. One would generally expect citizens with confidence in institutions in general to approve of the ruling party. Moreover, as noted in Chapter 3, the PDP largely left INEC alone in 2015 according to its commissioner, but the party failed to embrace electoral integrity as a campaign issue with a broad constituency. Confirmation of this hypothesis would support the notion that the PDP should have done so. Support for this hypothesis would appear as a positive coefficient on *Approve.INEC.*

Estimates and Statistical Tests

In this section, I test my hypotheses using survey data. Doing so introduces a few differences from the estimates in Chapter 4 using state-level data. Notably, the dependent variable is different here because I am examining the survey respondent's *intended* vote, rather than the actual observed vote that took place a few weeks later. The variable *Vote.tomorrow* is based on a question from the same survey which asks, "If elections were to take place tomorrow, which presidential candidate would you vote for?" After weighting the sample for whether the respondent was in an urban or rural area, the survey indicated that 47.3 percent said they would vote for Goodluck Jonathan, while 47.7 percent said Muhammadu Buhari, with the remainder either undecided or declaring for another candidate. Since this is a categorical variable, with an indication of support for one of the minor candidates[6] taking on a value ranging from 3 to 12, this would yield meaningless results. I therefore recode the variable so that 1 = support for Jonathan and 0 = support for Buhari. Since the dependent variable (the outcome we are explaining) is binary, I test the hypothesis using probit models. As explained by a popular econometrics textbook, probit models "are applicable in a wide variety of fields and are used extensively in survey or census-type data" where the dependent variable is limited to binary values (Gujarati 1995, 575). This procedure might have presented problems if other candidates had been more popular, but the candidates from the twelve other parties on the ballot received only a combined total of 5 percent of the votes.

---

[6] The other candidates mentioned by survey respondents received the remaining 5.0 percent of the votes. They are Ambrose Albert Owuru (Hope Party), Chekwas Okorie (United Progressive Party), Ganiyu Galadima (Allied Congress Party of Nigeria), Godson Okoye (United Democratic Party), and Rafiu Salawu (Alliance for Democracy). No respondent mentioned the other candidates listed on the ballot.

Bivariate Analysis

For the ethnic affinity hypothesis, I expect voters who self-identify as Hausa or Fulani to cast their lot with Buhari. As the authoritative biography of Buhari notes, his father was Fulani and his mother was a mixture of Hausa and Kanuri. Buhari's father, Adamu Buhari, had three wives. When he died, this set in motion an agreement with the Habe emir, one of the minor Islamic emirates in Katsina to care for Muhammadu's mother and for him. "This played a major role in the upbringing of Buhari," according to his biographer, including his (unenthusiastic) enrollment in a Qur'anic school (Paden 2016, 7). In short, these well-known facts mean that Buhari is ethnically and culturally associated with the north and its historical institutions. Support for this hypothesis would appear as a negative coefficient on the *HausaFulani* variable. Recall that this variable is based on a national survey in which respondents were asked, "Would you mind telling me to which ethnic group you belong?" and 99.1 percent of 3,953 respondents voluntarily identified themselves as belonging to a specific ethnic group (US State Department-sponsored poll 2015).

This approach complements the analysis in the previous chapter, where I controlled for ethnicity in all of the statistical tests of the economic voting and national in/security hypotheses. Taken together, this means that we have an understanding of the impact of ethnic identity on voting at different levels of analysis. In other words, I will ultimately have test results incorporating ethnicity using aggregated demographic data at state level as well as the individual level data from surveys used in the tests here. This provides a more comprehensive test of ethnic voting.

It is important to clarify some expectations for the results of the ethnic affinity tests. In a sense, it will not be terribly surprising to discover that Hausa-Fulani voted for Muhammadu Buhari. But the constitutional requirements for a connected plurality mean that neither ethnic group can win without a geographical distribution of support. This is consistent with Basedau's views about ethnic campaigning being a losing strategy for African political parties (Basedau et al. 2011). Evidence of inter-ethnic voting would also lend support to an institutionalist argument; the electoral system has an important role to play in national integration by creating incentives for politicians to build electoral coalitions across ethnic groups.

Figure 5.3 Voting intentions overall, by candidate.

Figure 5.4 Voting intentions of Islamic voters.

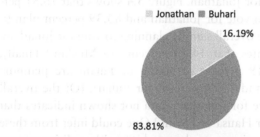

Figure 5.5 Voting intentions of Hausa and Fulani voters.

For the religious referendum hypothesis, we expect Islamic voters to support Buhari, recalling that Jonathan is a Christian from the south. This would appear as a negative coefficient on the *Muslim* variable. Rejection of this hypothesis would lend support to the notion that the choice of Yemi Osinbajo, a devout Christian, as vice president helped offset the perception of the election as a religious referendum. Finally, for the electoral integrity hypothesis, I expect voters who have lower

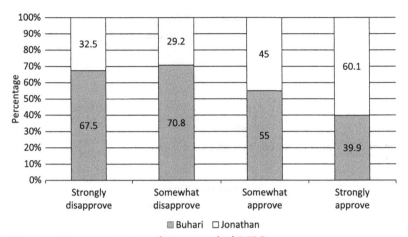

Figure 5.6 Voting intentions, by approval of INEC.

evaluations of INEC's performance to support Buhari. This would appear as a positive coefficient on the *Approve.INEC* variable. I test these hypotheses first on a bivariate level in the figures below, where *Vote.tomorrow* indicates voters' intensions as stated in the survey.

Figure 5.3 shows 51.62 of voters planned to vote for Buhari, while 48.38 planned to vote for Jonathan. Figure 5.4 shows that 16.61 percent of Muslims plan to vote for Jonathan and 83.39 percent plan to vote for Buhari. (Of the overall sample planning to vote for Jonathan, data not shown indicates that 14.53 percent are Muslim.) Finally, Figure 5.5 shows 16.19 percent of Hausa or Fulani are planning to vote for Jonathan, and 83.81 percent for Buhari. (Of the overall sample planning to vote for Jonathan, data not shown indicates that 10.64 percent are either Hausa or Fulani.) One could infer from these results that ethnic identity strongly overlaps with politics among Hausa-Fulani, and that Buhari therefore did in fact have strong ethnic appeal. But it is also important from four-way cross tabs that of support for Buhari, 48.37 percent comes from non-Hausa-Fulani.[7] Figure 5.6 shows that 67.6 percent of respondents who "strongly disapprove" of INEC planned to vote for Buhari, while 60.1 percent of those who "strongly approve" of INEC planned to vote for Jonathan.

---

[7] In light of the poor demographic data available on ethnicity in Nigeria, it of general interest that of non-Hausa-Fulani 18.7 percent are Muslims, and of all Muslims 69.31 are Hausa-Fulani.

The average citizens' opinion of INEC was a good predictor of voting intentions.

Multivariate Analysis with Control Variables

Next, I test the hypotheses on a multivariate level. I include some of the same control variables used for my tests of the national in/security and economic voting hypotheses in the previous chapter: *gender* and *income*, from the survey data. Recall that *income* is based on a survey question that asks about monthly household income and scoring on a scale of 1 to 5, with 5 indicating "plenty of disposable money." Because I am using the individual-level data for the ethnic affinity hypothesis, rather than the variables aggregated to the state-level above for cross-sectional tests across states, I am unable to use the *Literacy* variable, which measures literacy at the state level. Fortunately, the survey asked a question that offers a valid alternative. The survey first asked "Do you have any formal schooling, or not?" with 91.3 percent of the respondents said yes. Then the survey asked, "If yes, what is the highest level of schooling you have reached?" Answers were as follows: 1 = some primary schooling, 2 = primary schooling complete, 3= some secondary, 4 = secondary school complete, 5 = post-secondary qualifications, other than university; 6 = some university, and 7 = university complete. Only 11 out of 3,609 respondents said "don't know" or did not answer. I use this data to create the variable *Schooling*. Similarly, since I cannot use my existing controls for political conditions, I created the variable *ApproveGov* from a survey question measuring the approval rating of the governor. I recoded the variable from the original dataset, so that a value of 1 = strongly disapprove, 2 = somewhat disapprove, 3 = somewhat approve, and 4 = strongly approve. The 54 out of the 3,953 respondents who said "don't know" or declined to respond were dropped.

Finally, the variable *Age* controls for the possibility that the candidates appealed to different age cohorts. For example, it is plausible that Jonathan's campaign mobilized young people. According to Lewis and Kew's analysis of the election, "His backstory as a poor village youth from a minority group (he is an Ijaw) native to the Delta also inspired some admiration" (Lewis and Kew 2015, 98). It is also plausible that Buhari was the one who inspired many of the ten million youths who became eligible to vote for the first time in 2015 due to Nigeria's population boom. "The APC is determined to give a voice to the youth, *mekunu*, the *umu obenye*, and the *talakawa*," said a campaign manifesto document, adopting multilingual terms to refer to urban youth and working-class citizens left out of the PDP's patronage system (All Progressives Congress 2015a). The dependent variable is *Vote.tomorrow* and the base equation for the statistical models is expressed in Equation 5 as:

Equation 5:

$$Vote.tomorrow_i = \beta_0 + \beta_1 (Independent\ Variable) + \beta_2 (ApproveGov) +$$
$$\beta_3 (Income) + \beta_4 (Schooling) + \beta_5 (Gender) +$$
$$\beta_6 (Age) + \varepsilon$$

The results of the probit tests are displayed in Table 5.1. Since I am reporting marginal effects, this means I am describing the change in Y^* for each unit change in X. The ratio dy/dx is a discrete change of dummy variable from 0 to 1.

The test of the ethnic affinity hypothesis in column 1 indicates that almost 49 percent of those surveyed overall were willing to vote for Jonathan. The independent variables then describe how different characteristics affect that likelihood. The negative value of −.479 on *HausaFulani*, the primary variable of interest, means that a respondent's self-identification as either Hausa or Fulani corresponds with a nearly 48-percent difference in support for Goodluck Jonathan, the incumbent president from the Niger Delta Ijaw ethnic group, and Buhari, a northern Muslim with Fulani heritage. The coefficient is statistically significant at the 99-percent confidence interval. The positive coefficient on *ApproveGov* means that for each level of approval (based on the four categories) for the incumbent governor corresponded with a 3.1-percent increase in support for Jonathan. This makes sense since the PDP held most of the governorships going into the election. Similarly, the positive value estimated on *Income* means that an increase in the likelihood of an individual having disposable income (based on the variable's five categories) corresponded with a 3.6-percent increase in support for Jonathan. The coefficients are significant at the 99-percent confidence interval. This result is consistent with the previous chapter's analysis, where tests of the economic voting hypothesis and controls for economic performance both showed that better-off states were consistently more likely to support the PDP. Next, the

Table 5.1 *Probit Regressions for the Hypotheses.*

	(1) Ethnic Affinity		(2) Religious Referendum		(3) Electoral Integrity	
	dy/dx	X	dy/dx	X	dy/dx	X
		(.489)		(.488)		(.499)
HausaFulani	−.479***	.297				
	(−25.99)					
Muslim			−.558***	.404		
			(−33.63)			
Approve.INEC					.127***	3.188
					(9.93)	
ApproveGov	.031***	2.990	.033***	2.991	−.004	2.99
	(3.07)		(3.11)		(−.35)	
Income	.036***	2.012	.026*	2.103	.031**	2.01
	(2.61)		(1.79)		(2.34)	
Schooling	.015**	4.152	.004	4.15	.037***	4.15
	(2.04)		(.64)		(5.10)	
Gender	.010	.518	.013	.518	−.030	.518
	(.45)		(.60)		(−1.50)	
Age	−.002	31.11	.000	31.11	.002**	31.08
	(−1.45)		(.44)		(2.57)	
n (sample)	3,338		3,338		3,318	
N (population)	135,754,565		135,754,565		135,047,813	

Z scores in parentheses; *** p < .01, **p < .05, *p < .1

positive coefficient on *Schooling* means that more educated citizens were more likely to vote for Jonathan. Neither gender nor the age coefficient is significant. The results support the ethnic affinity hypothesis.

Column 2 shows the results of the religious referendum hypothesis, where the primary independent variable of interest is *Muslim*. The negative coefficient estimate of −.558 means that a respondent's self-identification as a Muslim corresponded with a nearly-56-percent decline in support for Goodluck Jonathan, the incumbent, Christian president. The coefficient is statistically significant at the 99-percent confidence interval. The positive coefficient on *ApproveGov* means that an increase in each level of approval for the incumbent governor corresponded with a 3.3-percent increase in support for Jonathan.

The positive values on *Income* similarly indicate that each categorical increase in the likelihood of an individual having disposable income corresponded with a 2.6-percent increase in support for Jonathan, though the coefficient is only weakly significant. This result is consistent with the state-level tests in the previous chapter, in which states that were better-off economically were more likely to support the PDP. The control variables *Gender* and *Age* are not significant. Notably, the level of education as measured by the *Schooling* variable loses significance in column 2. This means that education and religion are related, and that religion has a lot of explanatory leverage. The results offer strong support for the religious referendum hypothesis.

Finally, column 3 confirms the electoral integrity hypothesis. Each increased level of approval of INEC on a four-point scale corresponds with a 12.7-percent increase of support for Jonathan, and the coefficient is significant at the 99-percent confidence interval.[8] This is the only test where age is significant, with older voters throwing support for the PDP at a statistically significant level and perhaps suggesting that those voters also have more confidence in electoral institutions. Overall, the results of these tests clearly indicate that ethnic voting remains a part of Nigerian politics, but that religion was arguably even more important. And finally, voters skeptical about INEC's performance, especially among young people, voted for the opposition.

Analysis of Test Results

The findings from the qualitative analysis in Chapter 3 and the statistical support for economic voting in Chapter 4 offer encouraging evidence that issues and ideas are clearly part of political party campaigns and voter reactions to them. As a control variable, *HausaFulani* was not significant in any of those models. But the findings here clearly show that ethnic loyalties remain and the results with regard to religion are arguably disconcerting. Why was *HausaFulani* highly significant in the tests of the ethnic affinity hypothesis, but not significant in Chapter 4's tests of the national in/security and the economic voting

---

[8] Other tests, not shown here, indicate that opinion of Attahiru Jega, though firmly positive, did not correlate with support for either party at a statistically significant level. This "non-finding" suggests that he had an even better reputation than the institution he ran. Only 3.1 percent of respondents said they had never heard of him, suggesting extremely high national name recognition.

hypotheses? As mentioned earlier in this chapter, the answer relates to the different techniques used to measure ethnicity. Since the test of the ethnic affinity hypothesis here uses individual-level data, it offers a more precise measurement of the relationship between voter x and vote y. The statistical evidence of co-ethnic voting may come as no surprise, but the difference in results depending upon the unit of analysis used to measure ethnicity (individual-level data versus data aggregated to the state level) has important implications for Nigeria. The government has not kept track of ethnicity in official statistics for several decades now, and these results suggest that old assumptions that states can represent ethnic groups for purposes of federal character or any other reason are highly suspect. Decades of migration and intermarriage may be changing demographics, and the constitution may not have kept up with these social realities.

The strong effects of *HausaFulani* in the statistical tests of the ethnic affinity hypothesis were accented by agitation across the north for power to return to a president from the region. Any governor from the north probably would have won the election, complained a PDP leader about the party's loss in 2015. "There was a consideration that the north had been shortchanged … because of Jonathan's aspirations to run for a second tenure, this was the reason PDP lost" (Agbim 2017). This view is also relevant to the decay of the PDP outlined in previous chapters. Party elites felt that Jonathan had betrayed his understanding with them to *not* run in 2015. Under the concept of "power shift" as understood in terms of the 1999 pact, it was the north's "turn" to rule. When President Yar'Adua passed away in 2010, this set in motion a set of expectations in the north. When Jonathan became president in 2011, the north was "shortchanged with that arrangement," said a founding PDP member from Kano State in the north. This was "not so much because it had anything against the president, but because the arrangement should have provided a four year tenure for the north and then power would shift" (Lawan 2012). Voting along such cleavages is further facilitated by the weak party attachment, a situation generally lamented by Nigerian scholars (Obafemi et al. 2014). As evidence of this in the context of the 2015 elections, over 79 percent of survey respondents said it is more important to vote for the candidate than for a political party (US State Department-sponsored poll 2015).

The two maps illustrating the geographical distribution of electoral support tell a slightly more encouraging story, largely overlooked in existing analyses of the election. The APC, a party with a presidential candidate associated with the north, received over 4.3 million votes in the south, while the PDP candidate, hailing from the southern Niger Delta, received over 3.8 million votes in the north. This geographical spread of support is necessary to meet the connected plurality threshold, and it provides some evidence of voters crossing ethnic lines. Figure 5.1 shows that Buhari won twenty-one of the thirty-six states. But Figure 5.2 shows that Jonathan secured more than 25 percent, meeting the connected plurality threshold in twenty-six states.

The strong effect of *Muslim*, with even larger coefficients than *HausaFulani*, also has important implications for Nigeria's democratic future. One reason for the rise of religion in 2015 is an important but often overlooked shift in the years before the election: the PDP encouraged and took advantage of the politicization of the Christian Association of Nigeria (CAN) (Campbell 2013a). From its formation in the 1980s until 2010 (the year Jonathan was sworn in as president after the death of Yar'Adua), CAN had been dominated by a "conservative hierarchical" tradition. "For this group, their interaction with Islam is not just superficial; in most cases they have in-depth knowledge of Islam and its traditions" (Mang 2014, 99). This included the Nigerian Anglicans and the Catholics, both of whom were sympathetic to dialogue with Boko Haram, and who imposed a traditional hierarchy on priests and preachers in the lesser leadership. Pentecostals, until then, had primarily been focused on building a following. Once they had done so, Pastor Ayo Oritsejafor articulated a claim to their underrepresentation in politics. This especially resonated at an opportune time since he hailed from the same region as the new president, Jonathan. With his election to CAN, the Pentecostal influence turned a large slice of organized Christianity against dialogue with Boko Haram. As one politically active Catholic priest explained it, "CAN became like a Christian wing of the PDP" – going so far as Jonathan's government providing the president of the organization with a private jet (Ekeroku 2017). In Edo, a Niger Delta state hotly contested by the candidates, the APC accused hundreds of clergy of accepting up to 2 million naira (US$9,800) each. The attempted bribe was exposed, according to new accounts, when the state chair of CAN thought such payments were scandalous (Anonymous 2015b). In another incident, the president of CAN was implicated in a shady effort to import arms from South Africa using his private jet, a charge the president's political strategist denied on CAN's behalf (Eyoboka 2014). This is not to say that the PDP has become a "Christian" party. Nor is it religious in a comparable sense to Turkey's Justice and Development Party, which has propelled conservative Muslims to power, or to Chile's Christian Democratic Party, which mediated the difficult period of Chile's transition by bringing in the Catholic Church (Ozzano and Cavatorta 2013).

Religious influences in Nigeria's 2015 campaign were subtle but, as the test results show, systematic. A member of the Northern Elders Forum, a moderate group of elites that has favored negotiations with Boko Haram at various times, put it this way: "Two things have slowed down the end of the insurgency ... One is the political interest of president [Jonathan] to remain in power. They thought they could use Boko Haram to create an impression of Islamophbia feeling where the north should be treated as Islamic fundamentalists, jihadists" (Abdullah 2016). The APC's Vice Chair in Gombe State, Julius Ahaya, also blames the PDP. "They've been in charge, and they are the ones who introduced religion ... especially with the candidate of then General Muhammadu Buhari. They felt it was the only way they can pitch him against the non-Muslims." Ahaya, a minority Christian in a northern state, complained about the "propaganda" attempting to cast the APC as a religious party, especially in the southern part of the state where Christians are concentrated. The PDP told people "this party is owned by the Muslims and [it is] the Islamic party and things like that ... Just to discourage people and poison their minds." When other Christians in southern Gombe joined APC, they were labeled "sympathetic to Islam" and accused of "selling out" for joining an Islamic party. According to Ahaya, the traditional strategy is to elevate the profile of Christians in the party such as himself in order to undermine such propaganda (Ahaya 2016). The APC has thus far failed to do that, but the party could still fall victim to the public's stereotypes of it.

Religion is woven into the very fabric of Nigeria's political life in different ways. A 2006 survey by the Pew Research Center found that 76 percent of Christians and 91 percent of Muslims say that religion is more important to them than their nationality or their ethnic group. Pew called this "a sharp reminder of the religious divide" (Pew Research Center 2007). A few years later, another study reported that Africans generally rank unemployment, crime, and corruption as bigger problems than religious conflict. But Nigeria (and Rwanda) stood out because six-in-ten respondents said, "religious conflict is a very big problem" (Pew Research Center 2010).[9]

For a country with a long history of religious violence, and a largely secular constitutional compromise at the heart of its democratic authority, the insertion of religion into politics – whether by preachers, politicians, or ordinary people – is an alarming trend that INEC and other authorities would be wise to stem in future elections.

Conclusion

Nigerians should take the evidence of "economic voting" in Chapter 4 and issue-based campaigning in Chapter 3, as "good" news about politics. They should also be encouraged by the idea that an opposition party opened up its primaries, ran on a critique of existing electoral processes, and then managed to win power. There is an emerging electoral constituency for electoral integrity in an important African country. "A very significant thing is that PDP refused to be reformed over 16 years," a southeastern party leader reflected in an interview. "We took a lot of things for granted. You need to periodically do analysis of your weaknesses your strengths, we refused to carry out such reformation in the PDP" (Nnaji 2017). Less encouraging, if less surprising, is the ongoing political salience of ethnicity. Like Bratton, Bhavnani, and Chen (2013), I found that ethnicity mattered, even though economic welfare weighed heavily on voters' minds. Yet, we can remain hopeful that campaign appeals based on issues such as economic growth, job creation, security sector reform, or (perhaps one day) women's rights can dilute these divisive cleavages.

The evidence here of a religious divide is alarming, even if it is not so new. The statistical tests suggest that such thinking permeated not only Anambra State, among activists from the Movement for the Actualization of the Sovereign State of Biafra (MASSOB), but throughout the country wherever Christian communities reside. This was evident in Chapter 4's tests showing that fear of an increase

---

[9] The study also identified sub-Saharan Africa as "clearly among the most religious places in the world. In many countries across the continent, roughly nine-in-ten people or more say religion is very important in their lives."

in insurgent violence under Buhari mobilized PDP voters (model 4) more than the APC's promise of counter-terrorism (model 3). The PDP played to its core supporters by stoking fears of a Muslim president, and in doing so reinforced deepening religious polarization. As evident in the tests of the ethnic affinity hypothesis here, a voter's religion predicted her choice of presidential candidate even more reliably than her ethnic group.

Efforts to weaken the polarizing effects of politicized religion in Nigeria have been under way for several years in connection with insecurity related to Boko Haram's violence in northeast Nigeria and around Lake Chad. The Lake Chad basin includes Niger, Chad, and Cameroon, and is linked to ancient routes for the migration of people, products, and religious prophets for centuries (MacEachern 2018). Nigeria's historical traditions of Sufism and Muslim cultures of conflict resolution offer a theological basis for moderation in a region where terrorism has taken thousands of lives over the last decade (Paden 2005). Religious scholars have repeatedly pointed out the historical, indigenous basis for religious moderation. The Abuja Muslim Forum, for example, blames the lack of formal religious education for the misinformation that leads to radicalization. "Those who studied Islamic Studies as a degree, if checked the quantum of their knowledge is very little," and they tend to lack exposure to other relevant leadership training (Odemwingie and Gbadebo 2015). Underscoring the point, recent studies of the Islamic State, with whom Boko Haram has affiliated, report that that many recruits had a very poor understanding of Islam (Dearden 2017). Whatever indoctrination happens in Sambisa Forest and the group's hideouts near Lake Chad, it may have less to do with religious grievances than casual observations of Boko Haram indicate.

Foreign aid and programming by the government of Nigeria has attempted to increase the influence and capacity of religious moderates. The novel *Born on a Tuesday* offers a cautious warning about how such entreaties might be processed by *almajiris*, youth from poor families who enter religious schools under the tutelage of an imam. Listening to a peacebuilding education program, the main character reflects on how his mentor responded to his foreign visitors:

The man had said that Islam means peace and that all Muslims should be examples of peace in the community. Malam Abdul-Nur said he wanted to make a correction. "Islam does not mean peace," he began. All of us went quiet in the room apart from the boys who follow him everywhere he goes and shout Allahu Akbar after everything he says. They are very annoying, those boys.

The way he spoke English, I did not believe it was Malam Abdul-Nur speaking ... He sounded almost like the men from England, as if there was a small man inside him pushing the words out through his nose.

"Islam means submission. Submission to the will of Allah. And the will of Allah is not the will of the infidel or the will of America. Islam means that we do not submit to anything or anyone but Allah."

It is not that I do not agree with Malam Abdul-Nur. It was the way he tried to make them look like they did not know what they were saying. We all understood what they were saying. They were telling us to be good and kind to change the way the world sees us Muslims (John 2015, 86).

USAID and other donors provided US$43.6 million for a four-year program that established eighty "Nonformal Learning Centers" in two northern states, which aimed to "increase orphans' and vulnerable children's access to basic education, health and counseling" (Creative Associates International 2015, 15). The programs explicitly coordinated with local malams and the government of Nigeria. There is some evidence that such programs to spread the peacebuilding messages in the Qur'an are effective, especially where the proponents are not from England, as in the example from *Born on a Tuesday*. It may be more difficult to assess the lasting impact of more indirect interventions, such as the Northern Education Initiative funded by USAID. I leave these questions aside for empirical analysis of the work by implementers and practitioners. But I also hope such work will digest this chapter's intuitions about the political logic of extremist appeals in an electoral democracy. Electoral law has facilitated inter-ethnic cooperation; whether Nigeria's institutions are adequate to defuse the politicization of religion remains an open question.

The religious polarization is worrisome enough when read in the singular context of Boko Haram. It is even more alarming where it overlaps with a secessionist revival in the overwhelmingly Christian (and Catholic) southeast, and a new wave of tensions between farmers and northern-based pastoralists that is all too often viewed in religious terms. The intersection of these various challenges form the basis of the next chapter. There, I critique standard approaches to democratic consolidation and explore the challenges Nigeria now faces, which I characterize as "stress points." Handing over power from one civilian to the next was a first step, and electoral turnover with the defeat of an incumbent party in 2015 was an even bigger stride toward democracy. The next steps will be difficult for how they will challenge Nigerians' democratic mettle beyond the electoral arena, inviting a rethinking of the very basis of rights and representation.

Appendix 5.1
Descriptive Statistics for Individual-Level Data

Table 5.2 *Descriptive Statistics for Individual-Level Data.*

Variable	Number of Observations	Mean	Linearized Standard Error	95% Confidence Interval	
Vote.tomorrow	3,868	.483	.008	.466	.501
HausaFulani	3,952	.312	.008	.295	.329
Muslim	3,953	.419	.008	.401	.437
ApproveGov	3,952	3.324	.1933	2.944	3.702
Income	3,953	6.055	.354	5.361	6.749
Schooling	3,611	4.78	.157	4.465	5.084
GenderRatio	3,953	.502	.009	.484	.520
Age	3,952	31.53	.183	31.181	31.897

Note: Data has been weighted for whether the respondent was in an urban or rural area.

Appendix 5.2

Intended Vote, by State

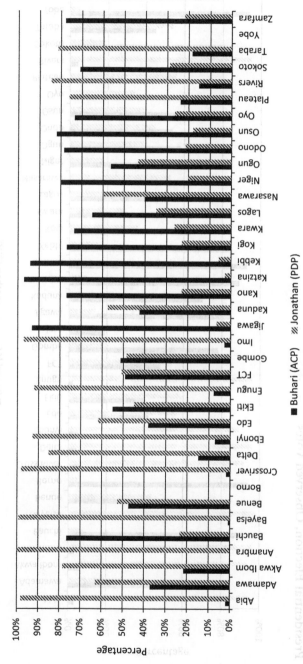

Figure 5.7 Voting intentions by state (*vote.tomorrow* variable).

Source: US State Department-sponsored poll. Nigeria pre-election survey. Washington, DC

Appendix 5.3

Presidential Election, Observed Votes

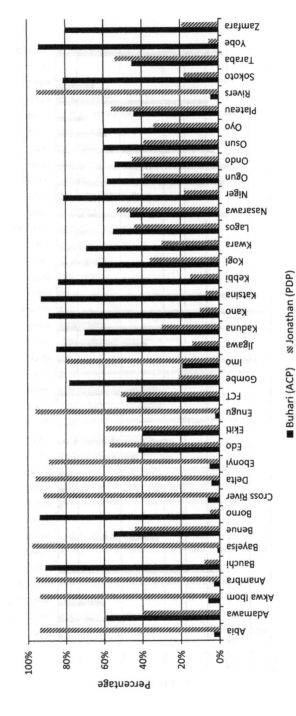

Figure 5.8 Presidential Election's observed votes, by state.
Source: Independent National Electoral Commission

Appendix 5.4

Information about the Variables

All the variables in this chapter are from State Department – sponsored pre-election surveys carried out in 2015 by a private contractor.

Vote.tomorrow, Dependent Variable

From a survey question asking, "If elections were to take place tomorrow, which presidential candidate would you vote for?" This variable represents self-identified individual voting preferences at the moment. A value of 1 indicates support for the incumbent, Jonathan. While the original question allowed respondents to choose minor candidates, the continuous variable is a valid measure as Jonathan and Buhari received 47.3 percent and 47.7 percent of the participants' responses, respectively.

HausaFulani, Independent Variable

From a question asking, "Would you mind telling me to which ethnic group you belong?" This variable is coded as a dummy dichotomous variable between self-identified Hausa or Fulani, coded as 1, with all other ethnic groups represented with 0.

Muslim, Independent Variable

From a question measuring self-reported religious affiliation. This is a dummy variable coded with 1 indicating individuals who self-identified as Muslims, with 0 representing individuals who self-identified with all other religions.

ApproveGov, Control Variable

From a question asking, "Do you approve or disapprove of the way [the state governor] is doing his job?" This measures political conditions or support of regional government. It is recoded as a categorical variable so that 1 = strongly disapprove, 2 = somewhat disapprove, 3 = somewhat approve, and 4 = strongly approve.

Income, Control Variable

From a question asking, "With regards to your monthly household income, please tell me which of the following phrases best suits your household situation?" This measures self-reported perceptions of purchasing power. It is coded as a categorical variable with the values of 1 = unable to meet basic needs without charity, 2 = able to meet basic needs, 3 = able to meet basic needs with some non-essential goods, 4 = able to purchase most non-essential goods, 5= plenty of disposable money.

Schooling, Control Variable

From a question asking, "If you have received formal schooling, what is the highest level of schooling you have reached?" This is coded as a categorical variable with the values 1 = some primary schooling, 2 = primary schooling complete, 3= some secondary schooling, 4 = secondary schooling complete, 5 = post-secondary qualifications, other than university, 6 = some university, and 7 = university complete.

Gender, Control Variable

The survey administrator discerned the gender of the survey participant. This measures individual-level gender status. Coded as dichotomous variable with 1= male and 0 = other.

Age, Control Variable

From a question asking, "Will you please tell me your exact age in years at your last birthday?" This measures self-identified age as a continuous variable.

6 | Subnational Subversion and Institutional Stress

Democratic transitions do not just transfer power from one set of rulers to another. They are formal processes that usher in an entirely new set of rules – what comparative politics refers to as a "regime." The boom of democratization research in the 1990s, like the modernization literature of the 1960s, made assumptions about transitions as linear processes moving toward democratic regimes. Scholars corrected for this by identifying a variety of regimes and noting the multi-directionality of transitions, including significant democratic backsliding in recent years (Bermeo 2016; Eisenstadt et al. 2017). Our appreciation of regimes and transitions has grown more complex, and the tools for measuring democracy have vastly improved (Coppedge 2012). Yet, our understanding of when (and whether) transitions end has changed little. Their status as finite processes remains murky because so many democratization processes reversed themselves in the 2000s, and there is little agreement on when they ended. Nigeria's 2015 election, analyzed in the previous three chapters, ended the country's transition. In doing so, a measure of power shifted from the elites who had stage-managed politics to voters and a new generation of democratic citizens alienated from the sixteen-year-old pact, detailed in Chapter 2.

This chapter advances the idea of "subnational stress points" as an alternative to democratic consolidation for analyzing post-transition politics. Rather than setting out to identify a threshold for when democratization is somehow complete, or assessing the quality of democracy, I compare the characteristics of three different security challenges in contemporary Nigeria. Adapting an idea used to understand the limited democratizing effects of the Arab Spring (Brownlee et al. 2015), I characterize stress points as tests of institutional resilience in the face of extra-institutional challenges. The question is thus whether political institutions can withstand pressures and grievances not articulated through elections, parties, or representatives.

First, I briefly discuss Linz and Stepan's well-known definition of consolidation: "democracy becomes the only game in town when no significant political group seriously attempts to overthrow the democratic regime or to promote domestic or international violence in order to secede from the state" (Linz and Stepan 1997, 15). This includes the absence of serious secessionist claims as well as the relatively uncontested legitimate exercise of violence (Linz and Stepan 1996; Englebert 2009). "Relatively" is a qualifier because most democracies endure fringe groups that challenge the state's monopoly on the use of force. In Nigeria's case, this monopoly is undermined in different ways, whether through the terrorism of Boko Haram, the impunity for electoral violence, or the state's toleration – or even encouragement – of local volunteer security forces. Informal security organizations, popularly known as "vigilantes," remain widespread due to the absence of state or local police (as noted in Chapter 4) and their usefulness in supplanting weak state capacity in areas facing security challenges (Ogbozor 2016).

Second, I compare three challenges that fragment state authority. Drawing on unusual field research, including interviews with secessionist activists in 2017, I analyze the return of Igbo nationalism in southeastern Nigeria and new movements demanding an independent republic of Biafra. The organizations at the heart of this movement have thus far relied on protests, propaganda (including a massive social media presence), and political mobilization against state repression. Next, I analyze the issues facing Nigeria's peripatetic pastoralists, including shrinking land for cattle grazing, disappearance of water sources, and tensions with farming communities. Finally, I examine Boko Haram, based in the far northeastern state of Borno. This violent insurgency embraces terrorism in the classic sense described in the book's Introduction. Its violence against schools, mosques, churches, marketplaces, and symbols of state power promotes a generalized sense of fear meant to compensate for an asymmetry of capacity vis-à-vis the state. All three subnational stress points are exacerbated by what I called in the book's Introduction the normalization of violence: Igbo activists inspire transnational organizing by honoring victims of pro-Biafra participation; farmers and pastoralists are supposedly caught in either an ancient cycle of retribution or shifting ecological conditions; and Boko Haram's terrorism somehow justifies massive state repression.

The chapter's conclusion summarizes how their various goals and tactics differ, associating them with different types of stress. I briefly discuss the Niger Delta insurgency, outlining the basis for potential alliances with eastern Biafran secessionists and explaining why this collaboration remains unlikely. I also summarize how the elite pact that shaped the transition outlined in Chapter 2 deepened the roots of these subnational stress points. The Fourth Republic's democratization by undemocratic means today impedes institutional development and accents popular doubts about governance.

Democratic Consolidation and Subnational Stress Points

Research on democratic consolidation since Linz and Stepan's (1996) classic work has explored both institutional and behavioral features. Survey research has considered how consolidation means that citizens' attitudes reflect an overwhelming faith in democratic procedures. Severe political or economic stresses constitute tests of this faith. Political actors internalize the underlying constitutional norms because violations would be both ineffective and costly. The Afrobarometer project provides an empirical basis for analyzing the extent to which Africans have internalized attitudes and norms conducive to democracy. One recent study using this data identifies gaps between demand and supply of democracy, as well as trends over time. Large majorities in Africa reject different forms of authoritarianism governance outright. But while demand for democracy increased in ten countries, it decreased in another fourteen. In many other countries, demand exceeds supply; people want democracy but do not characterize their government as sufficiently democratic (Bratton 2016).

Another approach to consolidation focuses on institutions rather than attitudes. The concept of alternation (or party turnover), referring to the ability of today's opposition to become tomorrow's incumbents, has emerged as a central institutional feature of consolidation. In 1990, alternation was almost entirely theoretical in Africa since opposition parties legally operated in only a handful of countries (Widner 1994). At the time, O'Donnell doubted the validity of virtually any comparative effort to operationalize these standards, insisting that alternation of power, stability during economic hardship, absence of anti-system movements, or other metrics all "suffer from extreme ambiguity" (O'Donnell 1997, 49). The supposed danger that alternation of power or other such indicators presented to any comparative analysis of democratic consolidation is what Carothers' labeled "feckless pluralism." Neither collusion among parties that limits competition, as in Nicaragua, nor entrenched parties that stabilize the polity through patronage, as in Nepal, should count toward consolidation. In effect, a range of elites compete for power but lack meaningful connections to citizen demands, argues Carothers (2002).

Such critiques may be fair, but they are based on a limited understanding of pluralism and competition. When he layed out his ideal of democracy, Dahl (1971) hardly had in mind the hegemonic politics that we see in contemporary Rwanda, Uganda, or Gabon, where the opposition is prevented from posing a viable threat to the incumbent party. Contestation implies that electoral defeat is entirely plausible because the political rights, civil liberties, and other contextual factors such as administrative neutrality necessary to making political competition vigorous are present. On these terms, the PDP's defeat in 2015 means that contestation is a meaningful feature of Nigeria's politics for the first time in its history. The recurring possibility of electoral defeat promotes accountability by stimulating a healthy sense of insecurity in politicians. This extends their time horizon, shifting from a utility calculation based on short-term payoffs such as corruption that collectively harms the nation (Hoffman and Patel 2017). Citizens feel that their vote matters, and weigh future outcomes rather than immediate needs.

Benchmarks for consolidation have stood the test of time, or at least remain useful for making cross-national comparisons. Huntington (1991) proposes a "two-turnover test" for consolidation. By this standard, consolidation occurs when the winners of founding elections are defeated and peacefully hand over power in a subsequent election, and the new winners themselves later peacefully turn over power through an election. Only a handful of countries in Africa, such as Ghana, Senegal, and Kenya, have achieved this. Research summarized by Cheeseman offers several answers as to why. First, he points to increasing respect for constitutional term limits. Some work suggests that such limits become a resource to hold politicians accountable (Kramon and Posner 2011), while cases such as Malawi and Zambia demonstrate the need for a shared goals among political elites, the media, and the military (Dionne and Dulani 2013). Second, turnover is more likely in electoral contests where the incumbent president is not running. For example, between 1990 and 2010, ruling parties lost only 15 percent of the time when the incumbent president was the candidate, but faced 50–50 odds when they ran a new candidate. Third, ruling parties lost in situations where the opposition and incumbent candidates had not worked closely together. "The impact of turnover has been varied," but evoking Linz and Stepan's phraseology, he says, "it is the most powerful symbol that parties are willing to play by the rules of the game" (Cheeseman 2015, 181–2). Other research points to business coalitions that increase the probably of opposition victory by providing private-sector financial backing and indirectly generating incentives for inter-ethnic coalitions (Arriola 2013).

Some have also argued that it might take even more than two elections for consolidation to take hold in African countries (Bratton 1999). Lindberg and various collaborators have thus emphasized the attitudinal and cultural effects of elections as a democratic ritual. For example, after at least four election cycles, citizens internalize expectations of democratic participation that make reversal less likely (Lindberg 2006). Where party turnover does happen at least twice, peaceful elections in Africa have a significant moderating effect on the political views of citizens, furthering the attitudinal component of democratic consolidation (Moehler and Lindberg 2009). Yet, it is increasingly clear that "democratization by elections" appears more likely in countries transitioning since the 1970s as opposed to earlier in the twentieth century, and that the relationship is weaker in the Middle East compared to Sub-Saharan Africa, Latin America, or many post-Soviet States (Edgell et al. 2017).

Conversely, compelling cross-national evidence indicates that the *absence* of alternation among rulers undermines citizen confidence that democracy will last. This is even further underscored by findings that citizens increasingly agree on the durability of democracy, whether they are supporters of the ruling party or the opposition, where alternations have taken place (Cho and Logan 2014). This good news about turnover may not extend to competitive authoritarian and hybrid regimes, and low party institutionalization may undermine the democratizing impact of alternation (Wahman 2014). Nigeria could easily fall in such a category once you look beyond electoral politics to corruption, widespread human rights violations by the police and military, and the weak organizational capacity of the parties. The biggest challenges to Nigeria's democracy today come not from the outcome or the administration of its elections, but from subnational contrarians questioning their limits entirely.

Subnational Stress Points in the Fourth Republic

Chapter 2 convincingly argued that Nigeria's transition, which began with the transfer of power from a military to a civilian regime, was completed with the nation's first ever party turnover in 2015. Yet, ongoing serious violent and nonviolent challenges to its legitimacy suggest that democratic consolidation inadequately captures the dys/functionality of the state. These stress points amount to tests of institutional resilience precisely because they amount to extra-institutional challenges. In each case, the political context of the 1999 transition's pact now complicates effective conflict resolution through democratic mechanisms.

First, I explore eastern secessionist agitation that has revived the imaginary of an independent Biafra, using pervasive but arguably undisciplined nonviolence. Where the movement's radicalism overlaps with legitimate critiques of the state articulated through elected representatives, traditional cultural organizations, and the diaspora, a discourse on "political restructuring" plays to ethnic Igbo demands for an independent Biafra. Short of secession, this rhetoric demands dialogue for improved representation either through portfolios at the center, the creation of new states, or the coalescence of states into five or six geopolitical "zones" and eventually an Igbo president. Next, I analyze growing conflicts between settled agriculturalists and pastoralists, tensions with deep structural roots exacerbated by institutional failures. Finally, I consider Boko Haram, the violent insurgency based in northeastern Nigeria. Its goals have evolved since its origins as an isolated religious sect during the early years of the Fourth Republic. Its chaotic violence against schools, urban markets, and symbols of the state aligned with its interest in power and control, rather than improved representation or increased resources. Mohammed Yusuf, its leader, who was captured and extra-judicially killed in 2009, had grown disappointed with the Sharia law permitted under the 1999 constitution and declared the group's intention to create some kind of Islamic state. In practical terms Sharia remained limited to civil cases, even after twelve northern state legislatures passed laws permitting its extension to the criminal code (Paden 2005). Undisciplined violence undermines support Boko Haram might generate support from the population it seeks to rule, and the government's crude counter-terrorism strategies have failed to capitalize on the tactical leverage generated by the organization's unpopularity.

Eastern Agitation against Nigeria's "Illegal Marriage"

Every secessionist movement – except those leading to the creation of South Sudan and Eritrea – has failed in Africa. Africa suffers from a "secessionist deficit," with failed agitations for independence in Cameroon, Congo, Senegal, and elsewhere (Englebert and Hummel 2005). Yet, separatism lives on in eastern Nigeria today under a resurrected banner of Biafra, the name adopted by the Igbo-dominated states that declared independence in 1967. After a series of ethnic pogroms against Igbos living in the north in the early 1960s, Igbos participated in a coup that was soon followed by a counter-coup that brought in a military government that immediately abolished federalism. "The idea of a unitary system of governance was the major fear of all the regions at the time, the north and west because they think that would make for an influx of people," recalls Yakubu Gowon, a general who took power in another coup and tried to address Igbo grievances by creating new states (Gowon 2010). The move to restore and expand federalism failed to appease the Igbos, plunging the country into one of Africa's bloodiest civil wars. A large literature on the civil war details its causes (Panter-Brick 1971; Nwankwo 1980), the wartime governance of Gowon's military regime (Muhammadu and Haruna 1979; LeVan 2015a), and the broader political and socio-cultural consequences of Nigeria's first long stretch of military rule (Osaghae 1998; Othman 1989). "The war discredited the political class and justified the rule of the military bureaucratic oligarchy as well as a technocratic approach to governance," says Egwu. General Gowon's "three R's" of Reconstruction, Reconciliation, and Rehabilitation married the Keynesian developmental state with the project of building post-colonial national unity (Egwu 2005, 104–5; Elaigwu 1988). In a speech on the fiftieth anniversary of the war, Obasanjo, who rose through the military ranks during its battles, said that the war happened because – and the three R's compensated for – post-independence leaders who emphasized development at the expense of unity (Shehu Musa Yar'Adua Foundation 2017).

The brief analysis here focuses on how important failures of the 1999 transition contributed to a resurrection of Biafran secessionism, a dire sign today that the project of unity remains incomplete. In particular, a centerpiece of the transition's pact alienated Igbo elites and contributed to the formation of the Movement for the Actualization of the Sovereign State of Biafra (MASSOB). After the military handover in 1999, MASSOB provided a mechanism for radical grassroots organizing of Igbo activists whose complaints about marginalization aligned with the interests of PDP politicians and Igbo elites, notably the pan-Igbo organization Ohanaeze Ndigbo. "The things that caused the war are still there, even double. We are not safe in a country called Nigeria," a MASSOB activist in Anambra State told me. "I am ashamed to call myself a Nigerian. I am Biafran" (Onuorah et al. 2017). The disincorporation of Igbos from the critical question of transition's success re-opened the wounds of the civil war. For MASSOB and the spinoff Indigenous People of Biafra (IPOB), post-transition Nigeria today feels a little too much like postwar Nigeria in the 1970s.

Igbo complaints about incomplete postwar reconciliation center on several recurring themes. The first asserts that all of the state governments after the war offered some reintegration into political life but held back economic reintegration. This critique has a strong a religious coloration because, with the exception of Obasanjo's three-year tenure in the late 1970s, every head of state from the start of the war in 1967 to the military handover in May 1999 was a northerner. Significant progress on reintegration occurred through federal character, Nigeria's version of affirmative action discussed in Chapter 2. It has roots in the postwar policies to reintegrate Igbos into the civil service and the military (Ekeh and Osaghae 1989), with some success. A Federal Character Commission compiles statistics on the ethnicity and origin of civil servants, while the media closely monitors cabinet composition, which the constitution requires to reflect the country's national diversity. Ex-president Obasanjo offers the election of Alex Ekwueme as Vice President of the Second Republic (1979–1983) as evidence that Igbo reintegration went beyond civil servants and cabinet seats (Shehu Musa Yar'Adua Foundation 2017). However, the treatment of Ekwueme in the early stages of the transition weakened the pact's deal, fragmented the newly formed PDP, and fueled Igbo frustration.

As noted in Chapter 2, Ekwueme's organization of elites under the rubric of the "G34" effectively terminated Abacha's "self-succession" bid in 1998, when the dictator planned to run in the transitional elections organized by his military junta (thus presenting a conflict of interest). As a former vice president and an heir apparent to Nnamadi Azikiwe's nationalist legacy, Ekwueme had the right credentials. And the election of an Igbo head of state would have closed the circle of postwar reconciliation; Igbos remain widely blamed for the country's first coup – a characterization that Ohanaeze leadership describes as a distortion of facts that point to northern involvement in the coup (Nwaorgu 2017; Osuntokun 1987). "The PDP had formed with Ekwueme in mind to become president. It was the northerners, headed by IBB [Ibrahim Badamosi Babangida] who pushed OBJ [Obasanjo] to pacify the Yorubas," claims a PDP state chair (Olotolo 2017). But then, in the words of a MASSOB activist, "Westerners and Northerners hijacked the party and organized it against the Igbos. PDP is not for the Igbos" (Onuorah et al. 2017). Even if these are overstatements, the PDP convention in Plateau State where they picked Obasanjo in the first primary was full of intrigue and devoid of transparency.

Ekwueme lost out in the end – decisively. "There was this military contraption; the retired generals wanted one of their own. Obasanjo was brought out from prison, dusted off, and hoisted on the party, the PDP," recalls the former President General of Ohanaeze. "Igbos were for Ekwueme since he was leader of G34. We hoped that Obasanjo, having experience with Nigeria would move to restructure the country. He had been presenting a front as a brave man. But he was frightened of the Fulani" (Nwaorgu 2017). A faction of Ohanaeze, led by lawyer Ben Nwabueze and its Council of Elders, attempted to turn the Igbo against the PDP after the selection of Obasanjo. "The democratic civilian government after the initial transition from more than 14 years of continuous military rule should not be headed by a military man," said their statement, hinting at Obasanjo's role in the civil war (Alli 1999). Ohanaeze soon retracted the statement, and news reports characterized the intrigue as a continuation of Nwabueze's dislike for Ekwueme stemming back to disputes in the early 1980s, during the Second Republic (Obenta and Agbese 1999). This may also be the reason why, under Nwabueze's leadership in 1998, the organization

Figure 6.1 Graffiti in Imo State referring to Igbo secessionists in 2017.
Source: Author's own photo

declined to take a position on either Abacha's "self-succession" plans
or the "June 12" question, i.e., whether a transition must address the
Yorubas' continuing anger over the annulled 1993 election (Eze 1998).[1]

Thus, at the moment of the transition, and throughout Obasanjo's
two presidential terms, Igbo grievances surfaced in the context of the
transition's pact that postponed their shot at power. Obasanjo was
selected for the first eight years (the assumption was that he would win
re-election, which he did) to mitigate Yoruba frustration over the 1993
election annulment and then a northerner would rule for eight years.
This situation gave long simmering complaints about the *economic*
failures of postwar reconstruction new salience, generating a "wedge"
issue for the Igbos within the PDP. "In the aftermath of the war, the
issue of appropriated properties in many cases was not addressed,"
said the chairman of the Privatization Committee in the House of

---

[1] Igbo ambiguity on these issues extended beyond Ohanaeze. In 2006, as
the governor of Abia State, Orji Uzor Kalu, positioned himself to succeed
Obasanjo, media reports reminded the public of his unwavering support for
Abacha in 1998. He took out a full-page advertisement, saying, "There is no
gain saying the fact that this nation needs a man of great vision like Abacha.
His courage is proverbial" (Opene 2006, 11).

Representatives at the time. "There was compensation but it was low, if at all. And Igbos are still not integrated into the civil service and the military. The PDP has failed on this. In reality, there is very little federal presence in the southeast" (Duru 2004). MASSOB today echoes these complaints. As one leader put it, "after the war, they tried to seize all our property. All our currency was taken" (Onuorah et al. 2017).

This rhetoric forms a central component of Ohanaeze Ndigbo's narrative of Igbo grievances. "At the end of the war, in an attempt to contain Igbo industry and entrepreneurship, Chief Awlowo as minister of finance under Gowon made a regulation by which every Igbo bank deposit that was transacted was reduced to 20 pounds" (Nwodo 2017). In the initial years of the Fourth Republic, news accounts and political rhetoric editorialized about the broader consequences of such economic and social marginalization. In 2000, the House of Representatives passed a vote of no confidence on the Minister of Works and Housing for the failure to repair a critical expressway linking Enugu to the Niger Delta. Over the four-year period of a Petroleum Trust Fund's road rehabilitation project, it repaired only 5.3 percent of the roads in the southeast. Perhaps most sensitively, none of the military service chiefs were Igbo at the time. "The marginalization of the Igbo has been complete," said a prominent chief. The next year, Senator Chuba Okadigbo pointed out that the southeast held the smallest share in the 2001 budget out of the six geopolitical zones (Okpaleke and Maduemesi 2001).

By implementing a core element of the 1999's pact, the transition – arguably unintentionally – validated a postwar Igbo narrative of economic and political marginalization. As one news account put it in 2006, Igbos seem content as "appendages to power – whether as vice president, Senate President, Speaker of the House of Representatives, Director General of *this* and Adviser *that*. They are ever so near; yet always so far away" (Opene 2006, 10). The PDP's corrupt party convention in 1999 in Plateau State generated continuity with these lingering Igbo resentments, fanning new flames of secession with MASSOB and IPOB.

Both of these Igbo nationalist groups have repeatedly stated commitments to nonviolence, but there are important differences in their tactics and broader strategies. MASSOB embraces classic tools of mass movements in Nigeria such as demonstrations, stay-at-home strikes, and targeted boycotts, including the 2006 census. It has also developed a cultural repertoire of resistance, including the circulation of new Biafran Pound notes as a challenge to the federal government's monopoly over the regulation of currency, neighborhood cleanups in cities such as Umuahia, and social welfare funded by a voluntary tax (Owen 2009). To the eventual embarrassment of the federal government, fifty-three youths were arrested during a 2004 soccer tournament organized by MASSOB in Lagos, charged with treason, and threatened with the death penalty (IRIN News Service 2005b). When the government arrested MASSOB's founder, Ralph Uwazurike, for treason in 2005, a strike across several southeastern states ended with about twenty activists killed (IRIN News Service 2005a). Confrontations between MASSOB and a transportation workers' union turned violent the following year, and President Obasanjo sent in the military, leading to further harassment and activist deaths. "We are a nonviolent organization," said a group spokesperson, "but the government became very nervous about our growing popularity in Igboland" (IRIN News Service 2006). The Civil Liberties Organization, a human rights groups that led the struggle against military government in the 1990s, condemned the violence, calling it "disproportionate and often lethal force against a group that bears no arms" (IRIN News Service 2005b). In one incident, police claimed that activists shot police officers, leading a spokesperson to announce, "Anybody who comes out in the name of MASSOB or any other banned organization will definitely be arrested" (IRIN News Service 2005c).

Imitating some of the successful propaganda efforts from the civil war era (see Achebe 2012), MASSOB has strong ties to a diaspora that has organized radio broadcasts and a massive online presence (Owen 2009; Englebert 2009). It has politically leveraged the state's repression to advocate for Igbo secession. In 2006, a coalition of Igbo organizations presented a petition to the United Nations listing arrests, "ambushes," and killings of named activists who carried flags, wore pro-Biafra t-shirts, or allegedly engaged in similarly innocuous activities (Nnorom and Okwukwu 2006). "They do whatever they like," said a Catholic priest in Anambra State who aligns himself with MASSOB. After a May 2016 massacre of up to 300 people (at least 150 of whom were confirmed by Amnesty International), "they loaded the bodies in front of my parish," he said (Onuorah et al. 2017; Amnesty International 2016). Sympathy for Biafra today in churches has roots in postwar retribution against eastern churches that supported the Biafran cause, notwithstanding Gowon's policy of "no victors, no vanquished." The federal government closed down church schools and hospitals, forcing students and patients into an ill-prepared public system and contributing to the low quality visible today (Campbell 2017).

In his sweeping study of corruption in Nigeria, Smith conducted deep ethnographic research in the early 2000s in Iboland, concluding that ordinary Igbos generally did not support secession (Smith 2007). Englebert came to a similar conclusion in his study of Africa's "secessionist deficit," noting that (like Niger Delta militant groups) MASSOB has generally called for a sovereign national conference and "separatist discourse remains marginal," with little sympathy among elites (Englebert 2009, 137). However, repeated cycles of large nonviolent protests being met with state repression, along with the return of power to the north in 2015, have altered the eastern political landscape and amplified calls for secession. While PDP politicians and Ohanaeze elites may have been able to advance Igbo interests at the center by capitalizing on eastern agitation, it is increasingly beyond their control. Ohanaeze formally takes no position on secession. But it is also increasingly concerned about the violence. The President General said in an interview, "So long as you don't respond to reasonable and constitutional demands of the Igbo nation, you arm the militant organizations in their minds with a clear message that the only option is secession" (Nwodo 2017). Governor Okezie Victor Ikpeazu of Abia State, a hotbed of secessionist agitation, takes a similar stance. "Igbos are for good reason beginning to feel excluded. Democracy thrives on inclusiveness." But, whether they are pursuing their goals in the right way, "is a question for another day" (Ikpeazu 2017).

Like MASSOB, IPOB works towards secession through nonviolent protest and an eventual referendum. "We believe in federalism, democracy. But not one Nigeria. Let's call it illegal marriage," an IPOB activist in Abia State told me (Indigenous People of Biafra 2017). The group originated in a split when a younger generation of youths grew frustrated with the incremental approach outlined by Unwazurike and broke off from MASSOB. As with Unwazurike's imprisonment, IPOB mobilization gathered momentum with the arrest of its founder, Nnamadi Kanu, in 2015, and the government's subsequent flirtation with proscribing the organization. The military unilaterally declared IPOB a terrorist organization, with the full endorsement of Governor Ikpeazu and the other four governors in the southeast in late 2017.

But then the Senate President explained that the military lacks the authority to do so, and questioned its rationale, given IPOB's goals and tactics (Adebayo 2017). Former President Jonathan also spoke out when Buhari's Minister of Information blamed Jonathan for the rise of IPOB as a tool deployed because the PDP lost the election (Akinkuotu 2017) – an assertion that seemed to ignore the steady repression against other pro-Biafra activists since 1999. Between August 2015 and November 2016 alone, the military killed at least 150 IPOB activists (Amnesty International 2016). Shortly thereafter, an unscientific but large survey of 489 respondents in the southeast in 2017 found Kanu's treatment by the government had increased his reputation as a freedom fighter among Igbos, and to some extent as an advocate for in the Niger Delta. Those who saw him as a freedom fighter amounted to 35.8 percent of respondents, while 21.7 percent saw him as "savior for all of Southern Nigeria," the second-largest category of responses. Only twenty percent saw him as either a "noisemaker" or a "traitor" (SB Morgan Intelligence 2017). "The issue of Biafran agitation is real," a Catholic priest in Enugu told me. "It is getting more followership every day and attracting more sympathy from other tribes, especially with the arrest of the IPOB leader" (Ekeroku 2017).

In late 2017, harsh military tactics escalated with "Operation Python 2," unleashing a new wave of harassment and violence across the east (shortly after field research for this book was conducted). IPOB technically remains a legal association, but the police proceeded as if the Senate President's clarification on IPOB never occurred (Anonymous 2017). "Our leader, Kanu, is committed to non-violence," said IPOB activists in Abia. "If people engage in violence there will be a lot of death everywhere" (Indigenous People of Biafra 2017). A coalition of civil rights groups, the Southeast Situation Room, urged activists to comply with the law and demanded that the military comply with international human rights law and desist from "intimidation, inhuman and degrading treatment" of citizens (Southeast Situation Room 2017). Ohanaeze's President General underscores the counter-productivity of President Buhari's over-militarized response to peaceful protest. "He has really created a mountain out of a molehill. He has given cannon fodder to MASSOB and IPOB … he has alienated a vast majority of the people who think restructuring is the way" (Nwodo 2017).

In his memoir of the Civil War, Nwankwo argues that Biafran propaganda was effective precisely because violence against Igbos validated their narrative as victims: "the Northern massacres lent credibility to the fear for the security of the Igbos which was the crux of Biafran propaganda" (Nwankwo 1980, 16). Those pogroms involved person-to-person violence, rather than state violence on display today. For this reason, the rising militancy of northern "Arewa Youths," organizing in the eastern states, constitutes another step in a dangerous escalation, with violence coming from multiple sides.[2]

The salience of religion in the roots of the Biafran revival, with the harassment of churches, and in the treatment of Arewa as a proxy for all things northern will further complicate the nation's efforts to fully reconcile with the east. Religion is also integral to the Biafran view of external relations. Both MASSOB and IPOB activists contend that the international community, appalled by the repression against them, will somehow push the federal government into holding a referendum. "We believe [Donald] Trump is not going to fail us," said an IPOB activist. "He hates what the Muslim is doing in Africa. He hates it. So we see him as a messiah" (Indigenous People of Biafra 2017). "We have got everything to be a nation. We are waiting for the world body to announce it," said a MASSOB leader on the Biafra Council of Elders (Onuorah et al. 2017). Though Ohanaeze had taken no formal position on a referendum at the time of this writing, the former Secretary General, Joe Nwaorgu, was unequivocal. Biafra should "definitely" be put to a vote, and "if there is a referendum at this time, Igbo will vote yes to opt out of Nigeria" (Nwaorgu 2017).

Pastoralism in Decline

"There is going to be a serious crisis that will destabilize West Africa," began Mohammed Bello, a professor involved with Pastoral Resolve (PARE), a Nigerian NGO seeking to address the challenges facing contemporary pastoralists. He was referring not to creeping violent extremism from Salafist movements, though. Instead, he had in mind a precarious convergence of ecological, political, and economic factors driving tensions between pastoralists and farmers (Bello 2016).

---

[2] On June 7, 2017, the Region of the Niger Delta (RONDEL) and the Rondel Solidarity Movement (RSM) announced themselves, saying they would fight for independence as an "aggressive but non-violent umbrella body" (Region of the Niger Delta 2017).

Pastoralism is an agricultural lifestyle associated with livestock, including camels, goats, sheep and cows, as well as animal husbandry. According to PARE, pastoralists "inhabit parts of the world where the potential for crop cultivation is limited due to lack of rainfall, steep terrain or extreme temperatures." Many pastoralists are transhumant, meaning nomadic, "in order to optimally exploit the meager and seasonally variable resources of their environment and to provide food and water for their animals" (Pastoral Resolve 2013, 2). A policy framework developed by the African Union succinctly sums up the difficulties facing the estimated 268 million pastoralists in every corner of the continent:

Pastoralism is changing. In the face of demographic trends, protracted conflicts, reduced access to grazing land and water, and in some regions, climatic changes, pastoralists are becoming increasingly vulnerable. Some pastoral areas are known for increasing levels of destitution and food insecurity, and the impacts of drought are worsening. These trends coincide with the limited political representation of pastoralists in the decision-making processes affecting their livelihoods, which in turn, is exacerbated by their physical position in remote areas, far from political and economic centres. There is also a tendency to overlook the suffering of pastoralists under the misconception that their hardships are self-inflicted by an apparent choice for a traditional life style which inhibits their ability for innovations and adaptation to change (African Union 2010, 5).

In Nigeria, pastoralists face declining access to water, increasingly insecure land rights, and underrepresentation that has fueled prejudice and undermined conflict resolution processes with farmers, who also face economic and social insecurity. The discussion that follows summarizes these challenges, suggesting that they are not symptoms of cultural decline, ancient rivalries, or caused by some global jihadist agenda. Pastoralism questions the essence of the Nigerian state because its spatially distributed economy (and loyalty) is at odds with the concentration of wealth and power in the capital since the onset of oil and authoritarianism. For cattle herders, democracy would mean citizenship without geographical fixity, rights to land entirely at odds with neoliberal notions of ownership, and new opportunities for economic integration amidst scarcity.

The troubles really began for transhumant agriculturists in the 1960s. In the decade prior, only 3 percent of an estimated six million

Figure 6.2 Cattle in Adamawa State, 2016.
Source: Author's own photo

Fulbe (Fulani) lived in their original homeland, and an ecology of relative harmony existed where the migrant pastoralists exchanged milk for grain, or manured fields in return for temporary grazing privileges (Isichei 1997). Though colonialism played no small role in disrupting pastoral lifestyles, British authorities also established the migration routes that today pastoralists now defend, even though they "are inadequate, and this brings about conflict with farmers." State officials have mixed feelings about grazing reserves, which are established by the federal government, "and this adds to insecurity" as well (Miyetti Allah 2016). Adamawa State offers a compelling example, where Governor Murtala Nyako claimed to use his state authority to "degazette" some of the official grazing areas, according to PARE (Bello 2016). This freed up valuable federal land for private investment, but it also pushed pastoralists off well-established paths that had been in use for centuries.[3]

The problems for pastoralists escalated due to several other factors. As noted by the African Union, the peripatetic nature of pastoralism is a cultural tool for adapting to ecological unpredictability.

[3] The State House of Assembly later impeached Nyako on corruption charges.

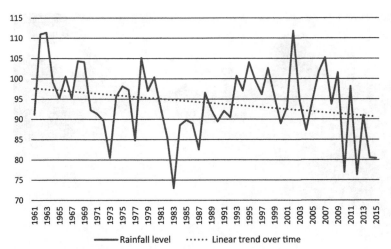

Figure 6.3 Rainfall levels for Nigeria, 1960–2015 (in millimeters).
Source: World Bank Climate Portal. www.climateknowledgeportal.worldbank.org/

However, rainfall levels have been declining for decades, as illustrated in Figure 6.3. This is even more dramatically illustrated visually in an analysis by the Environment Conflict and Cooperation platform, using images from the National Aeronautic and Space Administration that show that Lake Chad has shrunk by over 50 percent since 1963.[4] Thus, in addition to shrinking reserve areas, herders face fewer water sources and disappearing grasslands, meaning they have to wander farther in order to take care of their cattle. Herders also continued to use approximately forty grazing reserves that had long been in use but had never been officially "gazetted" (Bello 2016). This informality exacerbates the sense of insecurity that pastoralists feel today due to Nigeria's land tenure system, whereby customary freeholding is limited and state governors formally hold land "in trust" (LeVan and Olubowale 2014; Nwabueze 2009).

Population expansion and urban migration introduced at least four other complexities for relations between pastoralists and settled agriculturalists. First, by the 1970s, with the expansion of farms and topographical pressures on grazing areas, conflicts between farmers and pastoralists became increasingly confrontational and violent in northern Nigeria due to crop damage or the blockage of routes.

---

[4] https://library.ecc-platform.org/about-ecc (accessed September 24, 2017).

The military governments in the 1980s started to consider these tensions a national security issue, and by the 1990's they amounted to a "major" national security issue. In other words, today's tensions differ in scale, scope, and cause compared to historical environmental cycles and patterns of cross-cultural interactions. Focus groups with farmers and pastoralists in Katsina and Kano States in 2013 zeroed in on the erosion of traditions that had facilitated peaceful cross-cultural interactions. For example, up until the 1970s, grassland and water were seen as communal properties, pastoralists were generally granted free access to leftover crops and in return they left behind manure needed by farmers, and when farmers or cattle violated the migration routes, traditional authorities and the judiciary ruled against such encroachments. Since the 2010s, farmers and pastoralists alike have complained of people "assuming individualistic ownership and control of land," farmers rarely permit crop gleaning, pastoralists now "sell" manure, and farmers demand rent for use of land (Momale 2015b, 7). Pastoralists in interviews with me repeatedly acknowledged the problems presented by "herd boys," young men – often children – who wander carelessly onto farmland and inappropriately engage in "night grazing." A recent study based on over 250 interviews in two states (Zamfara and Kadunda) estimates that in the 1970s, herd boys constituted only about 20 or 30 percent of pastoralists in most local government areas. By 2015, herd boys constituted 50–80 percent of all herders (Momale 2015a). Pastoralists admit this is a growing problem, as the boys' parents adopt more sedentary and urban lifestyles. But they also complain; "all the cattle routes are blocked. On this side fifty cattle can pass," gestured a chief during an interview. "But other roads are deliberately made narrow in order to prevent passing, and this makes it impossible to avoid accident of trampling on crops … there is no way to graze or move around with cattle" (Chief of a village near Girei 2016). Organizations representing the interests of pastoralists take a strong line of defense for the historic cattle routes. Miyetti Allah's leaders, for example, insist, "those routes give us a right of way. So anybody who goes there is a trespasser" (Miyetti Allah 2016).

Second, as people moved into the cities, the price of beef increased while other agricultural commodities largely remained stable. Compared to other basic commodities, cattle today amounts to an agricultural enterprise worth entering – even as the resources and environment necessary to raise cattle shrink. Nigeria has undergone massive urbanization, especially with the movement of the capital from Lagos to Abuja. Whereas only 20 percent of Nigeria's population lived in cities in 1970, the United Nations Development Program estimates that 56 percent lived in cities by 2015 (LeVan and Olubowale 2014). This migration reflects a classic African story in many ways, with young people leaving rural areas in search of increased opportunities and greater access to the cash economy. Rising demand for beef combined with fewer people willing to wander with their cows drove prices up. This is evident in the herder/livestock ratio, which dropped from 1:0.23 in 1960 to 1:0.17 in 1987 and has continued to decline (Hassan and Jauro 2005). According to the Food and Agriculture Organization of the United Nations, Nigeria has been unable to keep up with demand for beef. Overall, population growth has far outpaced the rate of food production, so about 30 percent of slaughtered cattle is imported, along with other food.

Among Nigeria's pastoralists, who are overwhelmingly ethnic Fulani, transhumance remains the dominant mode of agriculture according to interviews and other sources (Pastoral Resolve 2013). However, urbanization has in a third way impacted the Fulani culturally as a group, leading some to embrace a semi-sedentary lifestyle, following cattle only seasonally. This has in turn created an important sociocultural cleavage among Fulani; in contrast to the more settled or urbanized Fulani, transhumance practitioners known as *Mbororo* generally insist on speaking Fulfulde to preserve their identity and distinguish themselves from the common hyphenated "Hausa-Fulani" label. "This distinction is important because conflicts between Fulani pastoralists and farmers are often politicised," according to Higazai. "They are often portrayed as being orchestrated by northern 'Hausa-Fulani' elites. In reality urbanised, sedentary Fulani and 'Hausa-Fulani' populations tend to have limited or no influence over nomadic Fulani pastoralists" (Higazi 2017, 6).

A fourth pressing complexity is that extensive powers over land tenure at the state level sets governors' political interests at odds with pastoralists, especially in the Middle Belt states or in southern states. The portrayal of pastoralist problems as broader religious or ethnic tensions weakens subnational obligations to federal grazing reserves and undermines a coordinated conflict resolution strategy across states. The governor of Ekiti State, for example, claimed to have abolished the grazing reserves, in response to farmers' frustration with herdsman encroachment. Abia, Taraba, and other states soon began exploring similar regulatory responses (Mkom et al. 2017). Though Nigeria is a federal system, it is unclear whether the states have such powers. As with the enactment of Sharia in 2000, this does not deter subnational politicians from embarking on experiments to make a popular political statement.

Regardless, such outbursts do undermine a coordinated effort to replicate models that work. For example, according to pastoralists in Gombe State, the state government wrote a letter to each Local Government Area chair to check encroachment on cattle routes. The police commissioner for the state organized a town hall meeting in June 2016 with herders, farmers, elders, and local government officials that greatly improved trust among stakeholders in the rural economy. Moreover, the state government took the initiative to establish small ranches with cattle dips, schools for nomadic children and water for the cattle, such as the one at Wawazinge Dukku. This has helped keep pastoralists from wandering off grazing routes but it has not been institutionalized. And replication of such efforts have in some ways become *more* complicated with the election of Buhari because state officials do not want to play into widespread perceptions that Buhari is helping his ethnic kin, the Fulani (Miyetti Allah 2016).[5] Other states have effectively utilized judicial commissions of inquiry, grassroots conflict resolution programs, and power-sharing mechanisms at the local government level (Thaut Vinson 2018).

By contrast, in neighboring Adamawa State, the governor eliminated some grazing areas as noted, and herders do not trust the state to serve as a neutral mediator in disputes. Since the arbitration structures do not function, a small violation by either side – such as herder boys straying off a narrow path or farmers planting crops less than 15 meters from the demarcated grazing route – quickly spirals out of control. Strong perceptions of corruption and bias also prevail; when fourteen pastoralists were killed in Song Local Government Area, PARE asserts that the government did not respond. "There is a coming conflict in the next several years over land" (Bello 2016). The failure in Song was replicated in

---

[5] Buhari reportedly does not speak much Fulfulde, suggesting that any primordial affinity to herders is overstated (Higazi 2017).

Taraba State, where media reports alleged fifty Fulani settlements had been burned, 20,000 cows slaughtered, and dozens killed in the Mambila Plateau areas (Sulaiman 2017). Months later, retaliation killings by pastoralists in Taraba and across the Middle Belt took on the appearance of unprovoked attacks.

Coordination of conflict resolution processes, or their replication in problematic places such as Adamawa, is also undermined by national-level politics and rhetoric. Pastoralist–farmer tensions are often conflated with communal tensions, Boko Haram's terrorism, or religious differences more generally (Higazi 2017; Mercy Corps 2015). No state offers a better example of this than Plateau, where local dispute resolution mechanisms worked effectively for decades until riots in urban Jos between Muslims and Christians in 2001 spilled into rural areas barely two years after the democratic transition. About 1,000 people died in the clashes, with riots on a lesser scale erupting again in 2008 and 2010. The historically cordial relations between the Fulani and the Christian Berom communities broke down when Fulani were expelled from Berom lands, and elites mobilized Berom farmers against Hausa and Fulani Muslims (Higazi 2016). Governor Jonah Jang provided the spark to ignite the flames when he first tapped into indigenous resentment over migrants by openly complaining about ethnic Jasawa from the north. He then interfered in local government power-sharing arrangements by attempting to impose a co-ethnic Berom politician, attempting to deny the Jasawa their turn to elect a candidate for the office. When the situation degenerated into violence, Jang organized an ethnic militia and vigilante groups under the banner of "Operation Rainbow" (Name withheld 2016).[6] According to a local government chair, the state PDP remained deeply divided between pro- and anti-Jang factions in 2016, a year after the governor left office (Akos 2016).

Conflict resolution is further complicated by the mischaracterization of farmer–herder herder tensions as ancient primordial hatreds, simplistic extensions of religious agendas (including Boko Haram's), or recasting herders as migrants in subnational governments' assertion

---

[6] It is worth noting that Boko Haram accused Governor Jang specifically of ethnic cleansing against Hausa and Fulani in Plateau State (Walker 2012). This is a good illustration of how the mischaracterization of farmer–herder differences not only impedes conflict resolution, but is also linked to otherwise-unrelated conflicts.

of legal indigeneity. As noted above, elites in Plateau State have advanced their own political agendas by creating a divisive constituency for policies of political exclusion. Evidence suggests that cattle rustling has grown. In the hardest-hit states, such as Plateau, Kaduna and Zamfara, the complexities of cattle rustling and rural banditry are amplified as local officials blame either herders or their way of life for the added insecurity. Though valid time series data are scanty, 21 percent of farmers and pastoralists in a survey said banditry became a concern of theirs between 2006 and 2010, but 55 percent said the problem peaked between 2011 and 2015; 54 percent claimed to have personally witnessed banditry. However, "the survey results contradict the popular notion that nomadic herdsmen are the major perpetrators of cattle rustling," with at least 50 percent of respondents identifying locals as the culprits, 25 percent mentioning criminal gangs, and 25 percent blaming herdsmen (Egwu 2015, 29).

Nigeria's pastoralists navigate their existence on the horns of a difficult dilemma captured by a Fulani myth of origin. In one variation, the prophet Muhammed sent disciples to spread Islam across West Africa. One proselytizer, Yacouba, married a king's daughter, who bore four children. But two of them were out of wedlock, and they invented their own language, Fulfulde. Blending Islam with traditional divination, Yacouba sent the three far away to a river to find their biological father. At the river, a handsome man emerged and gave them something never before seen in Africa as a gift: cattle. As long as they never looked back, and did not settle down in villages, the herd would keep growing. One child did look back, and his herd stopped growing (Belcher 2005). Being stationary today represents taking your eyes off the horizon and beginning the impossible task of looking back. Unlike Africa's settled agriculturalists, it is migration that brings adaptability for pastoralists and stationarity that introduces economic uncertainty and cultural crisis. As Nigeria looks to the future of its pastoralists, solutions such as nomadic education, grazing reserves, and coordinated conflict resolution are merely the mechanisms of hope where the nation's cows and their custodians seek meaning. Subnational resistance is a product of national failures: the failure in a hastily promulgated 1999 constitution to revisit citizenship laws decreed by the military that enable discrimination, and the political unpopularity of facing up to the ecological, demographic, and economic causes of stress.

Terrorism, Territory, and Boko Haram's Politics of Takfir

Boko Haram differs from the other subnational stress points considered here. It seeks neither secession, nor resources, nor representation. It opposes the Nigerian state's constitutional compromise between secular governance and religion, which since the colonial era has permitted the use of Islamic law to resolve civil disputes but otherwise protects freedom of worship. This ideological basis for insurgency hardened as the state's violent response drove the group underground and validated its narratives of victimization by the military (Thurston 2018). The overwhelming brunt of its violence has been regionally concentrated in the northeast, but its terrorism has shaken Nigeria's fragile sense of nationhood. Its Salafist ideology emerged in reaction to the instrumental treatment of northern politicians who, after the 1999 transition, sought to curry favor with conservative Muslim grassroots elements. When escalating state repression followed this betrayal, the turn to terrorism was a small step.

Between May 2011 and September 2017, Boko Haram was responsible for at least 16,488 deaths. At least another 7,151 deaths during this time can be attributed to government security forces, and an additional 14,299 deaths are blamed on some combination of Boko Haram and the security services (Council on Foreign Relations 2017). This level of violence places Boko Haram among the deadliest terrorist organizations in the world. Between 2009 and early 2014, at least 300,000 people fled the northeast (Scholz and Kriesch 2014). By the summer of 2017, the United Nations High Commission on Refugees said seven million people were struggling with food insecurity in northern Nigeria, with over five million people in Borno, Adamawa, and Yobe States facing some of the highest levels of food insecurity in the world (United Nations High Commissioner for Refugees 2017). Over the course of a decade, Boko Haram evolved from a small thorn in the lion's side to an adaptable and deadly threat.

Formally known in Hausa as *Jama'atu Ahlis Sunna Lidda'awati Wal-Jihad* ("People Committed to the Propagation of the Prophet's Teachings and Jihad"), Boko Haram seeks to establish Sharia in Nigeria, or at least in a large chunk of land in Borno State and around Lake Chad. How it would realize such a goal remains entirely ambiguous. Unlike other radical Salafist groups, "Boko Haram has no blueprint for the type of Islamic sharia it hopes to enthrone," writes a prominent northern scholar. "In areas where it attempted to experiment with some form of 'state' between 2014 and 2015, it could not establish any recognizable model of Islamic system based on the sharia" (Mohammed 2018, 590). In what follows, I briefly summarize the group's origins, the government's response to it, and various ideas advanced for ending its bloody reign.

Boko Haram originated in the early 2000's in Borno State as an isolated religious sect. Despite its reputation as "the Nigerian Taliban" in the popular media, its escalation to terrorism and suicide bombings was not entirely predictable. The charismatic young acolyte Mohammed Yusuf gradually upstaged elder imams, who many youths saw as too secular. Around this time, Ali Modu Sheriff, who was running for governor, and at least one senatorial candidate saw an opportunity and mobilized some Boko Haram youths as thugs. According to the former Vice President Atiku Abubakar, "that was the original militancy. They won elections and they abandoned those young men. Abandoned them to wither with their arms" (Abubakar 2016). The ruling PDP, seeing trouble ahead, dispatched a delegation to urge Borno politicians to disband the militias. While some politicians complied, Sheriff refused, according to Abubakar and at least two presidential investigations that remain secret (Abubakar 2016). Sheriff had supposedly promised the militias to implement a stricter form of Sharia law, but reneged after winning the election (Smith 2015). According to a senior politician from Kano, the whole movement by northern state legislatures in 1999 and 2000 to pass Sharia law was "a political weapon." Even the governor of Zamfara, the first state to do so, was not deeply religious; "he misunderstood the environment and what you can do" (Lawan 2012). In search of new acolytes, frustrated with harassment by the security services, and disappointed with the instrumentalization of faith by politicians, Boko Haram spread from Borno into neighboring Yobe and Bauchi States around 2004.

For the next several years Boko Haram engaged in small tit-for-tat skirmishes with local authorities over prayer services, funeral processions, and other minor issues that could be characterized as the first generation of its violence. It was during this time that its ranks grew for a variety of reasons. Some studies point to doctrinal rivalries among imams as a source of radicalization, as well as the expansion of Christian missionaries in the north inspiring feelings of Muslim defensiveness (Gow et al. 2013).

It is difficult to pin down how poverty contributed to Boko Haram's rise and radicalization at that point, but it did play some role. A landmark comparative study, *Guide to the Drivers of Violent Extremism*, concluded that, at best, there is an indirect connection between poverty and extremist recruitment, and that a variety of factors lead to violent extremism (US Agency for International Development, and Management Systems International 2009). A small but instructive collection of interviews with former Boko Haram combatants seems to confirm that ambiguous connection, with recruits coming from a range of socio-economic backgrounds, and some saying that Boko Haram offered them credit for small business start-ups. In the early iterations of its violence, recruits also say the organization's critique of governance failures was often sympathetically received (Mercy Corps 2016). Another survey of 119 former Boko Haram fighters found that less than 6 percent of them mentioned "employment opportunities" as a reason for joining, and only 15 percent mentioned poverty (Botha and Abdile 2016). One Nigerian survey found that poverty, alienation from families, and "roaming" preachers who distort religion were the primary drivers of radical youth recruitment in the north (CLEEN Foundation 2014). In addition, poor urban youths known as *almajiris* who live under the tutelage of imams have been recruited into Boko Haram (Mohammed 2014). However some studies say this is overstated, and it therefore fuels crude narratives of a Muslim "youth bulge" that is fertile for radicalization (Hoechner 2014; Hogan 2014). In the above survey, religious madrassas (attended by *almajiris*) played almost no role in recruitment (Botha and Abdile 2016).

In 2009, a series of altercations with the police escalated, culminating in the capture of Yusuf by the military and his extrajudicial killing by the police. According to human rights groups, hundreds of people were killed in a sprawling, massive exercise of military violence lasting several days (Amnesty International 2011). This turning point for Boko Haram ushered in its second generation of violence, when it went underground and its members sought to avenge Yusuf's death (Comolli 2015; LeVan 2013). After about a year in hiding, the group's new leader, Abubakar Shekau, emerged with attacks on police stations, military barracks, and prisons. In this second generation of violence, Boko Haram boldly bombed the police headquarters in the capital of Abuja, hundreds of miles from its own stronghold, and it then came to the world's attention with the bombing of the United

Nations offices in 2011. Suicide bombing, until then unheard of in Nigeria, had arrived – to the shock and dismay of countless media commentaries. Tactics also included kidnappings, which provided revenue for the group, and targeting of schools, churches, and mosques (Smith 2015; Mohammed 2014a; Sodipo 2013). The rise in terrorism raised the group's global profile, for example, by increasing American military assistance and prompting deeper military collaborations among Nigeria's neighbors.

A third generation of violence arrived in 2014. As discussed in Chapter 3, the group kidnapped 276 schoolgirls from Chibok, Borno State in April. That year it also bombed a bus depot just outside Abuja, which killed over seventy-five people. Other attacks followed. The randomness and brutality of these events shifted the public's attitudes about how to handle violent extremism. Over a three-month period, Boko Haram attacked over 200 towns and took control of at least twenty local government areas across three states. The group's success seizing and holding territory, though short-lived, reinforced the idea of Boko Haram as the African ISIL – an affiliation that had deepened a rift between Shekau and another faction led by Khalid al-Barnawi.[7] This put the military on the defensive as the nation headed into the contentious presidential elections studied in the previous three chapters. It also caught the attention of the international community, and the United Nations Security Council at this time formally listed Boko Haram as an al-Qaeda affiliate. Whether such ties represent opportunism or operational synchronization has remained a sharp subject of debate. Some studies emphasize the group's emergence at an opportune moment for Islamic extremism (Adesoji 2010). Other studies suggest that the rise of Boko Haram cannot merely be attributed to its international contacts; this oversimplifies the complex and localized nature of its origins (Omitola 2012; Mohammed 2018). While in power, the PDP used any evidence of Boko Haram's international ties to characterize the insurgency as externally inspired, rather than indigenous. This "inverted neocolonialism," which I discuss further in the conclusion, blamed foreign powers for Nigeria's failure to stem the

---

[7] The dispute stems from doctrinal differences about Islam, the virtues of negotiating with the government, and serious disagreements about the tactical utility of violence that alienates its potential followers (Barkindo 2017; Thurston 2018).

tide of terrorism and, as demonstrated in Chapter 3, helped give the APC the upper rhetorical hand in the presidential campaign.

The government has relied on a military response, with counterproductive results. "Tactics employed by government security agencies against Boko Haram have been consistently brutal and counterproductive," says a report by the United States Institute of Peace. "Their reliance on extrajudicial execution as a tactic in 'dealing' with any problem in Nigeria not only created Boko Haram as it is known today, but also sustains it and gives it fuel to expand" (Walker 2012, 1). A report published by the National Defense University in Washington drew the same conclusion. "Ordinary citizens fear both Boko Haram and the state security forces, with the latter accused of human rights abuses. With each battle between security forces and Boko Haram insurgents, civilian casualties mount. When security forces redeploy elsewhere claiming to have repelled Boko Haram, the militants return, regroup, and seek revenge" (Sodipo 2013, 1). Satellite photos in early 2014 displayed what appeared to be mass graves, and Amnesty International declared that both the security services and the terrorists may have committed crimes against humanity or even war crimes. The pan-Islamic group Jamatu Nasril Islam complained that the government's broad sweep led to extrajudicial killings of Muslims "on a mere whim of unsubstantiated suspicion" of belonging to Boko Haram (Tukur 2014). According to interviews with former members, security abuses provided Boko Haram with an effective basis for recruitment (Mercy Corps 2016). Vigilante groups, formed with the assistance of the security services, were also responsible for serious human rights violations, a problem highlighted by international groups (Amnesty International 2014; Matfess 2017) and local civil society activists alike (Borno and Yobe States Peoples Forum 2014). Where violence has subsided, mainly outside of Borno State, these groups pose challenges for demobilization and reintegration programs since government security services have declined to absorb them.

Both the insurgency and counter-insurgency have been economically disruptive. Hundreds of businesses have closed or been forced to relocate since 2009. Those that were willing to operate faced reduced hours of operation due to imposed curfews and interference from the security services (Idris et al. 2014). Amnesty International reported that the military rounded up 400 young men at Borno's Baga fish market in November 2012, and only seventy returned. Boko Haram has crippled economic activities in northern Nigeria, especially in the northeast. When northern governors (briefly) banded together in 2012 to address the insurgency, they described its negative effects on northern economies as very serious (Binniyat 2012). Following the state of emergency, farmers either abandoned their crops or faced other economic hardships. If the farmers remained in place, they had to pay bribes at military checkpoints when transporting food or were unable to obtain fertilizer and seed necessary for their crops in the first place. Insurgency-related violence has had a huge adverse impact on the rural poor, whose source of income depends upon what they are able to farm and then travel to sell. Over 5,000 women traders, mostly members of the Maiduguri Monday Market, have had to abandon their trade.

It was not until Boko Haram's third generation of violence – and especially the kidnapping of the Chibok girls – that the international community geared up for a full humanitarian response to the social dislocation and food security catastrophe. The United States played a significant role, directing nearly US$700 million to the Lake Chad region in Fiscal Year 2016–2017, with additional support coming from the World Food Program, the International Committee for the Red Cross, and others (US Agency for International Development 2017). Well past the election of Buhari in 2016, the humanitarian response continued to lack a centralized missing persons registry, an acknowledgement of widespread gender-based violence, and cooperation from national and state emergency management officials (Vigaud-Walsh 2016). Though figures vary estimates from a study carried out by the American University of Nigeria found that about 90 percent of the internally displaced persons in Adamawa State reside in informal "host communities" rather than registering as in IDP camps. Unlike such camps elsewhere in the world, Nigeria's are controlled by the military. Using satellite imagery and other technologies in 2018, Mercy Corps estimated that they were unable to reach 920,000 IDPs due to military requirements for an escort (in conflict with Mercy Corp's practice of maintaining humanitarian neutrality). In 2017, the military raided a camp, further eroding relations with the humanitarian agencies, including the United Nations, and undermining the fragile basis for bureaucratic coordination (Searcey 2017). Government reluctance to allow international organizations to play their usual roles has impeded the humanitarian response by forcing Boko Haram's victims to choose between life in a military camp and life as unregistered IDPs, and it has facilitated corruption (Page and LeVan 2016). Aid has also been affected by corruption, even before the humanitarian response scaled up (International Crisis Group 2014). There have been very few prosecutions, but in 2017 Nigeria's anti-corruption agency arrested an emergency management official for diversion of IDP assistance (Economic and Financial Crimes Commission 2017).

Whatever the end of Boko Haram looks like – the death or arrest of Shekau, the disintegration of its capabilities, etc. – the restoration of security would only be the beginning of the problems that the northeast, forever changed, now faces. As stated at the outset, the scope and scale of the humanitarian crisis is massive. Millions of IDPs have now been living away from home for so long, and they trust the security services so little to provide accurate information about the situation back home, that they do not want to return. And if they did return, it is not clear that the Nigerian Government is prepared to coordinate aid or spend on the scale necessary for reconstruction. Meanwhile, Demilitarization, Demobilization, and Reintegration ("DDR") programs began before the cessation of hostilities with few successful defection cases. Perhaps most frustrating of all for the humanitarian community, the Chibok girls who did not go abroad after escaping or being released in a 2017 negotiation lingered in government custody, unable to travel or visit their families (Sawab and Searcey 2017).

Nevertheless, the release of many of the Chibok girls distinguished Buhari from his predecessor's record with Boko Haram, and it possibly signaled an opening for broader dialogue. After Mohammed Yousef's death, there were clear indications that the group would de-escalate if the government prosecuted his killers, rebuilt destroyed places of worship, and compensated victims. Two presidential commissions, a major study by a Nigerian Government think tank (National Institute of Policy and Strategic Studies 2012), and various traditional rulers including the Borno Elders Forum urged the government to explore such avenues (African Examiner 2012; Mohammed 2014). However, the third generation of Boko Haram's violence reduced the political constituency for dialogue. The group's tactics, including a massive increase in the use of female suicide bombers (Warner and Matfess 2017) – even after the release of many of the Chibok girls – further undermined the basis for trust in its leadership. Similarly, the affiliation with ISIL and the seeming alienation from al-Qaeda made any ostensible demands, short of Sharia, increasingly murky.

An opportunity, rather than a complication, is an appreciation for the essential role of development and investment in the northeast region as central to addressing the underlying sources of the conflict. Donor countries have underscored the need for socio-economic development. "Military, law enforcement, and intelligence tools are vital to defend against these threats," said the US Under Secretary of State for Political Affairs, Tom Shannon, of Boko Haram and other terrorist groups threatening African security in 2017. "But military force alone is not enough for a sustained peace."[8] The National Institute of Policy and Strategic Studies in Nigeria noted regional development disparities and the need for expanded social policies (National Institute of Policy and Strategic Studies 2012). The US Institute of Peace (USIP) has funded a project by the Abuja-based Centre for Regional Integration and Development to expand vocational education and introduce a peace-based curriculum into northern Muslim schools, emphasizing Koranic messages of tolerance. The International Crisis Group calls for ending impunity for the security services in order to advance the rule of law and weaken the insurgency by responding to one of Boko Haram's principal demands. It also calls for international pressure to ensure that Nigeria's anti-corruption agencies followed through on prosecutions, enforced conditionalities on foreign aid being delivered to the north, and a development agency similar to the one created for the Niger Delta (International Crisis Group 2014) and not too different from the Presidential Initiative on the Northeast (PINE) that has since been created. In short, civil society, donors, and the government have all acknowledged the centrality of economic development to peace in the greater northeast.

The challenge that Boko Haram presents to Nigeria's democratic progress is much greater than generating this development, or providing security, as discussed in Chapter 4. There is also little question that representation has failed the northeast thus far. The ideological nature of the rebellion, rooted in a purity at odds even with other Nigerian Salafists (Thurston 2016), evident in the research mentioning the small number of recruits who joined for a job, adds a degree of intractability absent from all of the other stress points here. The constitutional compromise that has sustained Nigeria's unity since the colonial era

---

[8] Remarks at the US Institute of Peace, September 13, 2017. www.state.gov/p/us/rm/2017/274073.htm.

is premised on a secular basis for coercion, alongside a codified integration of religious practices such as government funding for the hajj, recognition of madrassas, and Sharia in northern civil courts. Boko Haram rejects that bargain entirely. In his book on African sovereignty, Englebert writes, "African rebels appear in general as conservative in matters of the state as everyone else. They might take issue with state authorities, but not with the authority of the state" (Englebert 2009, 48). Boko Haram, and the Caliphate alternative, ambiguous as it may be, has broken from that generalization in dramatic and deadly fashion. The task of reducing subnational stress and institutionalizing democracy must now proceed within an unconsolidated nation; the idea of Nigeria must win before violent insurgency can lose.

Concluding Comparisons

Nigeria's journey back to democracy that began in 1998 catalyzed each of the subnational stress points examined above. The transition did not cause crises presented by pastoralists, Igbo secessionism, or Boko Haram, but it did transform them by embedding their politics within the structure of the Fourth Republic's politics and institutions. How did this transformation occur, and how do the groups' varied goals and tactics strain democratic futures?

For the Igbo, the transition opened a new potential opportunity to address longstanding grievances about unsettled property restitution from the civil war era. Igbos went into 1999 hopeful about what lay ahead, even if they had been divided over Sani Abacha and how to resolve Yoruba frustration with the annulled 1993 election. When the latter issue was addressed in the PDP's transitional pact, it sidelined former Vice President Ekwueme and perpetuated a perception of perpetual under-enfranchisement. And if the Yoruba would get eight years (two terms) under the principle of "power shift" or zoning of the presidency, it meant that the northerners would have their turn next. The political events of 1999, and the pact that facilitated a successful handover to civilians, meant that Igbos were out for the next sixteen years. The transition also brought to power the same former general who had prosecuted the federal government's brutal war against the Biafra secessionists a generation earlier.

Next, the extension of Sharia to criminal matters through legislation passed by a dozen northern state assemblies antagonized Igbos, many of whom owned businesses throughout the north. "Ohanaeze is totally opposed to the adoption of Sharia," said the Secretary General of the Igbo group at the time. "We view it as fundamentally incompatible with our federal system" (Nwabueze 2001, 25). The rise of Boko Haram, too, is embedded within the Sharia movement, even if the state legislatures' actions have often been referenced in oversimplifications of the group's origins (Thurston 2018). It is also within the tradition of earlier Islamic reformist movements attempting to convert and radicalize northern Nigeria's moderate Sufi traditions (Adesoji 2011; Aghedo 2014; Isichei 1987), though one should be very cautious about attempting to establish explicit lineages, especially given the international contexts of Salafism today.

For pastoralists, the transition may seem less significant than the slow ecological crisis described earlier by the African Union. However, the Fourth Republic did disrupt efforts by previous military regimes to transform pastoralism and facilitate a transition to a more settled or mixed-commercial lifestyle. For example, after the civil war, Yakubu Gowon abolished the cattle tax as part of a broader effort to reduce beef imports and encourage pastoralists to stay within Nigeria (Gowon 2010). The government embarked on a First (1976–1986) and then a Second (1987–1995) Livestock Development Project to improve cattle productivity and address failures of the states to gazette their grazing laws as expected. A government program from 1996 to 1999 to rehabilitate livestock production facilities included recommendations for new reserves. It also set aside oil revenue from the Petroleum Trust Fund, which closed in 1999. A few years later, a study of pastoralism noted "all grazing reserves and traditional grazing areas of the country are in a deplorable state of disrepair," suffering from encroachment by small- and large-scale crops, poorly planned irrigation, uncontrolled bush fires, and overgrazing (Hassan and Jauro 2005, 132). In 2012 the Nigerian Senate failed to pass a National Grazing Rights and Reserves Bill (Matfess 2016), claiming that it lacked the authority to establish grazing reserves, despite the federal government's repeated record of doing just that. The political constituency for pastoralism changed in the Fourth Republic, where politicians had more to gain from large private land deals or mischaracterizing the farmer–herder tensions as religious. Geographical representation in the House and the Senate complicated interest aggregation for interests with little physical fixity.

Forged in the tumult of the 1999 transition, the Niger Delta militancy could easily be considered a fourth stress point alongside the others. Upset about decades of environmental destruction, development neglect, and state violence, hundreds of activists and organizations came together in 1998 to issue the Kaiama Declaration. Three years before, in 1995, the Abacha government shocked the world with the hanging of Ken Saro-Wiwa, a poet and environmental activist, galvanizing new transnational solidarity for the Niger Delta. Building on that momentum, the Declaration called for the withdrawal of oil companies and the military from the region, set up an Ijaw Youth Council (IYC), and rejected Abubakar's interim government, formed after the death of Abacha. "The way forward is a Sovereign National Conference of equally represented ethnic nationalities," said the authors, and this should precede any transition (United Ijaw 1998). As the transition was unfolding, an Ijaw chief (who participated in the Kaiama Declaration), said Ijaw youths do not seek secession. "All they are asking for is justice, fair play and equity in the allocation of resources and appointments" (Umanah 1999). Even amidst the discourse for a Sovereign National Conference, the call centered on "resource control" (meaning reallocation of oil money), environmental clean-up, and employment opportunities for youth – rather than secession (Adunbi 2015).

After President Obasanjo took office, the situation seemed to only get worse as the new democratic regime took desperate measures to keep the country's revenue source stable and assert sovereign control over the restless oil-producing areas. In June 1999, a local poet/activist wrote of military violence in Delta State, referencing a village that formed MEND's stronghold during its peak:

> I don't want to hear the voices of the red men
> who plunder the womb of my life,
> in search of death
> I want to hear the voices of the women of Gbaramatu
> in their new desire against death (Naagbanton 2015, 8).

Then, as if underscoring the flaws of putting a former military man in charge of the fragile democratic regime, came the brutal bombing of the village of Odi, not far from Kaiama in Baylesa State (Ikelegbe 2001; Human Rights Watch 1999). For the IYC and other activists, it signaled that the regime had changed, but their condition had not. By the end of Obasanjo's first term in 2003, attacks on oil pipelines and hostage-taking had begun.

"When we had militancy in the Niger Delta," said a (now-former) senior member of the National Assembly. "It was easy for people to see what the concerns were. Some people were agitating for improvement in environmental issues, some were just criminals ... but because it was easy to separate the criminal aspect of it from the activism, it was easy to dialogue and arrive at some kind of solution" (Lawan 2012). By generally not seeking secession, Delta militants lent themselves to a brand of radical democratic politics. And vastly unlike Boko Haram, the militants avoided harming civilians in pursuit of "resource control" in the country's oil-producing region (LeVan 2013). Groups used limited and tactical violence to take foreign oil workers hostage in return for ransom, attack oil infrastructure, and occasionally engage government security services. Militant grievances are embedded within a mainstream narrative of under-development, pollution, and foreign exploitation of the resources that account for approximately 90 percent of the country's export revenue. A government amnesty program demobilized tens of thousands of militants by effectively bribing them but failed to address the underlying causes of rebellion (Adunbi 2015; Abidde 2017). As a party official in the oil-rich Rivers State explained it, after President Jonathan was sworn in, an accompanying political program to address the underlying *causes* of the rebellion got forgotten (Finebone 2017). The amnesty program has therefore precipitated a bargaining dynamic that fosters local rivalries and new militancy. It has reduced violence but undermined confidence in Nigeria's democratic institutions as tools of conflict resolution, development, and equitable distribution. Soon after Buhari took office, a new group, the Niger Delta Avengers, emerged. Consistent with their predecessors in MEND and other militant groups, their demands centered on reallocation within the mainstream of political discourse. In particular, they sought a Maritime University in the Niger Delta (Niger Delta Militant Contact Group 2017).[9]

This highlights how these subnational stress points differ in their relationship to violence in ways that complicate democratic

---

[9] The location of the proposed university has been hugely divisive, since the former governor supposedly believes that it should not compete with the University of Port Harcourt.

consolidation. Nigeria's northeast may yet get the development it deserves, but an amnesty program along the lines of the Niger Delta's is unlikely. Not only is it difficult for Nigerians to forgive Boko Haram for Chibok, Baga, Nyanya, and hundreds of other horrific incidents, the country faced a fiscal crisis with the drop in oil prices in 2014, making it costly to pay off militants. Moreover, its ideological roots do no not lend themselves to a solution that bribes it into abandoning terrorism; Salafism does not lend itself to compromise. Pro-Biafra groups profess a commitment to nonviolence, and, as the President General of Ohanaeze said, state repression is radicalizing them. Recent academic work further suggests that most secessionist movements since 1960 have not used nonviolence, but those that did use it were more likely to achieve their goals. The reason why so few movements use nonviolence though, is because as resistance movements they tend to last a very long time – making organized nonviolent civil resistance difficult to sustain (Chenoweth and Stephan 2011; Cunningham 2017). Today's pro-Biafra organizations resemble other secessionist groups in other ways too, by providing public goods – however modest – in order to project themselves as worthy of state power (Stewart 2018). It is noteworthy that the latest research on Boko Haram is revisiting earlier portrayals of the group as lacking in such traditional guerrilla strategies. Some women are drawn to Boko Haram for the opportunity to obtain education and avoid hard physical labor; some men see it as a viable route to marriage and social status in a region of diminished opportunities (Matfess 2017).

MASSOB, agitating since the dawn of the transition, seems to be in for the long haul. But, as suggested by the comparative research, generating cooperation – and the international sympathy that the Biafra movements crave – runs up against norms for establishing external legitimacy; in the post-Cold War world, it is difficult to demonstrate the righteousness of your cause when carrying a gun.

Igbo secessionists invariably include the Niger Delta states in their vision of Biafra, in line with the historical boundaries sought in the civil war. But there are compelling reasons to avoid exaggerating any tactical similarities, and to question southeastern secessionists' calls for solidarity with Niger Delta rebels. "The mistrust between Igbo and Yoruba dates from 1953 between Zik [Nnamadi Azikiwe] and [Obafemi] Awolowo," explains the former Secretary General of

Ohanaeze, who insists the British rigged the independence elections in order to divide the south and enable a victory by the northern Fulani, the favored ethnic group under colonial rule. "The Nigerian problem is the Fulani problem ... how to contain the Fulani" (Nwaorgu 2017). An explicit goal of the PDP, according to some party leaders, was to reconcile the east and the Niger Delta (Olotolo 2017). On the one hand, this explains the electoral patterns of the two geopolitical zones in the Fourth Republic, consistently voting for the PDP. On the other hand, a Niger Delta–southeast alliance has conflicted with the PDP's pact for the transition: choosing a Yoruba in 1999, and then allowing the north eight years in power starting in 2007. Governor Ikpeazu of Abia State recalls the dilemma this way: "the PDP as a party crystallized as a result of the agitation of the west. But the north wanted to pacify the sentiments that were beginning to erupt, particular from the southeast as a result of the war experience," and PDP leaders also knew they had to address feelings of alienation across the Niger Delta (Ikpeazu 2017).

Perhaps the most explicit problem with a Niger Delta–Biafra collaboration is pragmatic; when the Niger Delta Avengers met with representatives of the Biafra movements, they failed to find sufficient common ground (Naagbanton 2017). Most of Nigeria's oil remains in the core Niger Delta states, which are full of a large plurality of Nigeria's ethnic minorities. These minorities are uneasy about political status in any vision of an independent Biafra. In other words, to Niger Delta militants, many of whom still have access to arms, the alliance proposed by the southeast sounds a bit too instrumental on the part of the Igbo secessionists (Niger Delta Militant Contact Group 2017). It is not clear what Niger Deltans would get out of the alliance. Meanwhile, Igbo politicians have warmed up to a northern president, at least at the time of this writing. Governors supported the military's attempt to ban IPOB and MASSOB, and Governor Dave Umahi of Ebonyi State praised Buhari for reaching out to the east. "You have no hatred for any state. You have treated all states with equality. What one state gets in the north, the other gets in the south" (Adesina 2017).

If the claims of under-development, political disenfranchisement, and social marginalization all sound a bit too familiar in tracing the origins of these democratic stress points, it is worth concluding by highlighting how impunity has fueled frustration. Even large-scale incidents that generate serious criticism, such as the bombing of Odi, torture in Borno State's Giwa Barracks, farmer–herder clashes that needlessly spiral out of control, or the shooting in Port Harcourt of Biafra supporters celebrating the election of Donald Trump, investigations may occur but prosecutions leading to convictions are practically unheard of. Nor has the state proven itself willing to operate under the rule of law against violent entrepreneurs worthy of conviction. As of late 2017, Nigeria's courts had concluded only thirteen cases linked to Boko Haram, yielding only nine convictions. Eight years into one of the world's deadliest waves of terrorism, the government finally announced that the trials of 1,600 other suspects would begin soon – but their trials would be done in secret (Agence France Press 2017). This will neither build confidence in democratic institutions nor will it provide an adequate demonstration effect to deter future insurgents. Though the drivers of violent extremism are complex and strongly influenced by context, government repression, the curtailment of civil liberties, and state illegitimacy or collapse are all rule-of-law issues (Robinson and Kelly 2017).

These problems of impunity are rooted in the very deals struck during the birth of the Fourth Republic outlined in Chapter 2: a graceful exit for military officials, no prosecutions, no truth-telling, and big defense budgets as "coup-proofing" in return for staying out of politics. Nigeria may have navigated the treacherous waters of party turnover for the first time in 2015. But competitive representation is an inadequate substitute for rule of law – an element in Linz and Stepan's democratic consolidation, formulated in the optimistic days of the Third Wave of Democratization when electoral defeats seemed to propel broader systemic transformations. Like other young democracies, Nigeria has yet to reconcile the bonds of its past with the liberal ambitions of its future.

7 | Conclusion

"If there is any assumption Nigerians made in the run up to the 2015 general elections, it is that given his experience and the long years spent seeking for the office, General Buhari is uniquely placed to run, perhaps, the most competent, organised and corrupt-free administration in Nigeria's history. However," the editorial continued, "two years after the PDP's defeat since ascending to the presidency, President Buhari has proved Nigerians wrong by running perhaps the most lethargic, chaotic, incompetent – and as it is now increasingly becoming obvious, a corrupt administration wrought with infighting, confusing, contest for power and authority and a shocking lack of grasp of the fundamentals of governance and administration" (Editorial 2017). What does this critique of Buhari's record tell us about democracy itself? Political science has defined and operationalized democracy for comparative analysis in a wide variety of ways and has become increasingly sensitive to different models and cultural understandings. But people actually experience politics in ways that transcend the operational technicalities of democracy as the electoral selection of rulers (Schumpeter, 1942), the "institutionalization of uncertainty" (Przeworski 1986, 58), or other approaches. For the Nigerians who read that editorial – and for most of us – democracy is a social experience of renewal in the face of new political challenges and recurring feelings of disappointment.

This book explained how the PDP came to power in 1999 and then how the APC defeated it in 2015. This is the beginning of a story not just about elections but about the elite politics of hope, the collective power of voters, and the boundaries of competition whose renegotiation forms the foundation of democratic renewal. In this concluding chapter, I summarize my core findings, elaborate on the book's contributions, and sketch out the limits of my analysis and the opportunities for rising scholars of African politics

217

and comparative democratization. I outline how overlapping elite bargains involving the transitional government, the exiting military, and the PDP facilitated the successful transfer to civilians in 1999. By showing how these bargains planted the seeds of democratization and undermined the PDP's competitiveness as 2015 approached, I add to our understanding of how elite pacts end. I also reiterate the main findings from my three chapters on the APC's electoral victory, the first party turnover in Nigeria's history. By articulating promises of economic renewal, anti-corruption, and electoral integrity, the APC capitalized on emerging electoral constituencies and correctly calculated that rational counter-terrorism could not flow from a shallow politics of fear. The PDP played to such prejudice, and failed. Robust evidence pointing to "economic voting" aligned with the winning party's platform. Ethnic identity is still salient in politics and the election also accented religious cleavages. But the findings about the importance of economic policy evaluations contribute to an emerging, encouraging literature on African voting behavior (Bratton et al. 2013; Gibson 2009). Finally, noting how flawed assumptions of transitions as unilinear processes "to" democracy have been largely abandoned, I introduced the notion of "stress points" as an analytic refresher to familiar but limited discourse on democratic consolidation. A secessionist revival in the southeast, ongoing violence from Boko Haram in the northeast, and geographically dispersed tensions between farmers and herders highlight the challenges ahead – both for Nigeria and for students of African politics.

Nigeria's Pacted Transition in Comparative Perspective

It is hard to overstate the size of the democratization literature, with long and lively debates about the causes of regime transitions and the contexts in which they succeed or fail. Chapter 2 offered a detailed examination of Nigeria's transition, and laid the groundwork for my later claim that the more undemocratic features of the transition continue to hold back democracy today. This analysis largely left aside the prior question of *why* the transition happened in the first place since numerous studies have already addressed that (LeVan 2011b; Kew 2016; Agbaje 2004). Instead, it highlighted the elite agreements known as "pacts" that operationalized core compromises between the exiting generals and the incoming democratic reformers, and then argued that the erosion of the transition's pact helped pave the way to the PDP's defeat in 2015.

I first noted how the 1999 transition is arguably Nigeria's *only* successful transition, since neither the First (1960–1966) nor the Second (1979–1983) Republics progressed beyond organizing a founding election, and both fell prey to military coups within a few years. These histories loomed large in the political memory of those present at the creation of the Fourth Republic, as the current political era is known. The pact that kept the 1999 transition on track actually involved two overlapping bargains. The first emerged from agreements between the military and the Provisional Ruling Council, which took over after Abacha's death and managed the transition. When Abubakar and the PRC met with the military in 1998, they reduced the military's fear of exit and shaped the political contours of competition for the remainder of the transition in three ways. First, the PRC promoted key Abacha loyalists, including hardliners who had resisted political liberalization. The legal legacy of their handiwork largely remained in place, with at least forty military decrees staying on the books (many of which can be found at http://carllevan .com/data/nigerias-military-decrees/). A second compromise involved Abubakar's reluctance to intercept or expose money stolen by Abacha and his family. Hundreds of millions of dollars of this "Abacha loot" is being discovered, recovered, and returned. The third compromise with the military concerned the PRC's tepid approach to transitional justice. Abacha's hardliners faced no meaningful consequences for their crimes, and those who jailed and hanged the playwright Ken Saro-Wiwa in 1995 actually did well for themselves after the PDP took power. For example, the Rivers State Attorney General who oversaw the military tribunal had a US$163 million football (soccer) stadium named after him, and the chief judge of the tribunal that sentenced Saro-Wiwa and his fellow pro-democracy activists to death was confirmed to serve as Chief Judge on the Federal High Court in 2011 (Pegg 2015). The peaceful transition of power from military generals to civilian elites on May 29, 1999 came at the cost of transparency, accountability, and legitimacy from a public largely cut out of the process (Eisenstadt, LeVan, & Maboudi 2017).

The other bargain, overlapping with the first, emerged from the PDP positioning itself for civilian power. Party elites knew that democracy depended on keeping the military happy – and in the barracks.

"We were transitioning from a long period of military rule to a democratic culture," recalled one PDP leader in an interview. "So it was the understanding that we need to come together ... in order to assure the military that we've come of age and that we would be able to control ourselves and be able to arrange ourselves in such a way that the military would not have any reason for incursion into political affairs" (Nnaji 2017). The new party settled on three founding principles to obtain power, and then adopted what I label a "dual strategy" to keep power. First, party elites agreed that picking a Yoruba presidential candidate would reduce anger in the southwest, where the annulled 1993 election results had derailed the previous transition and then divided Abacha's government. The party settled on Obasanjo, the former dictator who oversaw the 1979 transition. But in doing so they also shoved aside Alex Ekweume, an experienced politician from the Second Republic. This fanned the flames of Igbo frustration (discussed in Chapter 6) since Ekwueme had played a prominent role in defending democracy during its darkest days, and the process that eliminated him involved backroom deals and corruption. A second founding principle of the PDP was an agreement known as "power shift." In order to reassure northern elites, the party agreed to alternate the presidency between the north and south every eight years, after two presidential terms. This was necessary in light of the broad agreement that the 1999 presidential candidate should come from the south. Finally, the PDP sought to weaken the military's appetite and institutional capacity for politics. "One of the biggest problems we had in the past was military intervention in politics," a PDP leader told me. "So [President] Obasanjo made to remove all those military that had worked with politics in the past ... these were the ambitious people, who kept on organizing military coups" (Agbim 2017).

Once in power, Obasanjo – the ex-general and hero of the civil war – did just that. He purged the military officers who had been involved in politics, linking such efforts to a broader policy of professionalization so that the retirements would not be interpreted as retribution. But the PDP adopted a dual policy that involved weakening the military's capacity for politics while simultaneously embarking on "coup-proofing" measures. Nigeria's military budget drastically increased, even as security threats waned. Obasanjo's government also promoted 879 military officers just weeks before being sworn in for his second term in 2003; these promotions have received far less attention from historians than the dismissals and forced retirements in 1999–2000.

Finally, the party generated career opportunities for retired officers in its civilian ranks. This was not a new phenomenon in Nigerian civil–military relations, but it is notable that a post-transition generation of retired officers rose within the PDP after 2003. Their absorption into the PDP means that the party had partly institutionalized the military's influence, and that the pact with the military had survived those initial years of transition.

Finally, Chapter 2 also detailed how coup-proofing and the PDP's dual strategy imposed economic and political costs on the new democracy. The road to the APC's 2015 victory was paved by the elite divisions and the popular disappointments rooted in the pact. This is of broader comparative interest because, as noted above, existing research says little about when pacts actually end. In Nigeria's case, several factors eroded the 1999 transition's pact. First, the PDP's composition changed over time. More candidates joined politics without a personal stake in the transition and without a military background. A striking demographic dissonance fanned the flames of frustration as well. Using data on the age of politicians in the National Assembly, I showed how, as the country was getting younger, the average elected politician was getting older. A second problem concerned the party's internal rules to rotate power and limit eligibility for positions based on one's ethnographic background. When the northern president fell ill in 2009, and disappeared from public view until he passed away in 2010, power passed to his vice president, Goodluck Jonathan. But since he was a southerner, the party faced the dilemma of honoring the pact's principles of power shift or running an incumbent. By choosing the latter, the party won the 2011 elections but weakened the very basis of the bargain that had helped the party cohere. I then presented a variety of evidence from state-level contests, where politicians saw few reasons to honor rotational principles at the subnational level once they had been sacrificed at the national level. When party leaders tried, they further frustrated ambitions that would become a pipeline of defections to the APC (LeVan 2018; Agbaje, Akande, & Ojo 2018).

This analysis is of general interest because I showed how the transition ended later than the standard thresholds set by comparative studies (Linz 1996). It also occurred surprisingly quickly, and the process of elite bargaining limited public participation in ways that shaped the basis for subsequent political competition. Nigeria's democratization had decidedly undemocratic roots. In addition, unlike militaries in Latin America, for example, (Stepan 1988; Barros 2003), Nigeria's generals did not enjoy veto authority or privileged control over their policy domain – even as the PDP adopted its dual policy of coup-proofing and cleaning house.

From Transition to Party Turnover

Departing from the story of the pact's decay, the next three chapters explained the defeat of the PDP in 2015. Using mixed methods in three steps, I demonstrated through a qualitative content analysis that the APC and the PDP campaigned on different issues. Next I offered statistical evidence that electoral outcomes across states correspond with those differences. Finally, I used individual-level data in probit regressions to show that economic performance and electoral integrity motivated voters to support the opposition, even though ethnic and religious identities still have an allure.

The "Rational Counter-Terrorist" and Party Campaigns in the Age of Boko Haram

Chapter 3 pointed out that, until recently, research on African parties typically saw them as devoid of meaningful differences, campaigning either on ethnic appeals or staple issues such as anti-corruption, and rarely articulating any ideology (Obafemi, Egwu, Ibeanu, & Ibrahim 2014). The evidence from Nigeria's 2015 presidential election indicates that this picture is changing. Using a content analysis of 929 references coded with NVivo software and drawn from an original sample of 2,390 articles, I found that the APC referenced all five issue areas more frequently than the PDP. In fact, the old way of doing politics, leaving out discussion of substantive issues and getting press coverage for attending weddings and funerals, for example, seemed to work against the PDP's interests in 2015. The issues shaped the campaigns, and, as the next two chapters showed, shaped voting too.

There were compelling reasons to expect insecurity to dominate the successful presidential campaign: voters ranked it first among their priorities, and national surveys consistently demonstrated nationwide concern about the threat that terrorism posed. Yet, campaigning on counter-terrorism was hardly the rational strategy. I first found that the parties campaigned on the economy (and corruption) more often than any other issue, with 356 references. The content analysis also found, somewhat unexpectedly, that electoral integrity amounted to the second-most frequently mentioned issue. I interpret this to mean that the APC's rhetoric sought to capture an emerging voting constituency concerned about the quality of elections. Though I did not directly test for the effects of voter education, these findings are also consistent with research suggesting that it can work. Such efforts in Nigeria in 2015 included the "Vote Not Fight" campaign against election violence, workshops on "Curbing Youth Involvement in Electoral Violence" funded by the United Nations Development Programme, and the production of civic education materials. A related finding of interest in Chapter 3 concerns the significant *difference* between the parties; the APC mentioned electoral integrity 162 times while the PDP did so only 87 times. Since the APC held comparatively transparent primaries, they signaled a new way of doing business compared to the back-room deals that first formed the PDP and then inspired dozens of defectors.

Together, these findings provide an important empirical analysis of what African political parties actually talk about during campaigns. Since there were significant differences between the winning party and the losing party on the issues, this analysis also gives us ideas about how issues can propel electoral wins; even in the face of the bloodiest violence since the civil war, the APC consistently emphasized the economy and issues such as electoral integrity, betting that they would build a bigger electoral coalition. The PDP made a public relations display of its efforts to defeat Boko Haram, blaming Western countries for not intervening enough. But the opposition correctly calculated that rational counter-terrorism meant including security in a portfolio of issues that captured the political mood. I also found it interesting that neither party discussed social issues much, though the APC discussed them twice as much as the PDP. This was an unfortunate miscalculation for the PDP, I pointed out, since there had been several socio-economic improvements for women under President Jonathan's administration, but the PDP did little to electorally capitalize on them.

How Insecurity and Economic Conditions Shaped Electoral Outcomes in States

Chapter 4 shifted from an elite analysis of party leaders and campaigns to voting outcomes across states, measured in terms of the change in the PDP's vote share in the 2011 and 2015 presidential elections. First I tested an in/security hypothesis to determine if citizens actually acted upon their fears of terrorism, or their familiarity with subnational violence influenced voting. Recalling that democracies are 3.5 times more likely than other regimes to experience terrorism (Enders 2012), and that one would therefore expect to see many studies of elections and campaigns in these conditions, I noted there are few such studies outside the developed world. Terrorism could impact elections by shifting voter priorities to security. But the role of terrorism in shaping elections is conditioned by context (Oates 2006), including rhetoric such as that explored in Chapter 3. Polarization is one such likely effect, according to a number of comparative studies (Nanes 2016). Though, as pointed out in the book's Introduction, there is little basis for polarization in Africa – at least in ideological terms.

Violence had a weaker effect on the elections than anticipated, when I first sketched out my intuitions after observing the elections in 2015 as an international monitor. My results show that proximity to violence had no systematic correlation with voting outcomes across states. The same was true for the level of state penetration. Police presence, my proxy for this, could have influenced voting outcomes by reassuring people that the government was providing security. Alternatively, police presence could inspire cynicism, given the public's low esteem of the police and evidence of police partisanship in contested states. Neither appear to have been the case. Ideally both the results on proximity and state penetration should be tested with finer granularity than state-level data can offer, and I am hopeful such data will be available for future studies. I do find evidence, however, that terrorism promoted party polarization. The PDP mobilized voters with negatives: *fear* of how violent extremism would rise under a Muslim northerner. For APC voters, on the other hand, fears of an increase in "extremist attacks" with a Jonathan re-election simply didn't resonate the same.

These findings are important not simply because they suggest that violence played a smaller role in shaping the campaign and the election than expected, but because electoral violence constitutes a major focus of donors and domestic civil society in African elections. A joint report by the International Republican Institute and the National Democratic Institute for International Affairs on Ghana's 2016 presidential is illustrative. The pre-election mission noted "heightened competition and tensions," including "an increase in the number and visibility of youth vigilante groups that intimidate and harass citizens and potentially voters" as well as "inflammatory speech propagated by politically controlled media" and marginalization of minorities (National Democratic Institute for International Affairs, and International Republican Institute 2016, 1–2). Another example of practitioners' engagement on the issue is a course offered by the United States Institute of Peace, a US Government-funded think tank, entitled "Preventing Electoral Violence in Africa."[1] The United Nations alone funded at least ninety-nine programs between 2003 and 2015 designed to either raise public awareness about electoral violence or increase stakeholder capacity to reduce it (Birch 2017). Such efforts are worthwhile, and may help avert escalation to larger conflicts, but we also need to study violence's broader impact on parties, platforms, and voters.

Next, I find statistically significant evidence for the economic voting hypothesis under all statistical specifications. First, I demonstrated that more favorable views of the economy over the previous twelve months correlate with a nearly 15-percentage-point increase in support for the PDP. Second, I found that in states where more families have more disposable income (i.e., they are economically better off), they were generally more likely to support the PDP. Third, I demonstrated a strong, inverse correlation between the PDP's share of vote and the mean citizen assessment for whether Buhari would improve the economy. States where voters did not believe Buhari would improve the economy were overwhelmingly more likely to support for the PDP. In states where the average voter believed Buhari was better-positioned to improve the economy, they overwhelmingly cast their lot with him. Voters in both parties cared about the economy, but, as shown in Chapter 3, the APC hammered the hopeful message of reform home to voters. The PDP, which had a favorable economic record to run on, notwithstanding the downturn in late 2014, seems to have misread the possibilities for building a broad electoral coalition based on the salient issues of the day. These findings lend support to an emerging literature showing that African voters increasingly vote on evaluations of policy rather than ethnicity or candidate personality

---

[1] See www.usip.org/education-training/courses/preventing-electoral-violence-in-africa-tools-policymakers.

(Gibson 2009; Bratton 2013). For example, a recent cross-national study of African countries concluded, "(w)ithout denying that ethnic sentiments play a role in shaping vote choice, we note that rational calculations about material welfare are apparently at the forefront of voters' minds" (Bratton 2013, 96). This is also consistent with tests in some of my recent collaborative research. Using electoral results across most of Nigeria's 774 local governments in 2015, we found that neither patronage nor violence influenced electoral outcomes, but economic performance did (LeVan, Page, & Ha 2018).

Finally, I found that state debt levels were extremely reliable predictors of voting outcomes; the higher the level of debt, the more likely the state supported the ruling PDP. This makes sense since this debt increases the states' dependence on the center (even though state governments have some ability to borrow money). This represents a potentially important finding for the literature on fiscal federalism, which has long presumed that low levels of internally generated revenue (IGR) in Nigeria's states is a sign of weak federalism (Amuwo 2000; Ekpo 1994; Ikein 1998). IGR does predict some results, but it is subnational debt that drives political dependence on the ruling party.

I concede that I did not explicitly explore potential *mechanisms* that linked campaign appeals to voters. But the robust results across every model offer a good inferential basis for saying that the APC "primed" Nigerians to vote on the economy. I also note that these tests required aggregating some of the survey data to the state level. This requires some fairly strong assumptions of homogeneity within each state, but it also offers the advantage of including several objective measures of government performance and social conditions. Such assumptions are not required for the third round of tests with individual-level data, and my findings were also consistent with the interviews I conducted with officials in states such as Rivers, Abia, Enugu, Plateau, Gombe, and Bauchi.

Electoral Integrity, Ethnicity, and Religion in 2015

Chapter 5 used data from statistically sampled national surveys to explore how electoral integrity stacked up as issues alongside social cleavage strategies that appeal to ethnicity or religion. This means that I used *voter intentions*, rather than observed levels of change in the PDP's vote share, as the dependent variable. Overall, the results of these tests clearly indicate that ethnic voting remains a part of Nigerian politics, but that religion was arguably even more important. And finally, voters skeptical about INEC's performance – especially young people – voted for the opposition.

First, I found support for my electoral integrity hypothesis. Each increased level of approval of INEC on a four-point scale corresponds with a 12.7-percent increase of support for Jonathan at a statistically significant level. In this model, a control for age indicated that older voters supported the PDP. This outcome is consistent with evidence I presented in Chapter 2 that as the nation demographically got older, the average age of a PDP politician in the National Assembly increased consistently over time. Civil society campaigns such as the recent "Not too Young to Run" are founded on fact as much as on popular mythology about the underrepresentation of youth.

Next, I found statistical support for an "ethnic affinity" hypothesis predicting that citizens who self-identify as either Hausa or Fulani would vote for Buhari, a northern candidate of part-Fulani heritage. Any governor from the north probably would have won the election, complained a PDP leader about the party's loss in 2015. "There was a consideration that the north had been shortchanged ... because of Jonathan's aspirations to run for a second tenure, this was the reason PDP lost" (Agbim 2017). Under the concept of "power shift," as understood in terms of the 1999 pact, it was the north's "turn" to rule. When President Yar'Adua passed away in 2010, this set in motion a set of expectations in the north. Buhari represented the path for power to return to the north, after Jonathan's alleged abandonment of a gentlemen's agreement to not run in 2015 if he had run in 2011.

The geographical distribution of electoral support for both candidates tells a more encouraging story, if only slightly so. The APC, a party with a presidential candidate inextricably associated with the north, received over 4.3 million votes in the south, while the PDP candidate, hailing from the southern Niger Delta, received over 3.8 million votes in the north. This geographical spread of support is necessary to meet the connected plurality threshold, and it provides some evidence of voters crossing ethnic lines in their choice of presidential candidate. Buhari won twenty-one of the thirty-six states, but Jonathan secured more than 25 percent in twenty-six states. APC was in fact formed on the basis of such an inter-ethnic collaboration. "Alliances/coalitions, party splits and mergers have influenced the dynamics of political party competition in Nigeria since the First Republic," says a recent study. "Prior to the APC merger, each opposition group was viewed more as a regional or sectional party, representing narrow interests, a contrast to the outwardly nationwide appeal of the PDP. The [APC] coalition has thus brought together several major contending groups across the north-south divide" (Muhammed-Bande 2014, 69). Ethnicity might make you competitive, but in 2015 it was the issues that made you win.[2]

Less encouraging, and very worrisome, were the test results for my "religious referendum" hypothesis. Religious influences in Nigeria's 2015 campaign were subtle but, based on the statistical results, systematic. This implicit influence was evident a few weeks before the 2015 election, when the US Commission on International Religious Freedom expressed its concern about the ominous shadow cast over Nigeria's ballot boxes:

In an electoral context, the religious and ethnic affiliations of persons running for public office are important to most Nigerian voters and are always known to them; indeed many observers note that these are two of the most important bases on which people vote. If given a choice, Muslims tend to vote for Muslims and Christians for Christians. Both political parties understand the importance of the confluence of religious identity and politics, and both are highlighting religion in the campaign (US Commission on International Religious Freedom 2015, 4).

For a country with a long history of religious violence, and a largely secular constitutional compromise at the heart of its democratic authority, the insertion of religion into politics – whether by preachers, politicians, or ordinary people – is an alarming trend that INEC and other authorities would be wise to stem in future elections.

But I also hope such efforts will digest this chapter's related intuitions about the political logic of extremist appeals in an electoral democracy. Limiting the political salience of faith-based cleavages will likely constitute one of the next great challenges of Nigeria's long, meandering project of national integration. More than just civic

---

[2] I attribute this to Jennifer Dresden, who made this comment after reading Chapters 4 and 5.

education or attitude-shaping, this project will also require affirmation of the constitutional compromises over secularism at the heart of Nigeria's enduring unity (LeVan 2015b). Electoral law has facilitated inter-ethnic cooperation; whether it is adequate to defuse the politicization of religion remains uncertain.

Surviving Institutional Stress and Building a Democratic Future

As already noted earlier, the soaring optimism of the 1990s after the collapse of the Soviet Union tended to equate democracy with elections (Edozie 2009; Karl 1990). This aligned with modernization theory's understanding of democratization as a linear sequence from liberalization to transition and then democratic consolidation (Carothers 2002; Diamond, Fukuyama, Horowitz, & Plattner 2014). Linz and Stepan parsimoniously described consolidation as the moment when democracy becomes "the only game in town," meaning that it is routinized and deeply internalized in social, institutional, and psychological life. The utility in defining consolidation so broadly is that it makes it possible to include many types of democracy, as Linz and Stepan do. By including behavior, attitudes, and norms alongside processes and institutions, their definition helps overcome shallow definitions of democracy.

Yet, in Chapter 6 I argued that considering consolidation as the end point of a process has proven problematic. Not only did a huge number of stable, illiberal regimes emerge in the two decades after their work (Levitsky 2010), a recent resurgence of reactionary populism has raised the deeply troubling prospect of "de-consolidation," even among more developed nations (Foa 2017). I therefore experimented with "stress points" as an alternative terminology and as a tool to examine contemporary challenges to Nigeria's political institutions. Building upon recent analyses of the Arab Spring (Brownlee et al. 2015), I described how stress points are subnational case studies for examining whether a regime's institutions can weather extra-institutional pressures.

First, I analyzed the revival of Igbo nationalism in southeastern Nigeria, with many young activists and religious leaders demanding an independent republic of Biafra. The organizations at the heart of this movement have thus far relied on protests, propaganda, and political mobilization against state repression. MASSOB and the off-shoot movement IPOB both align themselves with demands for a referendum triggering secession. Buhari has treated their demands with detachment, but also offers a useful reminder for the new generation of radicals. "As a young Army Officer, I took part from the beginning to the end in our tragic civil war costing about 2m lives, resulting in fearful destruction and untold suffering," he said in a 2017 speech. "Those who are agitating for a re-run were not born by 1967 and have no idea of the horrendous consequences of the civil conflict, which we went through" (Buhari 2017). The subtle nods the secessionist activists receive from Igbo elites delicately balance memory of these wartime miseries with the lingering anger of the antebellum era.

Second, I explored the challenges facing pastoralists, including shrinking land for cattle grazing, disappearance of water sources, and tensions with farming communities. With the expansion of farms and topographical pressures on grazing areas, conflicts between farmers and pastoralists have become increasingly violent due to crop damage or blockage of routes. Also, as people moved into the cities, the price of beef increased compared to other agricultural commodities, meaning that cattle remains an enterprise worth entering despite the risks and limited resources. In addition, urbanization has impacted the Fulani culturally, leading some to embrace a semi-sedentary lifestyle, following cattle only seasonally. This has in turn created an important sociocultural cleavage among Fulani themselves as some seek to distinguish themselves from the commonly hyphenated "Hausa-Fulani" identity.

Finally, I examined Boko Haram based in the far northeastern state of Borno. This violent insurgency embraces terrorism in the classic sense described in the book's Introduction. Its violence against schools, mosques, churches, marketplaces, and symbols of state power promotes a generalized sense of fear meant to compensate for an asymmetry of capacity vis-à-vis the state. I summarized the group's origins, the government's response to it, and various ideas advanced for ending its bloody reign. Boko Haram's first generation of violence involved small skirmishes with local authorities over prayer services, funeral processions, and other minor issues. Its second generation of violence arrived in 2009, when a series of altercations with the police escalated and Boko Haram's leader was captured by the military and extrajudicially executed by the police (Amnesty

International 2011). This pushed the group underground and turned its members on to vengeance as well as some transnational terrorist ties. I pinpointed the start of the third generation of violence in 2014, with the kidnapping of 276 schoolgirls, as described in Chapter 3. That year Boko Haram also bombed a bus depot just outside Abuja, and engaged in other brutal and increasingly random acts of violence. This horror generally shifted the public's attitudes about how to handle violent extremism, and weakened the political constituency for dialogue and the viability of an amnesty program modeled after the Niger Delta's. Nigeria's contemporary radical movements have carefully constructed a "cannon" of theological teachings that offer little basis for compromise. These teachings "retroactively portray earlier figures as part of a cohesive community," ignoring differences in order to claim that the quest for purity is a continuous centuries-old struggle (Thurston 2016, 31).

Nigeria's journey back to democracy that began in 1998 catalyzed each of the subnational stress points examined above. The transition did not cause crises presented by pastoralists, Igbo secessionism, or Boko Haram, but it did transform them by embedding their politics within the structure of the Fourth Republic's politics and institutions.

For eastern Igbos, Biafran secessionism is a reminder that the project of nation building remains incomplete, and more specifically it reminds Igbos how the transition's pact marginalized the east. Alex Ekwueme, the former vice president from the Second Republic, seemed poised to win the PDP's primaries in 1999. But he lost out as party elites and the military set out to implement a core element of the pact by choosing Obasanjo, a Yoruba. This decision implicitly validated a postwar Igbo narrative of economic and political marginalization, and validated Igbos' perceived sense of perpetual under-enfranchisement – they were still being "punished" for the first coup. Not long after the military handover in 1999, MASSOB provided a radical mechanism to keep this critique alive, along with mainstream PDP politicians and other eastern elites. Today this is important for how religion could provide an especially toxic ingredient in eastern politics; the politicization of religion under electoral politics evokes the pivot to religion during the Biafran war of secession. As pointed out in a recent book on ethnic and religious politics in Africa, "the changing context of the war – in which local land and resources became secondary to moral and transnational support – made appeals to religion, rather than ethnicity, the new optimal strategy" (McCauley 2017, 165). "Northern Muslim" pastoralism provides a "wedge" issue for Igbos to divide their political adversaries, a move that closely resembles the playbook for international coalition building followed during the civil war (McCauley 2017). The transition contributed to Boko Haram as a stress point perhaps just as explicitly. Within months after the transition, twelve northern governors passed Sharia law. Harsh criminal measures never really took effect (Paden 2005), and some scholars now see it as a strategy for political "insurance" by northern elites fearful of the shift of power to the south with Obasanjo's presidency (Mohammed 2005). The moderation of Sharia served as a basis for Boko Haram's early complaints, and fed their sense of betrayal by politicians (Thurston 2018).

By considering Nigeria's subnational stress points alongside its electoral politics, this book has hopefully inspired new ways of thinking about regime transitions, advanced our understanding of electoral politics amidst deadly terrorism, and provided a hint of good news for presidential campaigns in Africa. What are the key contributions, and what work needs to be done? In the next section I mention some of the book's other implications and sketch out some ideas for future research.

Research Agendas on Terrorism and Electoral Politics in Africa

The political effects of terrorism on electoral politics in the United States, Europe, and Israel are well known. For example, leading up to America's 2016 elections, 80 percent of registered voters said that terrorism would be important to them in deciding who to vote for, with 84 percent mentioning the economy (Pew Research Center 2016). In 2017, just after a gruesome terror incident, the Conservative Party in the United Kingdom narrowly beat back an electoral challenge, and the far-right National Front nearly prevailed in France after brutal attacks in Nice, Paris, and elsewhere. But in the many developing democracies where terrorist groups are active, terrorism as a category of violence tends to be obscured by research on electoral violence, state failure, or other types of instability. One recent study of the multiparty elections in 166 countries tests for the impact of protests, international invasions, or economic downturns as regime threats, but not terrorism (Teorell 2017).

Terrorism implies intent to deliberately harm civilians, rather than seeing them as "collateral damage," to use the infamous phrase that entered popular lexicon during the Persian Gulf War of 1991. It also implies asymmetry; terrorists leverage the fear that violence is meant to generate because they have inferior military capabilities. The choice of targets may facilitate this by generating spectacle. This was seen with al-Qaeda's 2001 attack on the Pentagon in the United States, Islamic State sympathizers' attack on London Bridge in 2017, and Boko Haram's 2011 bombing of the United Nations building in Abuja. Spectacle strikes at symbols rather than achieving any significant tactical benefit in military terms. Such terrorism often aims to influence politics or democratic processes. This study examined how violence, evaluations of candidates' promises to provide security, and the broader cloud of fear amidst terrorism shapes those processes. Terrorism thus differs from electoral violence because its perpetrators defy and seek to circumvent or destroy the institutions of democracy; they challenge the very method, or premise, of acquiring state power. Terrorists do frequently seek to disrupt or undermine elections, but this is merely an element of a broader strategic repertoire for sowing a generalized sense of fear.

Comparative Perspectives on Nigeria's Insurgent Instability

This book sought to place this fear in comparative context. Judged against the comparative research outlined in the Introduction and used to inform my hypotheses in Chapters 3, 4, and 5, Nigerians are not alone. For starters, Boko Haram's violence has clearly sought to stimulate the generalized sense of fear associated with terrorism. Targets associated with people's everyday lives – markets, bus depots, and schools – amplify this fear as the violence acquires qualities of randomness because nowhere is safe. More than 200 people died in twenty different Boko Haram attacks on churches between 2010 and 2012, and hundreds of people disappeared in at least forty-two separate mass abductions – including the kidnapping of 276 girls from Chibok (discussed at greater length in Chapter 3). Boko Haram's strategy shifted with its dramatic increase in suicide attacks in 2014.

"Despite espousing an anti-Christian and anti-educational ideology," the attacks overwhelmingly focused on targets without any discernable ideological orientation or symbolism, says a recent West Point study. Suicide attacks "instead predominantly targeting innocent soft-civilian targets with no clear religious or political affiliation ... all of Boko Haram's largest attacks are not connected by any particular targeting trend" (Warner 2017, 16).

Nigeria also seems to fit Aksoy and Carter's (2014) expectations about the link between frustrated representation and violent claims articulated outside political institutions. Its rigid majoritarian electoral system has failed to give voice to frustrations. Other barriers to entry into politics include exorbitant candidate registration fees and powerful "godfathers" who fix primaries and further complicate peaceful expression of grievances. This is especially urgent with regard to secessionist demands in the east. As noted already, the head of the pan-Igbo organization Ohanaeze Ndibo explains, "So long as you don't respond to reasonable and constitutional demands of the Igbo nation, you arm militant organizations in their minds with a clear message that the only option is secession" (Nwodo 2017).

Third, and relatedly, whether under democracy or dictatorship, Nigeria's governments have responded to agitation, whether violent or nonviolent, with repression and disproportionate force. This reactive approach is rooted in a historical normalization of violence described in the Introduction. Yet, cross-national evidence suggests that even with regard to violence as extreme as terrorism, respecting human rights is the best strategy (Walsh and Piazza 2010). In addition, repression against terrorist groups – closing-off of nonviolent alternatives described by Aksoy – *increases* the level of domestic terrorism (Piazza 2017). One large survey of the literature concluded such repression can backfire by simply prompting terrorists to adopt new tactics and new insurgencies or criminal networks to emerge. Examples include French brutality in Algeria that increased international sympathy for the National Liberation Front, or Spain's "dirty war" against separatists that undermined the government's democratic legitimacy (Schneider 2015). Piazza's (2017) study linking such responses to an increase in terrorism aligns perfectly with the brutal crackdown on Niger Delta communities in 1999 that inspired the formation of MEND (Adunbi 2015) or Boko Haram's turn to violence after the public, extrajudicial execution of its leader in 2009 (Mohammed 2014). This may also come to pass in the case of the state violence against Islamic Movement of Nigeria, a minority Shiite sect, or the Biafra secessionists. The social movements literature arrived at similar conclusions long ago (Tarrow 1994; Chenoweth 2011).

Finally, leading up to the 2015 election, the ruling People's Democratic Party prioritized visible counter-terrorism at the expense of effective counter-terrorism, much as de Mesquita (2007) predicts. President Goodluck Jonathan embraced what could be called "inverted neocolonialism": rather than accusing the West – as Kwame Nkrumah and a generation of nationalists did – of continuing imperial rule through subtle interventions and sinister schemes, Jonathan blamed Western powers *for not intervening enough.* "Are they (the United States) not fighting ISIS? Why can't they come to Nigeria?" he asked the *Wall Street Journal* in an interview where he pleaded for American troops (Salvaterra 2015). His administration further complained the US was not sharing enough intelligence (Stewart 2016) or selling enough weapons (Agence France Press 2015). Jonathan embarked on a publicity campaign, sending his top two intelligence aides to Washington to show maps of territories regained. Meanwhile, foreign mercenaries – rather than the Nigerian military – took the fight to Boko Haram's front lines (Nossiter 2015b; Idris, Hamza, Mutum, & Doki 2015; Abubakar 2016).

In other regards, Nigeria presents a challenge to existing research on terrorism and elections. For example, findings by Kibris (2011) and Getmansky and Zeitzoff (2014) pointing to political polarization do little to help us understand the effects of terrorism on voting behavior in Africa. Like much of the literature on European political parties, it is premised on a left-right continuum that generally does not exist in Africa. This is not only due to the weak ideological coherence of most parties, it also stems from historical roots of African parties in liberation struggles, social movements, or ethnic appeals instead of Western cleavages in church versus state, or often a division of interests between labor and capital that emerged through industrialization (Elischer 2013).

Also, Boko Haram and its leader Abubakar Shekau push the boundaries of models of terrorists as rational actors making cost-benefit analyses. This "rational choice" approach has effectively applied economic principles for understanding terrorism, and has also withstood psychological analyses of individual perpetrators (Schneider 2015). Boko

Haram obviously shares a willingness to target civilians as a tactic to sow a generalized sense of fear that resembles most terrorist groups, including al-Qaeda. Osama bin Ladin infamously told the world in 1998: "We do not have to differentiate between military or civilian. As far as we are all concerned, they are all targets" (National Commission on Terrorist Attacks upon the United States 2004, 47). But for such violence to be effective or seen as such, it must be viewed as a way of achieving the organization's goals. As discussed in Chapter 6, Boko Haram's goals are difficult to discern beyond vague promises of establishing Sharia law either in Nigeria or in the region, or later on (when it facilitated its need for external affiliations) establishing a greater Islamic Caliphate. This differs markedly from bin Laden's comments before and after 9/11, when he demanded expulsion of American troops from Saudi Arabia, an end to US-led sanctions on Iraq, and a halt to US support for Israel; these goals were within mainstream critiques of American foreign policy and enjoyed support across the Arab world (National Commission on Terrorist Attacks upon the United States 2004).

With the wave of populism sweeping electoral democracies, we may see more of the paradox of democratic counter-terrorism. "Elites' preference for open societies is running up against growing public demands for new forms of economic, cultural, and political closure," commented an influential essay in the *Journal of Democracy* after Donald Trump's election (Galston 2017, 23). Politicians able to leverage popular culture or experience in show business to seek elected office are well-equipped to respond to this demand. According to Street, "the emergence of the celebrity politician is linked to the emergence of a post-democratic order in which politics is transmuted into a spectacle that is to be performed to an audience, not of citizens, but of spectators" (Street 2012, 350). Political science has invested heavily in exploring analogies between markets and politics, comparing citizens to consumers. The recent rise of celebrity politics and populists suggests that a more apt analogy would be citizens as audience and politicians as performers. If so, this relationship effectively conflates popularity with responsive government, weakening the relationship between accountability and representation in government. It accents the effects of the paradox of democratic counter-terrorism by rewarding politicians for adopting less-effective strategies.

Closing Thoughts

"We are going to reinforce and reinvigorate the fight not only against elements of Boko Haram which are attempting a new series of attacks on soft targets," said Buhari a few months before this book went to press, adding "kidnappings, farmers versus herdsmen clashes in addition to ethnic violence fueled by political mischief makers. We shall tackle them all" (Searcey 2017). The APC government may have already found itself mired in the paradox of democratic counter-terrorism by limiting its pursuit of Boko Haram to violence so narrowly construed. Repression effectively convinces determined groups that either there is no alternative to violence, or prompts already-violent groups to adapt their tactics, as Boko Haram has done.

Nigeria's problems of impunity, whether for torture in Giwa barracks, fraud at the polling unit, or for the theft of millions of dollars, have roots in the very deals struck during the birth of the Fourth Republic: a graceful exit for military officials, unlikely prosecutions, no truth-telling, and "coup-proofing." Nigeria may have navigated the treacherous waters of party turnover for the first time in 2015. But it has yet to prove its democratic constitutional mettle by asserting civilian control over the security services, reining in its politicians, and institutionally adapting to stress points facing the Fourth Republic. Nigeria has learned that electoral accountability is possible, but representation serves as an inadequate substitute for rule of law. The nation's next political awakening may begin with letting go of the undemocratic deals that hold back Nigeria's popular aspirations and economic potential, and impede its paths to sustainable peace.

Bibliography

Interviews

Abdullah, Ango (Member, Northern Elders Forum), A. Carl LeVan, September 20, 2016, Bauchi.

Abubakar, Atiku (Former vice president), A. Carl LeVan, September 25, 2016, Abuja.

Agbim, Ichie Ken (Member, Imo State PDP), A. Carl LeVan, March 26, 2017, Owerri, Imo State.

Ahaya, Julius (Vice Chair, Gombe State APC), A. Carl LeVan, September 21, 2016, Gombe.

Akos, Zaka (Chair, Bokkos Local Government Area), A. Carl LeVan, September 19, 2016. Jos, Plateau State.

Akun, Chief Jethro (Former PDP State Chair, Plateau), A. Carl LeVan, September 19, 2016, Jos.

All Progressives Congress (Senior Official), A. Carl LeVan, September 26, 2016, Abuja.

Amaechi, Rotimi (Rivers State Governor, 2007–2015), A. Carl LeVan, April 16, 2014, Port Harcourt.

Aminu, Jibril (Senator), A. Carl LeVan, March 8, 2010, Abuja.

Bello, Mohammed (Member, Pastoral Resolve), A. Carl LeVan, September 23, 2016, Yola.

Bindir, Umar (Secretary to the State Government of Adamawa), A. Carl LeVan, September 23, 2016, Yola, Adamawa.

Chief of a village near Girei (name withheld), A. Carl LeVan, September 24, 2016, Yola South Local Government Area, Adamawa State.

Duru, Chidi (Member, House of Representatives), A. Carl LeVan, May 28, 2004, Abuja.

Ebri, Clement (Former Governor of Cross River State) A. Carl LeVan, March 16, 2010, Abuja.

Ekeroku, Ambrose (Executive Director, Carmelite Prisoners' Interest Organisation), A. Carl LeVan, March 28, 2017, Enugu.

Emeana, Ray, Nnaji Chuma, and Ichie Ken Agbim (Imo State PDP Leaders), A. Carl LeVan, March 26, 2017, Owerri, Imo State.

239

Eze, Chukwumeka (Communications Director, Rivers State APC), A. Carl
    LeVan, April 15, 2014, Port Harcourt.
Finebone, Chris (APC Rivers State Publicity Secretary), A. Carl LeVan,
    March 31, 2017, Port Harcourt.
Gowon, Yakubu (Former Head of State), A. Carl LeVan, March 16,
    2010, Abuja.
Ijeohmah, Justine (Executive Director, Centre for Human Rights,
    Development and Environmental Foundation), A. Carl LeVan, March
    31, 2017, Port Harcourt.
Ikpeazu, Okezie Victor (Governor of Abia State), A. Carl LeVan, March 29,
    2017, Umuahia.
Indigenous People of Biafra (IPOB), A. Carl LeVan, March 29, 2017,
    Abia.
Lamido, Umar (Member of the Gombe State House of Assembly, All
    Progressives Congress), A. Carl LeVan, September 21, 2016, Gombe.
Lawan, Farouk (Member of the House of Representatives), A. Carl LeVan,
    February 24, 2012, Abuja.
Miyetti Allah (Cattle Breeders Association), A. Carl LeVan, September 21,
    2016, Gombe.
Naagbanton, Patrick (Executive Director, Centre for Environment, Human
    Rights and Development), A. Carl LeVan, March 25, 2017, Port
    Harcourt.
Name withheld (Reporter for a major daily national newspaper), A. Carl
    LeVan, September 20, 2016, Jos, Plateau State.
Ndigwe, Ralph (Director, Civil Resource and Development Documentation
    Centre), A. Carl LeVan, March 27, 2017, Anambra.
Niger Delta Militant Contact Group (member), A. Carl LeVan, March 31,
    2017, Port Harcourt.
Nnaji, Chuma (Member, State PDP), A. Carl LeVan, March 26, 2017,
    Owerri, Imo State.
Nwaorgu, Joe (Former President-General, Ohanaeze Ndigbo), A. Carl
    LeVan, March 29, 2017, Enugu.
Nwodo, John Nnia (President General of Ohanaeze Ndigbo), A. Carl LeVan,
    March 27, 2017, Enugu.
Nwodo, Okwesilieze (former Secretary General, People's Democratic Party),
    A. Carl LeVan, March 8, 2010, Abuja.
Olotolo, Martin (PDP Enugu State Chair), A. Carl LeVan, March 28,
    2017, Enugu.
Onuorah, A., and four MASSOB members (names withheld), A. Carl LeVan,
    March 27, 2017, Anambra.
Rapnap, Joyce (Former Deputy Speaker, Plateau State Assembly), A. Carl
    LeVan, September 19, 2016, Jost.

Wada, Tawar Umbi (Senator, National Assembly), A. Carl LeVan, June 3, 2004, Abuja.

Waku, Joseph K.N. (Vice Chair, Arewa Consultative Forum), A. Carl LeVan, March 10, 2010, Abuja.

Periodicals and Non-Academic Sources

Abbah, Theophilus, Isiaka Wakili, Turaki Hassan, and Musbahu Bashir. 2013. "Presidency, Senate Set for Showdown over Anti-Terrorism Law." *Daily Trust*, January 13.

Abdallah, Nuruddeen and Aliyu Machika. 2009. "Why I did Not Succeed Abacha as Head of State – Jeremiah Useni." *Daily Trust*, August 23.

Abubakar, Abdulsalam. 1998a. "Full Text of Abubakar's Speech." *Constitutional Rights Journal*, April–June, 14.

1998b. "The Way Forward." *Constitutional Rights Journal*, July–September, 12–14.

Adebanjo, Adegbenro. 2001. "Descent to the Abyss." *TELL*, January 22, 26–27.

Adebayo, Hassan. 2017. "Governors, Military Lack Power to Proscribe, Declare IPOB Terrorist Organisation – Saraki." *Premium Times*, September 18.

Adenusi, Owolabi, Ted Ogdogwu, and Justina Asishana. 2014. "Boko Haram Seizes More Territories." *Newswatch Times*, November 16.

Adeosun, Segun. 2015. "AIG Mbu Threatens to Kill Civilians in Retaliation." *TELL*, February 14.

Adesina, Femi. 2017. "#PMBinSE." Abuja, Nigeria: Office of the President.

Adeyemo, Wola. 1999. "We Are Fed Up." *TELL*, January 4, 16–21.

Adeyemo, Wola, Adejuwon Soyinka, and Olusegun Adeosun. 2015. "APC will Reform the Military." *TELL*, January 19.

Afolabi, Ayodele. 2014. "PDP Moves to Sanction Ihedioha, Others as Group Endorses Tambuwal for President." *African Examiner*, October 26.

Africa Confidential. 1984. "Nigeria: The Inevitable." January 4, 1–2.

Africa Network for Environment and Economic Justice. 2015. "Fight Corruption Now, ANEEJ Calls on Buhari." April 1.

Africa Research Bulletin. 2000. "Nigeria: From Urn to Barracks." October 1–31, 14163.

2001. "Military Heads Retired." April 1–30, 14381.

African Examiner. 2012. "Northern Leaders want FG to Dialogue with Boko Haram." February 2, 2012.

African Union. 2010. *Policy Framework for Pastoralism in Africa*, edited by Department of Rural Economy and Agriculture. Addis Ababa, Ethiopia: African Union.

Afrobarometer. 2006. "Performance and Legitimacy in Nigeria's New Democracy." *Afrobarometer Briefing Paper No. 46*, http://afrobarometer.org/files/documents/briefing_papers/AfrobriefNo46.pdf.

2009a. "Popular Perceptions of Shari'a Law in Nigeria." *Afrobarometer Briefing Paper No. 58*, http://afrobarometer.org/files/documents/briefing_papers/AfrobriefNo58.pdf.

2009b. "Summary of Results: Round 4 Survey in Nigeria." http://afrobarometer.org/files/documents/summary_results/nig_r4_sor.pdf.

Agande, Ben. 2014. "Chibok Girls, Parents Shun Meeting with Jonathan." *Vanguard*, July 15.

Agekameh, Dele. 1999. "Free at Last." *TELL*, March 15, 36–7.

2000. "The Riot Act." *TELL*, March 13, 14–18.

2001. "Dangers Ahead." *TELL*, January 22, 28–34.

2002. "Why There is Anger in the Barracks." *TELL*, January 21, 28–33.

Agence France Press. 2015. "B'Haram Calls for Election Boycott, Jonathan Seeks US Help." *Punch*, February 14.

2017. "Nigeria's Boko Haram Trials to be Held Behind Closed Doors." *Agence France Press*, September 29.

Akinkuotu, Eniola. 2017. "IPOB Jonathan Condemns Deployment of Soldiers, Slams Lai Mohammed." *Punch*, September 19.

All Progressives Congress. 2015a. "APC Road Map." Abuja, Nigeria: All Progressives Congress.

2015b. *A New Party, for a New Nigeria.* Abuja: Campaign Manifesto.

AllAfrica.com. 2014. "Residents Flee Mubi as Boko Haram, Troops Clash." *Vanguard*, October 29.

Alli, Akinola. 1999. "Ohanaeze Ndigbo Backs Falae." *Nigerian Tribune*, February 26.

Ameh, John, Jude Owuamanam, and Kayode Idowu. 2014. "Military Lied about Schoolchildren Rescue – Principal, Parents." *Punch*, April 18.

Amnesty International. 2011. "Killings by Security Forces in the North Must Stop." London: Amnesty International.

2014. "Nigeria: More than 1,500 Killed in Armed Conflict in North-Eastern Nigeria in Early 2014." London: Amnesty International.

2016. "Bullets were Raining Everywhere: Deadly Repression of Pro-Biafra Activists." London: Amnesty International.

2017. "Lake Chad Region: Boko Haram's Renewed Campaign Sparks Sharp Rise in Civilian Deaths." London: Amnesty International.

Anonymous. 2015a. "Buhari Approves N1.2 Trillion Rescue Plan for Bankrupt States." *Premium Times*, July 6.

2015b. "How Edo Pastors Shared N7 billion PDP Bribe." *Premium Times*, March 1.

2017. "IPOB Members will be Prosecuted for Murder, Arson." *Guardian*, September 17.

Ayonote, Louisa. 1999. "This is Something Else." *TELL*, March 22, 14–18.

Barkindo, Atta. 2017. "An Introduction to Boko Haram's Ideologues." In *Newsite*. Abuja, Nigeria: Africa Research Institute.

BBC. 2014. "Army Backtracks on Schoolgirls' Release." September 23.

Bernard, Bayo. 2014. "Walking a Tight Rope." *The Source*, April 14, 26–7.

Binniyat, Luka. 2012. "Boko Haram – Northern Governors Set up Committee on FG White Paper." *Vanguard*, March 9.

Blanchard, Lauren Ploch and Alexis Arieff. 2016. *Terrorism and Violent Extremism in Africa*. Washington, DC: Congressional Research Service.

Borno and Yobe States Peoples Forum. 2014. "Memorandum to the National Conference on the Security Challenges in Borno and Yobe States."

Botha, Anneli and Mahdi Abdile. 2016. *Getting Behind the Profiles of Boko Haram Members and Factors Contributing to Radicalisation versus Working Towards Peace*, edited by Kaiciid Dialogue Center. Finland: Finn Church Aid Act Alliance.

Bratton, Michael. 2016. "Do Africans Still Want Democracy?" Afrobarometer Policy Paper 36. East Lansing, MI: Afrobarometer.

Buhari, Muhammadu. 2015. "We will Stop Boko Haram." *New York Times*, April 14.

2017. "Nigerian Independence Day." *Vanguard*, October 1.

Business Day Online. 2017. "An Incompetent and Corrupt Government," October 17.

Campbell, John. 2013a. "Catholic Suspend National Activity in the Christian Association of Nigeria." In *Africa in Transition*. Washington, DC: Council on Foreign Relations.

2017. "The Distorted Memory of Biafra." In *Africa in Transition*, edited by John Campbell. New York: Council on Foreign Relations.

Carter Center, and National Democratic Institute for International Affairs. 1999. "Observing the 1998–99 Nigeria Elections, Final Report." Washington, DC: Carter Center and National Democratic Institute.

Civil Society Legislative Advocacy Centre. 2015. "CISLAC Statement on Electoral Violence." Abuja, Nigeria: Civil Society Legislative Advocacy Centre.

CLEEN Foundation. 2014. "Youths, Radicalisation and Affiliation with Insurgent Groups in Northern Nigeria." Lagos and Abuja, Nigeria: CLEEN Foundation.

2015. "Election Security Threat Assessment, No. 8." Lagos, Nigeria: CLEEN Foundation.

Clinton, Bill. 1998. "Press Conference by President Clinton and Nelson Mandela." Cape Town, South Africa, March 27. Washington, DC: White House.

Clottey, Peter. 2013. "Nigeria Leader Urges International Cooperation to Defeat Terrorism." *Voice of America*, September 25.

Cocks, Tim. 2013. "Nigeria President Pardons Ex-Governor Convicted of Graft." *Reuters*.

Cohen, Patricia. 2009. "A Writer's Violent End, and Legacy." *New York Times*, May 5.

Constitutional Rights Project. 1998a. "A Coup Plot or a Set Up?" *Constitutional Rights Journal*, January–March, 28–29.

1998b. "End of a Dictator: A New Beginning?" *Constitutional Rights Journal*, 6–14.

1998c. "Task for General Abubakar." *Constitutional Rights Journal*, April–June, 5.

1998d. "The Umpire Seeks to be the Winner." *Constitutional Rights Journal*, January/March, 22–23.

1998e. "Who's in Charge?" *Constitutional Rights Journal*, July–September, 6–11.

Council on Foreign Relations. 2017. *Nigeria Security Tracker*. Available from www.cfr.org/nigeria/nigeria-security-tracker/p29483 (accessed October 1, 2017).

Crabtree, Steve. 2012. "Almost All Nigerians Say Gov't is Corrupt." *Gallup*, January 16.

Creative Associates International. 2015. *Integrated Quar'anic Education: Nigeria Case Study*, edited by Semere Solomon. Washington, DC: Creative Associates.

Dalby, Alexa. 2014. "Nigeria's Rebased GDP Goes from 37th Largest to 26th Largest Economy Globally." *African Business*, May 1, 8.

Dearden, Lizzie. 2017. "ISIS: UN Study Finds Foreign Fighters in Syria 'Lack Basic Understanding of Islam'." *Independent*, August 4.

Dori, Gambo. 2015. "Rein in the First Lady, Don't Abolish the Office." *AllAfrica.com*, February 22.

Economic and Financial Crimes Commission. 2017. "EFCC Arrests Gombe SEMA Officials for Theft." Abuja, Nigeria.

European Union Election Observation Mission. 2011. Nigeria: Final Report, General Elections, April 2011. European Union.

Eyoboka, Sam. 2014. "US $15 Million Arms Deal – Why We Have been Silent, Says FG." *Vanguard*, October 13.

Eze, Chukwujama. 1998. "Who will Save Ohaneze?" *TELL*, March 2, 22.

Faul, Michelle. 2014. "Generals are Guilty of Arming Boko Haram." *Associated Press*, June 3.

Federal Office of Statistics. 1968. "Annual Abstract of Statistics 1968." Lagos, Nigeria: Federal Government of Nigeria.

Federal Republic of Nigeria. 2011. *Main Report of the Federal Government Investigative Panel on the 2011 Election Violence and Civil Disturbances*, edited by Sheikh Lemu. Abuja, Nigeria: Federal Republic of Nigeria.

French, Howard. 1998. "Democracy to Despotism: A Special Report; Nigeria in Free Fall Seethes Under General." *New York Times*, April 4.

Godwin, Ameh Comrade. 2013. "Shocker: Yar'Adua, Diya, Adisa were Pardoned Since 1998/99." *Daily Post*, March 15.

Higazi, Adam. 2017. *From Cooperation to Contention: Political Unsettlement and Farmer-Pastoralist Conflicts in Nigeria.* London: Accord Spotlight.

Hoffman, Leena Koni and Raj Navanit Patel. 2017. *Collective Action on Corruption in Nigeria: A Social Norms Approach to Connecting Society and Institutions.* London: Chatham House.

Hogan, Caelainn. 2014. "The Many Faces of Boko." *Harper's*, July 16.

House of Representatives Ad-Hoc Committee. 2012. "Report to Verify and Determine the Actual Subsidy Requirements and Monitor the Implementation of the Subsidy Regime in Nigeria." Abuja, Nigeria: National Assembly.

Human Rights Watch. 1999. "The Destruction of Odi and Rape in Choba." New York.

2011. "Nigeria: Post-Election Violence Killed 800." New York.

2012. "Spiraling Violence: Boko Haram Attacks and Security Force Abuses in Nigeria." New York.

Idonor, Daniel. 2012. "Strike Panicked Jonathan." *Vanguard*, January 21.

Idowu, Bukola, Chima Akwaja, and George Agba. 2014. "Outrage Trails Lamido Sanusi's Suspension." *Leadership*, February 21.

Idris, Hamza, Ismail Mudashir, and Hassan Ibrahim. 2014. "Violence Strangling Economy of Northern Nigeria." *Daily Trust*, April 19.

Idris, Hamza, Ronald Mutum, and Terna Doki. 2015. "South Africa: Pretoria's Secret Role in Boko Haram Battle." *Daily Trust*, February 14.

Ikhilae, Eric. 2014. "Why Court Must Stop Mark, Tambuwal, by 79 Defectors." *The Nation*, February 18.

International Crisis Group. 2014. "Curbing Violence (II): The Boko Haram Insurgency." Brussels: International Crisis Group.

IRIN News Service. 2005a. "At Least 12 Dead in Clashes Over Separatist Protest." December 12.

2005b. "Government Cracks Down on Biafra Secessionist Movement." April 19.

2005c. "Police Arrest 45 People in Violent Southeast Secessionist Protests." September 15.

2006. "Government Cracks Down on Biafra Separatist Resurgence." September 4.

Jega, Attahiru. 2015b. "Statement on the Timetable for 2015 General Elections." Abuja, Nigeria: Independent National Electoral Commission.

Jones, Barbara. 2014. "Hostage Schoolgirl Exclusive." *Daily Mail*, May 31.

Kendhammer, Brandon. 2014. "Nigeria's Moral Economy of Powersharing." In *Nigeria: What is to be Done?*, edited by Ebenezer Obadare. Africaisacountry.com.

Legal Defence Centre. 2000. *The Judiciary and Democratic Transition in Nigeria*, translated by Basil Ugochukwu and Chijioke Ononiwu. Lagos, Nigeria: Legal Defence Centre.

Lewis, Peter M. and Michael Bratton. 2000. *Attitudes Towards Democracy and Markets in Nigeria*. *Michigan State University*. Paper 3. Accra and Cape Town: Afrobarometer. Available from http://afrobarometer .org/sites/default/files/publications/Working%20paper/AfropaperNo3_ 0.pdf (accessed August 14, 2018).

Loschky, Jay. 2014. "Nearly All Nigerians See Boko Haram as a Major Threat." Washington, DC: Gallup.

2015. "Ahead of Poll, Few Nigerians Trust in Elections." Washington, DC: Gallup.

Loschky, Jay and Robin Sanders. 2015. "Nigeria's Big Chance." Washington, DC: Gallup.

MacEachern, Scott. 2018. *Searching for Boko Haram: A History of Violence in Central Africa*. Oxford and New York: Oxford University Press.

Madunagu, Emeka and Sesan Olufowobi. 2004. "Coup: 28 Officers, Civilians Quizzed." *Punch*, April 3, 8.

Mamah, Emeka and Rotimi Ajayi. 2006. "I Regret not Overthrowing Obasanjo." *Vanguard*, January 31.

Marama, Ndahi. 2014. "Boko Haram Captures Another Border Town, Banki, in Borno." *Vanguard*, September 4.

Mbah, Cyril. 2015. "Bama Wells Filled with Dead Bodies as Boko Haram Flees." *Newswatch Times*, March 20.

Mercy Corps. 2015. "The Economic Costs of Conflict: Evidence on Violence, Livelihoods, and Reslience in Nigeria's Middle Belt." In *Memo for Policy Makers*. Portland, OR.

2016. "Motivations and Empty Promises: Voices of Former Boko Haram Combatants and Nigerian Youth." Washington, DC: Mercy Corps.

Mkom, John, Anayo Okoli, and Samuel Oyandogha. 2017. "Herdsmen's New Threat: Stop Anti-grazing Law or There will be Trouble." *Vanguard*, June 25.

Mohammed, Lai. 2014b. "Politicisation of Boko Haram Insurgency, Bane of Nigeria's Anti-terror Fight." Speech to the House of Commons, September 8, edited by All Progressives Congress. London.

Mosadomi, Wole. 2017. "How we Formed PDP Military Wing – IBB." *Vanguard*, March 12.

Mumuni, Mikail. 1999. "Was Idiagbon Killed?" *TELL*, April 12, 30–1.

Mutum, Ronald and Maureen Onochie. 2014. "Girls' Parents Prefer to Meet with Jonathan in Chibok." *Daily Trust*, July 17.

N-Katalyst. 2015. "Message from the Nigeria Civil Society Situation Room." Abuja, Nigeria.

National Bureau of Statistics. 2012a. "Nigeria Poverty Profile 2011." Abuja, Nigeria: National Bureal of Statistics.

2012b. "Nigerian Economy in the First Half of 2012 and Revised Economic Outlook for 2012–2015." Abuja, Nigeria: Nigerian Bureau of Statistics.

2013. "Economic Outlook for the Nigerian Economy (2013–2016)." Abuja, Nigeria: Nigerian Bureau of Statistics.

2015. "The Millenium Development Goals Performance Tracking Survey 2015 Report."

National Commission on Terrorist Attacks upon the United States. 2004. *The 9/11 Commission Report*. Authorized Edition. New York and London: W.W. Norton.

National Democratic Institute for International Affairs. 2012. "Final Report on the 2011 Nigerian General Elections." Washington, DC: National Democratic Institute.

National Democratic Institute for International Affairs, and International Republican Institute. 2016. "Statement of the Joint IRI/NDI Pre-Election Assessment Mission to Ghana." Accra, Ghana: National Democratic Institute for International Affairs and International Republican Institute.

National Human Rights Commission of Nigeria. 2015. "Pre-election Report and Advisory on Violence in Nigeria's 2015 General Elections." Abuja, Nigeria: Federal Government of Nigeria.

National Institute of Policy and Strategic Studies. 2012. "Eminent Persons and Expert Group Meeting on Complex Insurgencies in Nigeria." Kuru, Nigeria: National Institute of Policy and Strategic Studies.

Ndege, Yvonne. 2015. "Poll Shift Upsets Borno Residents." *Al Jazeera*, February 8.

Nengak, Daniel, Raphael Mbaegbu, and Peter M Lewis. 2015. "Nigeria Heads for Closest Election on Record." *Afrobarometer*. Lansing, MI and Abuja, Nigeria: Michigan State University.

Niboro, Ima. 1998. "Walking a Tightrope." *TELL*, June 29, 12–19.

Nmodu, Danlami. 1998. "Interview with Colonel Yohanna Madaki: We Won't Allow Abubakar to be Hijacked." *TELL*, November 9, 32–6.

Nnochiri, Ikechukwu, Emmanuel Elebeke, and Abdulwahab Abdulah. 2014. "Chibok Girls – We Didn't Ban Rallies in Abuja – IG." *Vanguard*, June 4.

Nnorom, Ahamefula and Emmanuel Okwukwu. 2006. "Biafra at the United Nations," edited by Coalition of Igbo and Biafran Organizations. Ekwe Nche Organization.

Nossiter, Adam. 2015a. "In Nigeria's Election, Muhammdu Buhari Defeats Goodluck Jonathan." *New York Times*, March 31.

2015b. "Mercenaries Join Nigeria's Military Campaign against Boko Haram." *New York Times*, March 12.

2015c. "Prices and Anger Rise in Nigeria, Presaging More Strikes." *New York Times*, January 15.

Nwabueze, Ben. 2001. "Igbo Kwenu!" *TELL*, January 15, 24–5.

Nwabughiogu, Levinus. 2015. "Presidency Abolishes Office of First Lady." *Vanguard*, August 22.

Nwosu, Nduka and Madu Onuorah. 2004. "Govt Speaks of Security Breach, Army Denies Arrests." *Guardian*, April 3, 1–2.

Obenta, Okechukwe and Andrew Agbese. 1999. "Ohaneze Re-states Support for PDP, Denies Backing APP." *The Post Express*, date unknown, 3.

Obi, Comfort. 2015. "Zakari Biu: Neither Buhari nor APC." *Daily Trust*, September 26.

Odebode, Niyi. 2017. "National Assembly will Publish its Budget Soon, Says Dogara." *Punch*, March 30.

Odemwingie, Edegbe and Bode Gbadebo. 2015. "Half Knowledge of Islam Fuels Boko Haram Insurgency." *Leadership*, October 22.

Ogah, David, Bukky Olajide, and Wole Shadare. 2012. "Strike Causes N733b Loss to Economy (about 3.8bn)." *Guardian*, January 17.

Ogbozor, Ernest. 2016. "Understanding the Informal Security Sector in Nigeria." In *Special Report*. Washington, DC: United States Institute of Peace.

Okafor, John. 2000. Trouble for Politicians-in-Uniform. *TELL*, October 2, 30–1.

Okenyodo, Kemi. 2017. "Non-state Security Actors and Security Provisioning in Nigeria." *Rule of Law and Empowerment Initiative*. Abuja, Nigeria: Partners West Africa.

Okenyodo, Oluwakemi. 2016. "Governance, Accountability, and Security in Nigeria." *Africa Security Brief*. Washington, DC: Africa Center for Strategic Studies. June, no. 30.

Okocha, Chuks. 2013. "57 House Members Cross Over to New PDP." *This Day*, September 4.

Okolo, Anselm. 2000. "Now, a Slim, Smart Force." *TELL*, January 31, 33.

Okpaleke, Declan and Uche Maduemesi. 2001. "Echoes of Biafra." *TELL*, January 15, 20–8.

Olaleye, Olawale. 2013. "Jonathan's Job Approval Rating Drops, Say Polls." *This Day*, May 1.

Olatunji, Daud. 2015. "Jonathan Squandered $55bn Oil Money – OBJ." *Vanguard*, January 6.

Olin, Laura. 2014. "#BringBackOurGirls: Hashtag Activism is Cheap – and That's a Good Thing." *Time Magazine*, May 9.

Olowolabi, Yemi. 1998a. "Abubakar's Stewardship." *TELL*, September 21, 24.

1998b. "Out from the Cold." *TELL*, August 31, 28.

Onwuemenyi, Oscarline. 2011. "Post-election Survey Lays Bare Frailties of 2011 Polls." *Vanguard*, June 30.

Opene, Onyechi. 2006. "The Nigerian Project: How Igbos Lost Out." *The Source*, April 10, 10–14.

Oyeyipoa, Shola. 2015. "Nwabueze: No Constitutional Provision for Tenure Elongation." *This Day*, March 11.

Page, Matthew T. 2016. "Improving U.S. Anti-corruption Policy in Nigeria." New York: Council on Foreign Relations.

Page, Matthew T. and A. Carl LeVan. 2016. "Donors Dither as Bureaucrats Exploit Nigeria's Humanitarian Crisis." *AllAfrica.com*, October 16.

Partnerships in the Niger Delta. 2017. "History Never Quite Repeats: Militancy in the Niger Delta." Washington, DC: Fund for Peace.

Pastoral Resolve. 2013. "Strategic Plan, 2014–2018." Abuja, Nigeria: Pastoral Resolve.

Pew Research Center. 2007. Available from www.pewresearch.org/fact-tank/2007/04/16/nigerian-muslims-self-identify-first-with-their-religion/ (accessed September 26, 2017).

2010. Available from www.pewforum.org/2010/04/15/executive-summary-islam-and-christianity-in-sub-saharan-africa/ (accessed September 26, 2017).

2016. "Top Voting Issues in 2016 Election." Washington, DC: Pew Research Center. Available from www.people-press.org (accessed January 10, 2018).

2017a. "Nigerian Muslims Self-identify First with their Religion." Washington, DC: Pew Research Center.

2017b. "Tolerance and Tension: Islam and Christianity in Sub-Saharan Africa." Washington, DC: Pew Research Center.

Querouil, Manon. 2014. "Gone Girls." *Marie Claire*, August 1.

Region of the Niger Delta. 2017. "A Demand for the Independence of Rondel from Nigeria in 2018." June 17.

Rhodan, Maya. 2014. "'Bring Back Our Girls' Protests Banned in Nigerian Capital." *Time Magazine*, June 2.

Robinson, Nicholas and Catherine Lena Kelly. 2017. "Rule of Law Approaches to Countering Violent Extremism." *ABA ROLI rule of Law Issue Paper*. Washington, DC: American Bar Association.

Sahara Reporters. 2008. "Bamaiyi Discharged and Acquitted." *Sahara Reporters*, April 2.

Salvaterra, Neanda and Drew Hinshaw. 2015. "Nigerian President Goodluck Jonathan Wants US Troops to Fight Boko Haram." *The Wall Street Journal*, February 13.

Sawab, Ibrahim and Dionne Searcey. 2017. "A Long, Slow Homecoming for Chibok Schoolgirls Freed by Boko Haram." *New York Times*, May 13, A7.

Sayne, Aaron, Alexandra Gilles, and Christina Katsouris. 2015. "Inside NNPC Oil Sales: A Care for Reform in Nigeria." New York: Natural Resource Governance Institute.

SB Morgan Intelligence. 2017. "The Prospects of Biafra 2.0." Lagos, Nigeria: SBM Intelligence.

Scholz, Jan-Philipp and Adrian Kriesch. 2014. "Boko Haram have Displaced Hundreds of Thousands." *DW*, March 17.

Searcey, Dionne. 2017. "Nigerian Military Raids United Nations Camp for Unclear Reason." *New York Times*, August 11, A5.

Searcey, Dionne and Tony Iyare. 2017. "President Buhari Returns to Nigeria, Facing Serious Challenges." *New York Times*, August 22, A6.

Semenitari, Ibim. 1999. "Exit of the Smileless General." *TELL*, April 5, 13.

Siollun, Max. 2008. "Can a Military Coup Ever Succeed Again in Nigeria?" In maxsiollun.wordpress.com/ (accessed April 11, 2017).

———. 2015. "How Goodluck Jonathan Lost the Nigerian Election." *Guardian*, April 1.

Sodipo, Michael Olufemi. 2013. "Mitigating Radicalism in Northern Nigeria." In *Africa Security Brief* no. 26. Washington, DC: Africa Center for Strategic Studies. August 31.

"Soldiers Seize Power." 1984. *Africa Research Bulletin*, January 7, 109–16.

Soriwei, Fiddles, Olalekan Adetayo, Allwell Okpi, and Kayode Idowu. 2014. "Jonathan Under Pressure to Accept B'Haram's Offers." *Punch*, May 19.

Southeast Situation Room. 2017. "Communique at the End of the South East Human Rights Situation Room Meeting." Enugu, Nigeria: Southeast Situation Room.

Stakeholder Democracy Network. 2013. "Communities not Criminals: Illegal Oil Refining in the Niger Delta." Port Harcourt, Nigeria and London: Stakeholder Democracy Network.

———. 2015. "Worrying Increase in Role of Military for Elections." *Flashpoints: the 2015 Elections in Nigeria* no. 7. London and Port Harcourt: Stakeholder Democracy Network. February 24.

Stewart, Phil and Warren Strobel. 2016. "U.S. Seeks to Approve Attack Aircract for Nigeria in Boko Haram Fight." *Reuters*, May 6.

Sulaiman, Ibrahim. 2017. "Dozens Massacred, 50 Fulani Settlements Razed down in Taraba Carnage – Senator." *Daily Nigerian*, June 22.

The Economist. 2014. "Africa's New Number One." April 12.

The Punch. 2015. "Jonathan Rains Dollars on South-West Obas." March 15.

Tijani, Aminu. 1998. "Go, Abacha, Go." *TELL*, April 13, 18–24.

Tukur, Sani. 2014. "Islamic Organization Condemns Killings of Muslims by Nigerian Soldiers." *Premium Times*, April 8.

Udo, Bassey. 2014. "Corruption Charges against Ministers Politically Motivated." *Premium Times*, May 5.

Ukpong, Cletus. 2016. "How Buhari Sparked Internet Debate with 'My Wife Belongs to my Kitchen' Comment." *Premium Times*, October 17.

Umanah, Ofonime. 1999. "Abacha's Loot Ignited Ijaw Crisis." *Punch*, January 14, 1–2.

Umoru, Henry. 2015. "PDP Wants Buhari Sanctioned for 2011 Election Bloodletting." *Vanguard*, March 2.

United Ijaw. 1998. "Kaiama Declaration." Bayelsa State.

United Nations High Commissioner for Refugees. 2017. "UNHCR Says Death Risk from Starvation in Horn of Africa, Yemen, Nigeria Growing, Displacement Already Rising." Geneva: UNHCR.

US Agency for International Development. 2017. "Lake Chad Basin – Complex Emergency." Washington, DC: Office of Foreign Disaster Assistance.

US Agency for International Development, and Management Systems International. 2009. "Guide to the Drivers of Violent Extremism." Washington, DC.

US Commission on International Religious Freedom. 2015. "Religious Freedom and Nigeria's 2015 Elections." Washington, DC.

US Commission on International Religious Freedom. 2017. "Annual Report 2016." Washington, DC.

US Department of Justice. 2014. "US Forfeits More than $480 Million Stolen by Former Nigerian Dictator." Washington, DC: Office of Public Affairs.

US State Department – Sponsored Poll. 2015. "Nigeria Pre-Election Survey." Washington, DC.

Usman, Evelyn and Ben Agande. 2015. "APC Jabs Jonathan Again!" *Vanguard*, January 3.

Vigaud-Walsh, Francisca. 2016. "Nigeria's Displaced Women and Girls: Humanitarian Community at Odds, Boko Haram's Survivors Forsaken." *Field Report*. Washington, DC: Refugees International. April 21.

Walker, Andrew. 2012. "What is Boko Haram?" *Special Report*, 308.

Warner, Jason and Hilary Matfess. 2017. "Exploding Stereotypes: the Unexpected Operational and Demographic Characteristics of Boko Haram's Suicide Bombers." United States Military Academy, West Point, NY: Combating Terrorism Center at West Point.

Books, Journal Articles, and other Academic Sources

Abidde, Sabella Ogbobode. 2017. *Nigeria's Niger Delta: Militancy, Amnesty and the Postamnesty Environment*. Lanham, MD and Boulder, CO: Lexington Books.

Acemoglu, Daron and James A. Robinson. 2012. *Why Nations Fail: The Origins of Power, Prosperity, and Poverty, Crown Business*. New York: Random House.

Achebe, Chinua. 2012. *There was a Country: A Personal History of Biafra*. New York: Penguin Press.

Adebanwi, Wale. 2014. *Yorùbá Elites and Ethnic Politics in Nigeria: Ọbáfẹ́mi Awólówò and Corporate Agency*. New York: Cambridge University Press.

Adekanye, J. 'Bayo. 1999. *The Retired Military as Emergent Power Factor in Nigeria*. Ibadan, Nigeria: Heinemann.

Adeniyi, Olusegun. 2011. *Power, Politics and Death: A Front-Row Account of Nigeria under the Late President Yar'Adua*. Lagos, Nigeria: Prestige & This Day Books.

Adesina, Olutayo. 1998. "Revenue Allocation Commissions and the Contradictions in Nigeria's Federalism." In *Federalism and Political Restructuring in Nigeria*, edited by Kunle Amuwo, Adigun Agbaje, Rotimi Suberu, and Georges Herault, 232–46. Ibadan, Nigeria: Spectrum Books.

Adesoji, Abimola. 2010. "The Boko Haram Uprising and Islamic Revivalism in Nigeria." *Africa Spectrum* no. 2:95–108.

 2011. "Between Maitatsine and Boko Haram: Islamic Fundamentalism and the Response of the Nigerian State." *Africa Today* no. 57 (4):89–119.

Adunbi, Omolade. 2015. *Oil Wealth and Insurgency in Nigeria*. Bloomington and Indianapolis: Indiana University Press.

Afigbo, A.E. 1989. "Federal Character: Its Meaning and History." In *Federal Character and Federalism in Nigeria*, edited by Peter P. Ekeh and Eghosa Osaghae, 19–46. Ibadan, Nigeria: Heinemann Educational Books Ltd.

African Development Bank. 2013. *Federal Republic of Nigeria Country Strategy Paper, 2013–2017*. Edited by West Africa Regional Department. Abidjan, Côte d'Ivoire: African Development Bank.

Afrobarometer and Practical Sampling International. 2016. "Afrobarometer Round 6 Results." Abuja, Nigeria and Lansing, MI: Afrobarometer.

Agbaje, Adigun. 1997. "Mobilizing for a New Political Culture." In *Transition without End: Nigerian Politics and Civil Society Under Babangida*, edited by Larry Diamond, Anthony Kirk-Greene, and Oyeleye Oyediran, 143–70. Boulder, CO and London: Lynne Rienner Publishers.

——. 2010. "Whose Catalyst? Party Politics and Democracy in the Fourth Republic: From Theory to Denial." In *Governance and Politics in Post-military Nigeria: Changes and Challenges*, edited by Said Adejumobi, 61–88. New York: Palgrave Macmillan.

Agbaje, Adigun, Adeolu Akande, and Jide Ojo. 2018. "The People's Democratic Party: from the 1999 Transition to the 2015 Turnover." In *Oxford Handbook of Nigerian Politics*, edited by A. Carl LeVan and Patrick Ukata, 353–68. Oxford and New York: Oxford University Press.

Agbaje, Adigun, Larry Diamond, and Ebere Onwudiwe. 2004. *Nigeria's Struggle for Democracy and Good Governance.* Ibadan, Nigeria: University of Ibadan Press.

Aghedo, Iro. 2014. "Old Wine in a New Bottle: Ideological and Operational Linkages Between Maitatsine and Boko Haram Revolts in Nigeria." *African Security* no. 7 (4):229–50.

Ahmad Khan, Sarah. 1994. *Nigeria: The Political Economy of Oil.* Oxford: Oxford University Press.

Aina, Ayandiji Daniel. 2004. "Party and Electoral Politics." In *Nigeria's Struggle for Democracy and Good Governance*, edited by Adigun Agbaje, Larry Diamond, and Ebere Onwudiwe, 82–100. Ibadan, Nigeria: University of Ibadan Press.

Akhaine, Sylvester Odion. 2011. "Nigeria's 2011 Elections: The 'Crippled Giant' Learns to Walk?" *African Affairs* no. 110 (441):649–55.

Akinola, Anthony. 1996. *Rotational Presidency.* Ibadan, Nigeria: Spectrum Books, with Safari Books Ltd. (UK) and African Books Collective (UK).

Akinterinwa, Bola. 1997. "The 1993 Presidential Election Imbroglio." In *Transition without End: Nigerian Politics and Civil Society under Babangida*, edited by Larry Jay Diamond, Oyeleye Oyediran, and A.H.M. Kirk-Greene, 257–80. Boulder, CO: Lynne Rienner Publishers.

Aksoy, Deniz. 2014. "Elections and the Timing of Terrorist Attacks." *The Journal of Politics* no. 76 (4):899–913.

Aksoy, Deniz and David B. Carter. 2014. "Electoral Institutions and the Emergence of Terrorist Groups." *British Journal of Political Science* no. 44 (1):181–204.

Al-Ississ, Mohamad and Samer Atallah. 2014. "Patronage and Ideology in Electoral Behavior: Evidence from Egypt's First Presidential Elections." *European Journal of Political Economy* no. 37:241–8.

Alapiki, Henry, Eme Ekeke, and Sofiri Joab-Peterside. 2015. *Post-amnesty Conflict Management Framework in the Niger Delta*. Port Harcourt, Nigeria: Faculty of the Social Sciences.

Almond, Gabriel and Sidney Verba. 1963. *The Civic Culture*. Princeton, NJ: Princeton University Press.

Amuwo, 'Kunle. 2001. "Transition as Democratic Regression." In *Nigeria During the Abacha Years, 1993–1998*, edited by Kunle Amuwo, Daniel C. Bach, and Yann Lebeau, 1–56. Ibadan, Nigeria: Institut Francais de Recherche en Afrique.

Amuwo, 'Kunle, Adigun Agbaje, Rotimi Suberu, and Georges Herault. 2000. *Federalism and Political Restructuring in Nigeria*. Ibadan, Nigeria: Spectrum.

Anyanwu, Chris N.D. 1999. *The Lawmakers: Federal Republic of Nigeria, 1999–2003*. 1st ed. Abuja, Nigeria: Startcraft International.

2003. *The Lawmakers: Federal Republic of Nigeria, 2003–2007*. 2nd ed. Abuja, Nigeria: Startcraft International.

2007. *The Lawmakers: Federal Republic of Nigeria, 2007–2011*. 3rd ed. Abuja, Nigeria: Startcraft International.

2011. *The Lawmakers: Federal Republic of Nigeria, 2011–2015*. 4th ed. Abuja, Nigeria: Startcraft International.

Arriola, Leonardo. 2008. "Ethnicity, Economic Conditions, and Opposition Support: Evidence from Ethiopia's 2005 Elections." *Northeast African Studies* no. 10 (1):115–44.

2013. *Multi-ethnic Coalitions in Africa: Business Financing of Opposition Election Campaigns*. New York: Cambridge University Press.

Asuni, Judy. 2009. *Understanding the Armed Groups of the Niger Delta*. New York: Council on Foreign Relations.

Ayoade, John A.A. 2013. "Zoning of Political Offices in Nigeria: Patriotism or Plunder?" In *Nigeria's Critical Election, 2011*, edited by John A.A. Ayoade and Adeoye A. Akinsanya, 17–56. Lanham, MD: Lexington Books.

Ayoade, John A.A. and Adeoye A. Akinsanya. 2013. *Nigeria's Critical Election, 2011*. Lanham: Lexington Books.

Azikiwe, Nnamdi. 1961. *Zik: A Selection of Speeches of Nnamdi Azikiwe*. Cambridge: Cambridge University Press.

Baba, Yahaya. 2018. "Executive Power and Hyper-Presidentialism." In *Oxford Handbook of Nigerian Politics*, edited by A. Carl LeVan and Patrick Ukata, 258–74. Oxford and New York: Oxford University Press.

Bach, Daniel C., Yann Lebeau, and 'Kunle Amuwo. 2001. *Nigeria During the Abacha Years, 1993–1998*. Ibadan: Institut Francais de Recherche en Afrique.

Badejo, Babafemi A. 1997. "Party Formation and Party Competition." In *Transition without End: Nigerian Politics and Civil Society Under Babangida*, edited by Larry Diamond, Anthony Kirk-Greene, and Oyeleye Oyediran, 171–92. Boulder, CO and London: Lynne Rienner Publishers.

Bamiduro, Joseph and Segun Oshewolo. 2014. "Understanding Government and Politics in Nigeria." In *Understanding Government and Politics in Nigeria*, edited by Rotimi Ajayi and Joseph Yinka Fashagba, 301–16. Omu-Aran, Nigeria: Landmark University.

Barros, Robert. 2002. *Constitutionalism and Dictatorship: Pinochet, the Junta, and the 1980 Constitution*. Cambridge and New York: Cambridge University Press.

——— 2003. "Dictatorship and the Rule of Law: Rules and Military Power in Pinochet's Chile." In *Democracy and the Rule of Law*, edited by Jose Maria Maravall and Adam Przeworski, 188–222. Cambridge: Cambridge University Press.

Basedau, Matthias, Gero Erdmann, and Andreas Mehler. 2007. *Votes, Money and Violence: Political Parties and Elections in Sub-Saharan Africa*. Uppsala, Sweden: Nordiska Afrikainstitutet.

Basedau, Matthias, Gero Erdmann, Jann Lay, and Alexander Stroh. 2011. "Ethnicity and Party Preference in Sub-Saharan Africa." *Democratization* no. 18 (2):462–89.

Bates, Robert H. 1981. *Markets and States in Tropical Africa: the Political Basis of Agricultural Policies*. Berkeley: University of California Press.

——— 1989. *Beyond the Miracle of the Market*. Cambridge: Cambridge University Press.

Bekoe, Dorina Akosua Oduraa. 2012. *Voting in Fear: Electoral Violence in Sub-Saharan Africa*. Washington, DC: United States Institute of Peace.

Belcher, Stephen. 2005. "Fulbe Stories of Cattle: A Muslim Version from Northern Nigeria." In *African Myths of Origin*, edited by Stephen Belcher, 55–56. New York: Penguin.

Bermeo, Nancy. 2016. "On Democratic Backsliding." *Journal of Democracy* no. 27 (1):5–19.

Berrebi, Claude and Esteban F. Klor. 2008. "Are Voters Sensitive to Terrorism? Direct Evidence from the Israeli Electorate." *American Political Science Review* no. 102 (3):279–301.

Birch, Sarah and David Muchlinski. 2017. "Electoral Violence Prevention: What Works?" *Democratization* no. 25 (3):385–403.

Blattman, Christopher. 2009. "From Violence to Voting: War and Political Participation in Uganda." *American Political Science Review* no. 103 (2):231–47.

Braji, Ibrahim. 2014. *The Nigerian Military: Origin, Politics and Capital Accumulation*. Revised ed. Ibadan, Nigeria: University Press PLC.

Bratton, Michael. 1999. "Second Elections in Africa." In *Democratization in Africa*, edited by Larry Diamond and Marc Plattner, 18–33. Baltimore and London: Johns Hopkins University Press.

Bratton, Michael and Nicolas Van de Walle. 1997. *Democratic Experiments in Africa: Regime Transitions in Comparative Perspective*. Cambridge and New York: Cambridge University Press.

Bratton, Michael, Ravi Bhavnani, and Tse-Hsin Chen. 2011. "Voting Intentions in Africa: Ethnic, Economic, or Partisan?" *Afrobarometer Working Paper* no. 127.

   2013a. "Voting and Democratic Citizenship in Africa." In *The Global Barometers Series*, edited by Michael Bratton, 79–100. Boulder, CO: Lynne Rienner Publishers.

   2013b. "Vote Buying and Violence in Nigerian Election Campaigns." In *Voting and Democratic Citizenship in Africa*, edited by Michael Bratton, 121–38. Boulder, CO: Lynne Rienner Publishers.

   2013c. *Voting and Democratic Citizenship in Africa*. Boulder, CO: Lynne Rienner Publishers.

Brownlee, Jason, Tarek Masoud, and Andrew Reynolds. 2015. *The Arab Spring: Pathways of Repression and Reform*. New York: Oxford University Press.

Bueno de Mesquita, Bruce, Alastair Smith, Randolph M. Siverson, and James D. Morrow. 2003. *The Logic of Political Survival*. Cambridge, MA and London: MIT Press.

Bunce, Valerie. 2003. "Rethinking Recent Democratization: Lessons from the Postcommunist Experience." *World Politics* no. 55:167–92.

Burchard, Stephanie M. 2015. *Electoral Violence in Sub-Saharan Africa: Causes and Consequences*. Boulder, CO: FirstForumPress, A Division of Lynne Rienner Publishers.

Bush, George W. 2001. "Address to a Joint Session of Congress and the American People," September 20. Washington, DC: The White House.

Campbell, John. 2013b. "Nigeria." In *Pathways to Freedom: Political and Economic Lessons from Democratic Transitions*, edited by Isobel Coleman and Terra Lawson-Remer, 201–26. New York: Council on Foreign Relations.

   2013c. *Nigeria: Dancing on the Brink*. 2nd ed. Lanham, MD: Rowman and Littlefield.

Carothers, Thomas. 2002. "The End of the Transition Paradigm." *Journal of Democracy* no. 13 (1):5–21.

Carter Center, and National Democratic Institute for International Affairs. 1999. *Observing the 1998–99 Nigeria Elections, Final Report*. Atlanta and Washington, DC.

Chang, Eric C.C. and Nicholas N. Kerr. 2016. "An Insider-Outsider Theory of Popular Tolerance for Corrupt Politicians." *Governance* no. 30 (1):67–84.

Cheeseman, Nicholas. 2015. *Democracy in Africa: Successes, Failures, and the Struggle for Political Reform, New Approaches to African History.* New York: Cambridge University Press.

Cheibub, Jose Antonio. 2007. *Presidentialism, Parliamentarism, and Democracy.* Cambridge and New York: Cambridge University Press.

Chenoweth, Erica and Maria J. Stephan. 2011. *Why Civil Resistance Works: The Strategic Logic of Nonviolent Conflict.* New York: Columbia University Press.

Cho, Wonbin and Carolyn Logan. 2014. "Looking Toward the Future." *Comparative Political Studies* no. 47 (1):30–54.

Chouin, Gerard, Manuel Reinert, and Elodie Apard. 2014. "By the Numbers: The Nigerian State's Efforts to Counter Boko Haram." In *Boko Haram: Islamism, Politics, Security and the State in Nigeria*, edited by Pierre Perouse de Montclos, 213–36. Ibadan, Nigeria: French Institute for Research in Africa.

Chowanietz, Christophe. 2011. "Rallying Around the Flag or Railing against the Government? Political Parties' Reactions to Terrorist Acts." *Party Politics* no. 17 (5):673–98.

Coleman, Isobel and Terra Lawson-Remer. 2013. "Political and Economic Lessons from Democratic Transitions." In *Pathways to Freedom: Political and Economic Lessons from Democratic Transitions*, edited by Isobel Coleman and Terra Lawson-Remer, 1–19. New York: Council on Foreign Relations.

Collier, Paul. 2009. *Wars, Guns, and Votes: Democracy in Dangerous Places.* New York: Harper.

Collier, Paul and Jan Willem Gunning. 2008. "Sacrificing the Future: Intertemporal Strategies and their Implications for Growth." In *The Political Economy of Economic Growth in Africa, 1960–2000*, edited by Benno Ndulu, Stephen O'Connell, Robert Bates, Paul Collier, and Chukwuma Soludo, 202–24. Cambridge: Cambridge University Press.

Colomer, Josep M. 1994. "Transitions by Agreement: Modeling the Spanish Way." *American Political Science Review* no. 85 (4):1283–302.

Comolli, Virginia. 2015. *Boko Haram: Nigeria's Islamist Insurgency.* London: C. Hurst & Co.

Conroy-Krutz, Jeffrey and Carolyn Logan. 2013. "Museveni and the 2011 Ugandan Election: Did the Money Matter?" In *Voting and Democratic Citizenship in Africa*, edited by Michael Bratton, 139–58. Boulder, CO: Lynne Rienner Publishers.

Constitutional Rights Project. 2002. *Confronting Abuses of the Past: Issues at the Oputa Commission.* Lagos and Abuja, Nigeria.

Coppedge, Michael. 2012. *Democratization and Research Methods, Strategies for Social Inquiry*. Cambridge: Cambridge University Press.

Cunningham, Kathleen Gallagher. 2017. "The Efficacy of Nonviolence in Self-determination Disputes." Paper presented at the American Political Science Association Annual Meeting, San Francisco.

Dahl, Robert. 1971. *Polyarchy: Participation and Opposition*. New Haven, CT and London: Yale University Press.

Datau, Polycarp Dama. 2014. *Political Party Primaries*. Jos, Nigeria: Manifold Strategy Centre.

De Mesquita, Ethan Bueno. 2007. "Politics and the Suboptimal Provision of Counterterror." *International Organization* no. 61 (1):9–36.

Diamond, Larry. 1982. "Cleavage, Conflict, and Anxiety in the Second Nigerian Republic." *Journal of Modern African Studies* no. 20 (4):629–68.

——— 1984. "Nigeria in Search of Democracy." *Foreign Affairs* no. 4 (62):905–27.

——— 1988. *Class, Ethnicity and Democracy in Nigeria: The Failure of the First Republic*. Houndmills, Basingstoke: Macmillan Press.

——— 1997. "Introduction: In Search of Consolidation." In *Consolidating the Third Wave Democracies*, edited by Larry Jay Diamond, Marc Plattner, Yun-han Chu, and Hung-mao Tien, xiii–xlvii. Baltimore: Johns Hopkins University Press.

Diamond, Larry, Francis Fukuyama, Donald L. Horowitz, and Marc F. Plattner. 2014a. "Reconsidering the Transition Paradigm." *Journal of Democracy* no. 25 (1):86–100.

Diamond, Larry Jay and Marc F. Plattner. 1999. *Democratization in Africa*. Baltimore: Johns Hopkins University Press.

Diamond, Larry Jay, Marc Plattner, Yun-han Chu, and Hung-mao Tien. 1997. *Consolidating the Third Wave Democracies, a Journal of Democracy Book*. Baltimore: Johns Hopkins University Press.

Diamond, Larry Jay, Oyeleye Oyediran, and A.H.M. Kirk-Greene. 1997. *Transition without End: Nigerian Politics and Civil Society Under Babangida*. Boulder, CO: Lynne Rienner Publishers.

Diamond, Larry, Francis Fukuyama, Donald Horowitz, and Marc Plattner. 2014b. "Discussion: Reconsidering the Transition Paradigm." *Journal of Democracy* no. 25 (1):86–100.

Dionne, Kim Yi, and Boniface Dulani. 2013. "Constitutional Provisions and Executive Succession: Malawi's 2012 Transition in Comparative Perspective." *African Affairs* no. 112 (446):111–37.

Douglas, Oronto. 2014. *Before and After: President Goodluck Jonathan and the Transformation of Nigeria*. Abuja: Office of the Special Adviser to the President.

Dudley, Billy J. 1973. *Instability and Political Order: Politics and Crisis in Nigeria*. Ibadan, Nigeria: University of Ibadan Press.

Edgell, Amanda B., Valeriya Mechkova, David Altman, Michael Bernhard, and Staffan I. Lindberg. 2017. "When and Where do Elections Matter? A Global Test of the Democratization by Elections Hypothesis, 1900–2010." *Democratization* no. 3 (25):422–44.

Edozie, Kiki. 2009. *Reconstructing the Third Wave of Democracy: Comparative African Democratic Politics*. Lanham, MD: University Press of America.

Edozie, Rita Kiki. 2002. *People Power and Democracy: The Popular Movement against Military Despotism in Nigeria, 1989–1999*. Trenton, NJ and Eritrea: Africa World Press.

Egwu, Samuel. 2005. "The Civil War and Federalism in Nigeria." In *Nigerian Federalism in Crisis: Critical Perspectives and Political Options*, edited by Ebere Onwudiwe and Rotimi T. Suberu, 100–13. Ibadan, Nigeria: Program on Ethnic and Federal Studies.

2007. "The Context and Lessons of the 2003 Elections in Nigeria." In *Perspectives on the 2003 Elections in Nigeria*, edited by Isaac Albert, Derrick Marco, and Victor Adetula, 10–29. Abuja, Nigeria: IDASA.

2014. "Internal Democracy in Nigerian Political Parties." In *Political Parties and Democracy in Nigeria*, edited by Olu Obafemi, Samuel Egwu, Okechukwu Ibeanu, and Jibrin Ibrahim, 192–216. Kuru, Nigeria: National Institute for Policy and Strategic Studies.

2015. "The Political Economy of Rural Banditry in Contemporary Nigeria." In *Rural Banditry and Social Conflicts in Northern Nigeria*, edited by Mohammed J. Kuna and Jibrin Ibrahim, 14–68. Abuja, Nigeria: Centre for Democracy and Development.

Eisenstadt, Todd A., A. Carl LeVan, and Tofigh Maboudi. 2017. *Constituents Before Assembly: Participation, Deliberation, and Representation in the Crafting of New Constitutions*. New York: Cambridge University Press.

Ekeh, Peter. 1975. "Colonialism and the Two Publics in Africa: A Theoretical Statement." *Comparative Studies in Society and History* no. 17 (1):91–112.

Ekeh, Peter P. 1989. "The Structure and Meaning of Federal Character in the Nigerian Political System." In *Federal Character and Federalism in Nigeria*, edited by Peter P. Ekeh and Eghosa Osaghae, 19–44. Ibadan, Nigeria: Heinemann Educational Books.

Ekeh, Peter P. and Eghosa Osaghae. 1989. *Federal Character and Federalism in Nigeria*. Ibadan, Nigeria: Heinemann Educational Books Ltd.

Ekpo, Akpan H. 1994. "Fiscal Federalism: Nigeria' Post-Independence Experience, 1960–90." *World Development* no. 22 (8):1129–46.

Elaigwu, J. Isawa. 1988. "Nigerian Federalism Under Civilian and Military Regimes." *Publius: The Journal of Federalism* no. 18 (1):173–88.

Elischer, Sebastian. 2013. *Political Parties in Africa: Ethnicity and Party Formation*. New York: Cambridge University Press.

Elkins, Zachary, Tom Ginsburg, and James Melton. 2009. *The Endurance of National Constitutions*. Cambridge and New York: Cambridge University Press.

Enders, Walter and Todd Sandler. 2012. *The Political Economy of Terrorism*. 2nd ed. Cambridge: Cambridge University Press.

Englebert, Pierre. 2009. *Africa: Unity, Sovereignty, and Sorrow*. Boulder, CO: Lynne Rienner Publishers.

Englebert, Pierre and Rebecca Hummel. 2005. "Let's Stick Together: Understanding Africa's Secessionist Deficit." *African Affairs* no. 104 (416):399–427.

Falola, Toyin. 2009. *Colonialism and Violence in Nigeria*. Bloomington: Indiana University Press.

Falola, Toyin and Julius Omozuanvbo Ihonvbere. 1985. *The Rise and Fall of Nigeria's Second Republic, 1979–84*. London: Zed Books.

Fashagba, Joseph Yinka. 2015. "Subnational Legislatures and National Governing Institutions in Nigeria, 1999–2013." In *African State Governance: Subnational Politics and National Power*, edited by A. Carl LeVan, Joseph Yinka Fashagba, and Edward McMahon, 93–120. Houndmills, Basingstoke and New York: Palgrave Macmillan.

Fayemi, Kayode. 2002. "Nigeria's Security Sector and the Dilemma of Civilian Control." *Conflict, Security & Development* no. 2 (1):111–20.

Ferree, Karen E., Clark C. Gibson, and James D. Long. 2014. "Voting Behavior and Electoral Irregularities in Kenya's 2013 Election." *Journal of East African Studies* no. 8 (1):153–72.

Foa, Roberto Stefan and Yascha Mounk. 2017. "The Signs of Deconsolidation." *Journal of Democracy* no. 28 (1):5–16.

Forrest, Tom. 1995. "Politics and Economic Development in Nigeria." Updated edition. *African Modernization and Development Series*. Boulder, CO: Westview Press.

Fukuyama, Francis. 1992. *The End of History and the Last Man*. New York: Free Press.

Galadima, Habu. 2014. "Party Manifestoes and Programmes." In *Political Parties and Democracy in Nigeria*, edited by Olu Obafemi, Samuel Egwu, Okechukwu Ibeanu, and Jibrin Ibrahim, 100–29. Kuru, Nigeria: National Institute for Policy and Strategic Studies.

Galston, William A. 2017. "The Populist Moment." *Journal of Democracy* no. 28 (2):21–33.

Gberevbie, Daniel Eseme and Faith Osasumwen Oviasogie. 2013. "Women in Governance and Sustainable Democracy in Nigeria, 1999–2012." *Economics & Sociology* no. 6 (1):89–107.

Gboyega, Alex. 1989. "The Public Service and Federal Character." In *Federal Character and Federalism in Nigeria*, edited by Peter P. Ekeh and Eghosa Osaghae, 164–87. Ibadan, Nigeria: Heinemann Educational Books Ltd.

Getmansky, Anna and Thomas Zeitzoff. 2014. "Terrorism and Voting: The Effect of Rocket Threat on Voting in Israeli Elections." *American Political Science Review* no. 108 (3):588–604.

Gibson, Clark C. and James D. Long. 2009. "The Presidential and Parliamentary Elections in Kenya, December 2007." *Electoral Studies* no. 28:497–502.

Gigerenzer, Gerd. 2006. "Out of the Frying Pan into the Fire: Behavioral Reactions to Terrorist Attacks." *Risk Analysis* no. 26 (2):347–51.

Gow, James, Funmi Olonisakin, and Ernst Dijxhoorn. 2013. *Militancy and Violence in West Africa, Contemporary Security Studies*. Boulder, CO: Routledge.

Gujarati, Damodar. 1995. *Basic Econometrics*. 3rd ed. New York: McGraw-Hill.

Haggard, Stephan, and Robert R. Kaufman. 2016. *Dictators and Democrats: Masses, Elites and Regime Change*. Princeton, NJ: Princeton University Press.

Harbeson, John W., Donald S. Rothchild, and Naomi Chazan. 1994. *Civil Society and the State in Africa*. Boulder, CO: Lynne Rienner Publishers.

Hart, Austin. 2013. "Can Candidates Activate or Deactivate the Economic Vote? Evidence from Two Mexican Elections." *The Journal of Politics* no. 75 (4):1051–63.

2016. *Economic Voting: A Campaign-centered Theory*. New York: Cambridge University Press.

Hassan, Umaru and A.B. Jauro. 2005. "Grazing Reserves and Permanent Resettlement of Pastoralists." In *A Compendium of Studies and Issues in Pastoralism in Nigeria*, edited by Mohammed Bello and Sahabo Mahdi, 123–39. Yola, Nigeria: Paraclete Publishers.

Herbst, Jeffrey. 2000. *States and Power in Africa: Comparative Lessons in Authority and Control, Princeton Studies in International History and Politics*. Princeton, NJ: Princeton University Press.

Herskovits, Jean. 2007. "Nigeria's Rigged Democracy." *Foreign Affairs* no. 86 (4):115–130.

Higazi, Adam. 2016. "Farmer-Pastoralist Conflicts on the Jos Plateau, Central Nigeria: Security Responses of Local Vigilantes and the Nigerian State." *Conflict, Security & Development* no. 16 (4):365–85.

Higley, John, and Richard Gunther. 1992. *Elites and Democratic Consolidation in Latin America and Southern Europe*. Cambridge and New York: Cambridge University Press.

Hills, Alice. 2012. "Lost in Translation: Why Nigeria's Police don't Implement Democratic Reforms." *International Affairs* no. 88 (4):739–55.

Hoechner, Hannah. 2014. "Traditional Quaranic Students (Almajirai) in Nigeria: Fair Game for Unfair Accusations?" In *Boko Haram: Islamism, Politics, Security and the State in Nigeria*, edited by Pierre Perouse de Montclos, 9–32. Ibadan, Nigeria: French Institute for Research in Africa.

Hoffman, Barak and James D. Long. 2013. "Parties, Ethnicity and Voting in African Elections." *Comparative Politics* no. 45 (2):127–46.

Horowitz, Donald. 1985. *Ethnic Groups in Conflict*. Berkeley: University of California Press.

Human Rights Watch. 2007. *Election or Selection?* New York: Human Rights Watch.

Hunter, Lance Y., David J. Bennett, and Joseph W. Robbins. 2016. "Destabilizing Effects of Terrorism on Party System Stability." *Terrorism and Political Violence* no. 30 (3):503–23.

Huntington, Samuel P. 1991. *The Third Wave: Democratization in the Late Twentieth Century*. Norman, OK: University of Oklahoma Press.

1997. "Democracy for the Long Haul." In *Consolidating the Third Wave Democracies*, edited by Larry Jay Diamond, Marc Plattner, Yun-han Chu, and Hung-mao Tien, 3–13. Baltimore: Johns Hopkins University Press.

Hyden, Goran. 2013. *African Politics in Comparative Perspective*. 2nd ed. Cambridge and New York: Cambridge University Press.

Ibeanu, Okechukwu. 2003. "Aguleri-Umuleri Conflict in Anambra State." In *Civil Society and Ethnic Conflict Management in Nigeria*, edited by Thomas A. Imobighe, 167–222. Ibadan, Nigeria: Spectrum Books Ltd.

Ibeanu, Okey. 2014. "Regulating Nigerian Political Parties: The Role of the Independent National Electoral Commission." In *Political Parties and Democracy in Nigeria*, edited by Olu Obafemi, Samuel Egwu, Okechukwu Ibeanu, and Jibrin Ibrahim, 45–59. Kuru, Nigeria: National Institute for Policy and Strategic Studies.

Ibrahim, Jibrin. 2014. "Introduction: Engaging Political Parties for Democratic Development." In *Political Parties and Democracy in Nigeria*, edited by Olu Obafemi, Samuel Egwu, Okechukwu Ibeanu, and Jibrin Ibrahim, 1–11. Kuru, Nigeria: National Institute for Policy and Strategic Studies.

Ibrahim, Jibrin and Okechukwu Ibeanu. 2009. *Direct Capture: The 2007 Nigerian Elections and the Subversion of Popular Sovereignty*. Abuja, Nigeria: Centre for Democracy and Development.

Ikein, Augustine A. and Comfort Briggs-Anigboh. 1998. *Oil and Fiscal Federalism in Nigeria: The Political Economy of Resource*

Allocation in a Developing Country. Aldershot and Brookfield, VT: Ashgate.

Ikelegbe, A. 2001. "Civil Society, Oil, and Conflict in the Niger Delta Region of Nigeria." *Journal of Modern African Studies* no. 39 (3):437–69.

Indridason, Indridi H. 2008. "Does Terrorism Influence Domestic Politics? Coalition Formation and Terrorist Incidents." *Journal of Peace Research* no. 45 (2):241–59.

Isaksson, Ann-Sofie, Andreas Kotsadam, and Måns Nerman. 2014. "The Gender Gap in African Political Participation: Testing Theories of Individual and Contextual Determinants." *The Journal of Development Studies* no. 50 (2):302–18.

Isichei, Elizabeth. 1987. "The Maitatsine Risings in Nigeria, 1980–1985." *Journal of Religion in Africa* no. 17 (3):194–208.

Isichei, Elizabeth Allo. 1997. *A History of African Societies to 1870.* Cambridge: Cambridge University Press.

Jega, Attahiru. 2015a. "Nigeria's 2015 Elections." Paper read at Nigeria's 2015 Elections: What Have We Learned? June 10, at Washington, DC.

John, Elnathan. 2015. *Born on a Tuesday.* New York: Black Cat.

Kalu, Ogbu. 2008. *African Pentecostalism: An Introduction.* Oxford and New York: Oxford University Press.

Kamrava, Mehran. 2014. *Beyond the Arab Spring: The Evolving Ruling Bargain in the Middle East.* London: Hurst & Company.

Kandeh, Jimmy D. 2004. *Coups from Below: Armed Subalterns and State Power in West Africa.* New York and Houndmills: Palgrave Macmillan.

Karl, Terry Lynn. 1990. "Dilemmas of Democratization in Latin America." *Comparative Politics* no. 23 (1):1–21.

Kew, Darren. 2004. "The 2003 Elections: Hardly Credible but Acceptable." In *Crafting the New Nigeria: Confronting the Challenges*, edited by Robert I. Rotberg, 139–73. Boulder, CO: Lynne Rienner Publishers.

——— 2016. *Civil Society, Conflict Resolution, and Democracy in Nigeria.* First edition. *Syracuse studies on peace and conflict resolution.* Syracuse, NY: Syracuse University Press.

Kibris, Arzu. 2011. "Funerals and Elections: The Effects of Terrorism on Voting Behavior in Turkey." *Journal of Conflict Resolution* no. 55 (2):220–47.

Kramon, Eric. 2016. "Electoral Handouts as Information: Explaining Unmonitored Vote Buying." *World Politics* no. 68 (3):454–98.

Kramon, Eric and Daniel Posner. 2011. "Kenya's New Constitution." *Journal of Democracy* no. 22 (2):89–103.

Kukah, Matthew Hassan. 2003. *Religion, Politics and Power in Northern Nigeria.* Ibadan, Nigeria and UK: Spectrum Books and Safari Books Ltd.

Laakso, Liisa. 2007. "Insights into Electoral Violence in Africa." In *Votes, Money and Violence: Political Parties and Elections in Sub-Saharan Africa*, edited by Matthias Basedau, Gero Erdmann, and Andreas Mehler, 224–52. Uppsala, Sweden: Nordiska Afrikainstitutet.

Laitin, David. 1982. "The Sharia Debate and the Origins of Nigeria's Second Republic." *Journal of Modern African Studies* no. 20 (3):411–30.

Laitin, David D. 1986. *Hegemony and Culture: Politics and Religious Change among the Yoruba*. Chicago: University of Chicago Press.

Lange, Matthew. 2009. *Lineages of Despotism and Development: British Colonialism and State Power*. Chicago: University of Chicago Press.

LeVan, A. Carl. 2011a. "Power Sharing and Inclusive Politics in Africa's Uncertain Democracies." *Governance: A Journal of Policy, Administration, and Institutions* no. 24 (1):31–53.

2011b. "Questioning Tocqueville in Africa: Continuity and Change in Nigeria's Civil Society During Democratization." *Democratization* no. 18 (1):135–59.

2013. "Sectarian Rebellions in Post-transition Nigeria Compared." *Journal of Intervention and Statebuilding* no. 7 (3):335–52.

2015a. *Dictators and Democracy in African Development: The Political Economy of Good Governance in Nigeria*. New York: Cambridge University Press.

2015b. "Parallel Institutionalism and the Future of Representation in Nigeria." *Journal of Contemporary African Studies* no. 33 (3): 370–90.

2018. "Reciprocal Retaliation and Local Linkage: Federalism as an Instrument of Opposition Organising in Nigeria." *African Affairs* no. 117 (466):1–20.

LeVan, A. Carl and Josiah Olubowale. 2014. "'I am Here Until Development Comes': Displacement, Demolitions, and Property Rights in Urbanizing Nigeria." *African Affairs* no. 113 (452):387–408.

LeVan, A. Carl and Yahya Baba. 2017. "Politics in Nigeria." In *Comparative Politics Today*, edited by G. Bingham Powell, Russell J. Dalton, and Kaare Strom, 550–93. London: Pearson.

LeVan, A. Carl, Matthew T. Page, and Yoonbin Ha. 2018. "From Terrorism to Talakawa: Explaining Party Turnover in Nigeria's 2015 Elections." *Review of African Political Economy* no. 45 (155):1–19.

LeVan, A. Carl, Titi Pitso, and Bodunrin Adebo. 2003. "Elections in Nigeria: Is the Third Time a Charm?" *Journal of African Elections* no. 2 (2):30–47.

Levitsky, Steven and Lucan Way. 2010. *Competitive Authoritarianism: Hybrid Regimes After the Cold War, Problems of International Politics*. Cambridge and New York: Cambridge University Press.

Lewis, Peter M. 2011. "Nigeria Votes: More Openness, More Violence." *Journal of Democracy* no. 22 (4):60–74.

Lewis, Peter M. and Darren Kew. 2015. "Nigeria's Hopeful Election." *Journal of Democracy* no. 26 (3):94–109.

Lewis, Peter M., Pearl T. Robinson, and Barnett Rubin. 1998. *Stabilizing Nigeria: Sanctions, Incentives, and Support for Civil Society*. New York: Century Foundation Press.

Lijphart, Arend. 1999. *Patterns of Democracy: Government Forms and Performance in Thirty-six Countries*. New Haven, CT: Yale University Press.

2012. *Patterns of Democracy: Government Forms and Performance in Thirty-six Countries*. 2nd ed. New Haven, CT: Yale University Press.

Lindberg, Staffan I. 2004. "The Democratic Qualities of Multiparty Elections: Participation, Competition and Legitimacy in Africa." *Journal of Commonwealth and Comparative Politics* no. 39 (1):28–53.

Lindberg, Staffan I. 2006. *Democracy and Elections in Africa*. Baltimore: The Johns Hopkins University Press.

2009. *Democratization by Elections: A New Mode of Transition*. Baltimore: Johns Hopkins University Press.

Lindberg, Staffan I. and M.K.C. Morrison. 2008. "Are African Voters Really Ethnic or Clientelistic? Survey Evidence from Ghana." *Political Science Quarterly* no. 123 (1):95–122.

Linz, Juan J. and Alfred Stepan. 1996. *Problems of Democratic Transition and Consolidation*. Baltimore: Johns Hopkins University Press.

1997. "Toward Consolidated Democracies." In *Consolidating the Third Wave Democracies*, edited by Larry Jay Diamond, Marc Plattner, Yun-han Chu, and Hung-mao Tien, 14–33. Baltimore: Johns Hopkins University Press.

Lipset, Seymour Martin. 1959. "Some Social Requisites of Democracy: Economic Development and Political Legitimacy." *American Political Science Review* no. 53 (1):69–105.

Lubeck, Paul M. 1986. *Islam and Urban Labor in Northern Nigeria: The Making of a Muslim Working Class, African Studies Series*. Cambridge: Cambridge University Press.

Mang, Henry Gyang. 2014. "Christian Perceptions of Islam and Society in Relation to Boko Haram and Recent Events in Jos and Northern Nigeria." In *Boko Haram: Islamism, Politics, Security and the State in Nigeria*, edited by Pierre Perouse de Montclos, 85–109. Ibadan, Nigeria: French Institute for Research in Africa.

Mansfield, Edward D. and Jack Snyder. 1995. "Democratization and the Danger of War." *International Security* no. 20 (1):5–38.

Marcus, George E., W. Russell Neuman, and Michael MacKuen. 2000. *A ffective Intelligence and Political Judgment*. Chicago: University of Chicago Press.

Matfess, Hilary. 2016. "Fulani Militants in Nigeria: Mischaracterization Obscures Threat and Impedes Response." *Institute for Defense Analysis Africa Watch* no. 12.

2017. *Women and the War on Boko Haram: Wives, Weapons, Witnesses, African Arguments*. London: Zed Books.

Mbanefoh, Gini A. and Festus O. Egwaikhide. 1998. "Revenue Allocation in Nigeria: Derivation Principle Revisited." In *Federalism and Political Restructuring in Nigeria*, edited by Kunle Amuwo, Adigun Agbaje, Rotimi Suberu, and Georges Herault, 213–31. Ibadan, Nigeria: Spectrum.

McCauley, John. 2017. *The Logic of Ethnic and Religious Conflict in Africa*. Cambridge and New York: Cambridge University Press.

Mehler, Andreas. 2007. "Political Parties and Violence in Africa." In *Votes, Money and Violence: Political Parties and Elections in Sub-Saharan Africa*, edited by Matthias Basedau, Gero Erdmann, and Andreas Mehler, 195–223. Uppsala, Sweden: Nordiska Afrikainstitutet.

Meredith, Martin. 2011. *The Fate of Africa: A History of Fifty Years of Independence*. Revised and updated ed. New York: Public Affairs.

Merolla, Jennifer L. and Elizabeth J. Zechmeister. 2009. "Terrorist Threat, Leadership, and the Vote: Evidence from Three Experiments." *Political Behavior* no. 31 (4):575.

Moehler, Devra C. and Staffan I. Lindberg. 2009. "Narrowing the Legitimacy Gap: Turnovers as a Cause of Democratic Consolidation." *The Journal of Politics* no. 71 (4):1448–66.

Mohammed, Habu. 2010. "Human Rights NGOs and the Politics of Constructive Engagement in Nigeria's Fourth Republic." In *The Left and the Human Rights Struggle in Nigeria*, edited by Jibrin Ibrahim and Y.Z. Ya'u, 105–34. Kano, Nigeria: Centre for Research and Documentation.

Mohammed, Kyari. 2005. "Religion, Federalism and the Shari'a Project in Northern Nigeria." In *Nigerian Federalism in Crisis: Critical Perspectives and Political Options*, edited by Ebere Onwudiwe and Rotimi T. Suberu, 147–64. Ibadan, Nigeria: Program on Ethnic and Federal Studies.

2014. "The Message and Methods of Boko Haram." In *Boko Haram: Islamism, Politics, Security and the State in Nigeria*, edited by Pierre Perouse de Montclos, 9–32. Ibadan, Nigeria: French Institute for Research in Africa.

2018. "The Origins of Boko Haram." In *Oxford Handbook of Nigerian Politics*, edited by A. Carl LeVan and Patrick Ukata, 585–606. Oxford and New York: Oxford University Press.

Momale, Saleh. 2015a. "Changing Methods of Animal Husbandry, Cattle Rustling and Rural Banditry in Nigeria." In *Rural Banditry and Social Conflicts in Northern Nigeria*, edited by Mohammed J. Kuna and Jibrin Ibrahim, 69–110. Abuja, Nigeria: Centre for Democracy and Development.

2015b. Pastoralists – Farmers Relations and Implications to Food Security in the Kano-Katsina-Maradi Region. In *International Symposium on Intercommunity Co-existence and Peace Building in the History of the Maradi Region, Niger Republic*. L'Universite dan Dicko Dankoulodo de Maradi, Niger Republic.

Momoh, Abubakar. 2014. "Party System and Democracy in Nigeria, 1999–2010." In *Political Parties and Democracy in Nigeria*, edited by Olu Obafemi, Samuel Egwu, Okechukwu Ibeanu, and Jibrin Ibrahim, 78–99. Kuru, Nigeria: National Institute for Policy and Strategic Studies.

Muhammadu, Turi and Mohammed Haruna. 1979. "The Civil War." In *Nigerian Government and Politics under Military Rule, 1966–1979*, edited by Oyeleye Oyediran, 25–46. New York: St. Martin's Press.

Muhammed, Lai. 2014. "Parties and Nigeria's Electoral Process." Paper read at Parties and Nigeria's Electoral Process. Washington, DC.

Muhammed-Bande, Tijani. 2014. "Dynamics of Political Party Competition in Nigeria: Origins and Evolution." In *Political Parties and Democracy in Nigeria*, edited by Olu Obafemi, Samuel Egwu, Okechukwu Ibeanu, and Jibrin Ibrahim, 60–77. Kuru, Nigeria: National Institute for Policy and Strategic Studies.

Mutua, Makau. 2008. *Kenya's Quest for Democracy: Taming Leviathan*. Boulder, CO and London: Lynne Rienner Publishers.

Naagbanton, Patrick. 2015. *Fury of the Fisher Woman*. Lagos, Nigeria: Creektown Books.

Nanes, Matthew J. 2016. "Political Violence Cycles: Electoral Incentives and the Provision of Counterterrorism." *Comparative Political Studies* no. 50(2): 171–99.

National Bureau of Statistics. 2010. *The Report of National Literacy Survey 2010*. Abuja, Nigeria: Federal Government of Nigeria.

National Consortium for the Study of Terrorism and Responses to Terrorism (START). 2016. Global Terrorism Database [data file]. Available from www.start.umd.edu/gtd (accessed June 1, 2018).

Nigerian Bureau of Statistics. 2012. *Annual Abstract of Statistics 2012*. Abuja, Nigeria: Federal Government of Nigeria.

Nnoli, Okwudiba. 1995. *Ethnicity and Development in Nigeria*. Alershot, Hong Kong, and Singapore: Avebury.

Norris, Pippa and Robert Mattes. 2013. "Does Ethnicity Determine Support for the Governing Party?" In *Voting and Democratic Citizenship in*

Africa, edited by Michael Bratton, 41–60. Boulder, CO: Lynne Rienner Publishers.

Nwabueze, Remigius. 2009. "Alienations Under the Land Use Act and Express Declarations of Trust in Nigeria." *Journal of African Law* no. 53 (1):59–89.

Nwala, T. Uzodinma. 1997. *Nigeria: Path to Unity and Stability, Abuja National Constitutional Conference 1994–1995: A Critical Review*. Enugu, Nigeria: Novelty Industrial Enterprises.

Nwankwo, Arthur A. 1980. *Nigeria: The Challenge of Biafra*. 3rd ed. Enugu, Nigeria: Fourth Dimension Publishers. Original edition, 1972.

O'Donnell, Guillermo. 1997. "Illusions about Democratic Consolidation." In *Consolidating the Third Wave Democracies*, edited by Larry Jay Diamond, Marc Plattner, Yun-han Chu, and Hung-mao Tien, 40–53. Baltimore: Johns Hopkins University Press.

O'Donnell, Guillermo A. and Philippe C. Schmitter. 1986a. *Transitions from Authoritarian Rule. Tentative Conclusions about Uncertain Democracies*. Baltimore: Johns Hopkins University Press.

1986b. *Defining Some Concepts (and Exposing Some Assumptions)*. Edited by Guillermo O'Donnell, Philippe C. Schmitter, and Lawrence Whitehead. Vol. 4, *Transitions from Authoritarian Rule: Prospects for Democracy*. Baltimore and London: Johns Hopkins University Press.

1986c. "Negotiating (and Renegotiating) Pacts." In *Transitions from Authoritarian Rule: Prospects for Democracy*, edited by Guillermo O'Donnell, Philippe C. Schmitter, and Lawrence Whitehead, 37–47. Baltimore and London: Johns Hopkins University Press.

Oates, Sarah. 2006. "Comparing the Politics of Fear: The Role of Terrorism News in Election Campaigns in Russia, the United States and Britain." *International Relations* no. 20 (4):425–37.

Obafemi, Olu, Samuel Egwu, Okechukwu Ibeanu, and Jibrin Ibrahim. 2014. *Political Parties and Democracy in Nigeria*. Kuru, Nigeria: National Institute for Policy and Strategic Studies.

Obi, Cyril. 2011. "Taking Back Our Democracy? The Trials and Travails of Nigerian Elections Since 1999." *Democratization* no. 18 (2):366–87.

Obianyo, Nkolika. 2013. "Sour Friendship: Electoral Politics in Imo and Abia States, 2007–2011." In *Nigeria's Critical Election, 2011*, edited by John A.A. Ayoade and Adeoye A. Akinsanya, 117–56. Lanham, MD: Lexington Books.

Odinkalu, Chidi. 2001. "Transition to Civil Rule by the Military." In *Nigeria During the Abacha Years, 1993–1998*, edited by Kunle Amuwo, Daniel C. Bach, and Yann Lebeau, 1–56. Ibadan, Nigeria: Institut Francais de Recherche en Afrique.

Odior, Ernest Simeon O. 2014. "Government Expenditure on Education and Poverty Reduction: Implications for Achieving the MDGs in Nigeria: A Computable General Equilibrium Micro-simulation Analysis." *Asian Economic and Financial Review* no. 4 (2):150–72.

Ogujiuba, Kanayo Kingsley and Kizito Ehigiamusoe. 2014. "Capital Budget Implementation in Nigeria: Evidence from the 2012 Capital Budget." *Contemporary Economics* no. 8 (3):293–314.

Ohiomokhare, Senami. 2013. "Presidential Media Chat #5." In *President Explains: Transcripts of Presidential Media Chats with Dr. Goodluck Ebele Jonathan*, edited by Documentation and Strategy Special Advisor to the President on Research, 205–54. Abuja, Nigeria: Office of the Special Adivser to the President.

Ojo, Emmanuel O. 2004. "The Military and Political Transition." In *Nigeria's Struggle for Democracy and Good Governance*, edited by Adigun Agbaje, Larry Diamond, and Ebere Onwudiwe, 63–82. Ibadan, Nigeria: University of Ibadan Press.

Okonjo-Iweala, Ngozi. 2012. *Reforming the Unreformable: Lessons from Nigeria*. Cambridge, MA: MIT Press.

Okoye, Chudi. 1999. "Blocked Transition in Nigeria: Democracy and the Power of Oligarchy." In *Voting for Democracy: Watershed Elections in Contemporary Anglophone Africa*, edited by John Daniel, Roger Southall, and Morris Szeftel, 158–82. England and Burlington, VT: Ashgate Publishing.

Olaitan, 'Wale Are. 2000. "Rotational Presidency and State-Building in Nigeria." In *Federalism and Political Restructuring in Nigeria*, edited by 'Kunle Amuwo, Adigun Agbaje, Rotimi Suberu, and Georges Herault, 137–46. Ibadan, Nigeria: Spectrum.

Olukoshi, Adebayo O. 1993. *The Politics of Structural Adjustment in Nigeria*. London, Ibadan, and Portsmouth, NH: James Currey, Heinemann Educational Books, and Heinemann.

Omitola, Bolaji. 2012. "Terrorism and the Nigerian Federation." *African Security Review* no. 21 (4):4–16.

Omoruyi, Omo. 1999. *The Tale of June 12: The Betrayal of the Democratic Rights of Nigerians*. London: Press Alliance Network.

Omotola, J. Shola. 2010. "Elections and Democratic Transition in Nigeria Under the Fourth Republic." *African Affairs* no. 109 (437):535–53.

Onwudiwe, Ebere and Rotimi T. Suberu. 2005. *Nigerian Federalism in Crisis: Critical Perspectives and Political Options*. Ibadan, Nigeria: Program on Ethnic and Federal Studies.

Osaghae, Eghosa E. 1998. *Crippled Giant: Nigeria Since Independence*. Bloomington: Indiana University Press.

Osaghae, Eghosa, Onigu Otite, Francis O. Egbokhare, Chris O. Ikporukpo, and Isola Williams. 2001. *Ethnic Groups and Conflicts in Nigeria*. Edited by Programme on Ethnic and Federal Studies. Vol. 1, *Ethnic Groups and Conflicts in Nigeria*. Ibadan, Nigeria: The Lord's Creations.

Oseni, Michael. 2013. "Internally Generated Revenue (IGR) in Nigeria: A Panacea for State Development." *European Journal of Humanities and Social Sciences* no. 21 (1):1050–66.

Osori, Ayishi. 2017. *Love Does not Win Elections*. Lagos, Nigeria: Narrative Landscapes Press.

Osuntokun, Akinjide. 1987. *Power Broker: A Biography of Sir Kashim Ibrahim, Spectrum records*. Ibadan, Nigeria: Spectrum Books.

Othman, Shehu. 1989. "Nigeria: Power for Profit–Class, Corporatism, and Factionalism in the Military." In *Contemporary West African States*, edited by Donal B. O'Brien, John Dunn, and Richard Rathbone, 113–44. Cambridge and New York: Cambridge University Press.

Ottaway, Marina. 2003. *Democracy Challenged: The Rise of Semi-authoritarianism*. Boulder, CO: Lynne Rienner Publishers.

Owen, Olly. 2009. "Biafran Pound Notes." *Africa* no. 79 (4):570–94.

Owen, Olly and Zainab Usman. 2015. "Briefing: Why Goodluck Jonathan Lost the Nigerian Presidential Election of 2015." *African Affairs* no. 114 (456):455–71.

Oyediran, Oyeleye. 1979. *Nigerian Government and Politics Under Military Rule, 1966–1979*. New York: St. Martin's Press.

Ozzano, Luca and Francesco Cavatorta. 2013. "Conclusion: Reassessing the Relation between Religion, Political Actors, and Democratization." *Democratization* no. 20 (5):959–68.

Paden, John. 1997. "Nigerian Unity and the Tensions of Democracy: Geo-cultural Zones and North-South Legacies." In *Dilemmas of Democracy in Nigeria*, edited by P. Beckett and C. Young, 243–64. Rochester, NY: University of Rochester Press.

⸻ 2016. *Muhammadu Buhari: The Challenges of Leadership in Nigeria*. Zaria, Nigeria: Huda Huda Publishing.

Paden, John N. 2005. *Muslim Civic Cultures and Conflict Resolution: The Challenge of Democratic Federalism in Nigeria*. Washington, DC: Brookings Institution Press.

⸻ 2012. *Postelection Conflict Management in Nigeria: The Challenges of National Unity*. School for Conflict Analysis and Resolution, *Monograph Series*. Arlington, VA: George Mason University.

Panter-Brick, S.K. 1971. *Nigerian Politics and Military Rule: Prelude to the Civil War, Institute of Commonwealth Studies*. London: Athlone Press University of London [original edition, 1970].

Pape, Robert Anthony. 2006. *Dying to Win: The Strategic Logic of Suicide Terrorism*. New York: Random House Trade Paperbacks.

Pegg, Scott. 2015. "Introduction: On the 20th Anniversary of the Death of Ken Saro-Wiwa." *The Extractive Industries and Society* no. 2:607–14.

Pew Research Center. 2007. *Nigerian Muslims Self-identify First with their Religion*. Washington, DC: Pew Research Center. Available from www.pewresearch.org/fact-tank/2007/04/16/nigerian-muslims-self-identify-first-with-their-religion/ (accessed September 26, 2017).

——— 2010. *Tolerance and Tension: Islam and Christianity in Sub-Saharan Africa*. Washington, DC: Pew Research Center. Available from www.pewforum.org/2010/04/15/executive-summary-islam-and-christianity-in-sub-saharan-africa/ (accessed September 26, 2017).

Piazza, James A. 2017. "Repression and Terrorism: A Cross-national Empirical Analysis of Types of Repression and Domestic Terrorism." *Terrorism and Political Violence* no. 29 (1):102–18.

Posner, Daniel. 2005. *Institutions and Ethnic Politics in Africa*. Cambridge and New York: Cambridge University Press.

Powell, Jonathan. 2012. "Determinants of the Attempting and Outcome of Coups d'état." *Journal of Conflict Resolution* no. 56 (6):1017–40.

Przeworski, Adam. 1986. "Some Problems in the Study of the Transition to Democracy." In *Transitions from Authoritarian Rule: Prospects for Democracy*, edited by Guillermo O'Donnell, Philippe C. Schmitter, and Lawrence Whitehead, 47–63. Baltimore and London: Johns Hopkins University Press.

——— 1991. *Democracy and the Market: Political and Economic Reforms in Eastern Europe and Latin America, Studies in Rationality and Social Change*. Cambridge and New York: Cambridge University Press.

Przeworski, Adam, Michael E. Alvarez, Jose Antonio Cheibub, and Fernando Limongi. 2000. *Democracy and Development: Political Institutions and Material Well-being in the World, 1950–1990*. Cambridge and New York: Cambridge University Press.

Randall, Vicky. 2007. "Political Parties in Africa and the Representation of Social Groups." In *Votes, Money and Violence: Political Parties and Elections in Sub-Saharan Africa*, edited by Matthias Basedau, Gero Erdmann, and Andreas Mehler, 82–104. Uppsala, Sweden: Nordiska Afrikainstitutet.

Reno, William. 2011. *Warfare in Independent Africa*. New York and Cambridge: Cambridge University Press.

Riedl, Rachel Beatty. 2014. *Authoritarian Origins of Democratic Party Systems in Africa*. New York and Cambridge: Cambridge University Press.

Robbins, Joseph, Lance Hunter, and Gregg R. Murray. 2013. "Voters versus Terrorists: Analyzing the Effect of Terrorist Events on Voter Turnout." *Journal of Peace Research* no. 50 (4):495–508.

Rodden, Jonathan. 2004. "Comparative Federalism and Decentralization: On Meaning and Measurement." *Comparative Politics* no. 36 (4): 481–500.

Rouquie, Alain. 1986. "Demilitarization and the Institutionalization of Military-dominated Polities in Latin America." In *Transitions from Authoritarian Rule: Prospects for Democracy*, edited by Guillermo O'Donnell, Philippe C. Schmitter, and Lawrence Whitehead, 108–30. Baltimore and London: Johns Hopkins University Press.

Saldaña, Johnny. 2015. *The Coding Manual for Qualitative Researchers.* 2nd ed. Los Angeles and London: Sage.

Sandra, Julie. 2005. "Institutional Processes of Conflict Management." In *The Military and Management of Internal Conflict in Nigeria*, edited by Amos G. Adedeji and Istifanus S. Zabadi, 39–55. Abuja, Nigeria: National War College.

Schedler, Andreas. 2006. *Electoral Authoritarianism: The Dynamics of Unfree Competition.* Boulder, CO and London: Lynne Rienner Publishers.

Schneider, Friedrich, Tilman Brück, and Daniel Meierrieks. 2015. "The Economics of Counterterrorism: A Survey." *Journal of Economic Surveys* no. 29 (1):131–57.

Schumpeter, Joseph Alois. 1942. *Socialism, Capitalism and Democracy.* New York: Harper and Brothers.

Serrano, Rafael and Zacharias Pieri. 2014. "By the Numbers: The Nigerian State's Efforts to Counter Boko Haram." In *Boko Haram: Islamism, Politics, Security and the State in Nigeria*, edited by Pierre Perouse de Montclos, 192–212. Ibadan, Nigeria: French Institute for Research in Africa.

Shehu Musa Yar'Adua Foundation. 2017. "Memory and Nation Building: Biafra 50 Years After." Paper presented at Memory and Nation Building: Biafra 50 Years After, May 25, Abuja.

Shin, Jae Hyeok. 2015. "Voter Demands for Patronage: Evidence from Indonesia." *Journal of East Asian Studies* no. 15 (1):127–51.

Shugart, Matthew S. and John Carey. 1992. *Presidents and Assemblies.* Cambridge: Cambridge University Press.

Simbine, Antonia T. 2002. *Political Parties and Democratic Sustenance in Nigeria's Fourth Republic, NISER Monograph Series.* Ibadan, Nigeria: Nigerian Institute of Social and Economic Research.

Sisk, Timothy D. and Andrew Reynolds. 1998. *Elections and Conflict Management in Africa.* Washington, DC: US Institute of Peace.

Sklar, Richard. 2001. "An Elusive Target: Nigeria Fends Off Sanctions." In *Nigeria During the Abacha Years, 1993–1998*, edited by 'Kunle Amuwo, Daniel C. Bach, and Yann Lebeau, 259–288. Ibadan, Nigeria: Institut Francais de Recherche en Afrique.

Sklar, Richard L. 2004 [1963]. *Nigerian Political Parties: Power in an Emergent African Nation*. Trenton, NJ and Eritrea: Princeton University Press and Africa World Press, Inc.

Sklar, Richard, Ebere Onwudiwe, and Darren Kew. 2006. "Nigeria: Completing Obasanjo's Legacy." *Journal of Democracy* no. 17 (3):100–15.

Smith, Daniel Jordan. 2007. *A Culture of Corruption: Everyday Deception and Popular Discontent in Nigeria*. Princeton, NJ: Princeton University Press.

Smith, Mike. 2015. *Boko Haram: Inside Nigeria's Unholy War*. London and New York: I.B.Tauris.

Special Advisor to the President on Research, Documentation and Strategy. 2014. *Sure and Steady Transformation: Progress Report of President Goodluck Jonathan's Administration*. 2 vols, Vol. 2. Abuja, Nigeria: Office of the Special Adviser to the President.

Stepan, Alfred. 1988. *Rethinking Military Politics: Brazil and the Southern Cone*. Princeton, NJ: Princeton University Press.

Stewart, Megan A. 2018. "Civil War as State-Making: Strategic Governance in Civil War." *International Organization* no. 72 (1):205–26.

Stockholm International Peace Research Institute. 2016. *SIPRI Military Expenditure Database*. Stockholm: SIPRI.

Stokes, Susan C. 2007. "Political Clientelism." In *The Oxford Handbook of Comparative Politics*, edited by Carles Boix and Susan C. Stokes, 604–27. New York: Oxford University Press.

Strauss, Scott and Charlie Taylor. 2012. "Democratization and Electoral Violence in Sub-Saharan Africa, 1990–2008." In *Voting in Fear: Electoral Violence in Sub-Saharan Africa*, edited by Dorina Bekoe and Akosua Oduraa, ix. Washington, DC: United States Institute of Peace.

Street, John. 2012. "Do Celebrity Politics and Celebrity Politicians Matter?" *The British Journal of Politics & International Relations* no. 14 (3):346–56.

Suberu, Rotimi. 1991. "The Struggle for New States in Nigeria, 1976–1990." *African Affairs* no. 90:499–522.

2001. *Federalism and Ethnic Conflict in Nigeria*. Washington, DC: United States Institute of Peace Press.

Suberu, Rotimi T. 1997. "Crisis and Collapse: June–November 1993." In *Transition without End: Nigerian Politics and Civil Society Under Babangida*, edited by Larry Diamond, Anthony Kirk-Greene, and Oyeleye Oyediran, 281–99. Boulder, CO and London: Lynne Rienner Publishers.

2008. "The Supreme Court and Federalism in Nigeria." *The Journal of Modern African Studies* no. 46 (3):451–85.

Tarrow, Sidney. 1994. *Power in Movement: Social Movements, Collective Action, and Politics.* New York: Cambridge University Press.

Teorell, Jan and Michael Wahman. 2017. "Institutional Stepping Stones for Democracy: How and Why Multipartyism Enhances Democratic Change." *Democratization* no. 25 (1):78–97.

Thaut Vinson, Laura. 2017. *Religion, Violence and Power-Sharing: Local Government Institutions and Patterns of Inter-Religious Violence in Nigeria.* Cambridge and New York: Cambridge University Press.

2018. "Pastoralism, Ethnicity and Subnational Conflict Resolution in the Middle Belt." In *Oxford Handbook of Nigerian Politics*, edited by A. Carl LeVan and Patrick Ukata, 681–98. Oxford and New York: Oxford University Press.

Throup, David W. 1985. "The Origins of Mau Mau." *African Affairs* no. 84 (336):399–433.

Thurston, Alexander. 2016. *Salafism in Nigeria: Islam, Preaching, and Politics.* New York and Cambridge: Cambridge University Press.

2018. *Boko Haram: The History of an African Jihadist Movement.* Princeton, NJ: Princeton University Press.

Tripp, Aili Mari. 2010. *Museveni's Uganda: Paradoxes of Power in a Hybrid Regime, Challenge and Change in African politics.* Boulder, CO: Lynne Rienner Publishers.

Tyoden, Sonni Gwanle. 2013. "The Electoral System, Political Parties and Democracy in Nigeria: Critical Issues for Policy." *Nigerian Journal of Policy and Strategy* no. 18 (1):1–18.

Uddhammar, Emil, Elliott Green, and Johanna Söderström. 2011. "Political Opposition and Democracy in Sub-Saharan Africa." *Democratization* no. 18 (5):1057–66.

Ujo, A.A. 2000. *Understanding the 1998–99 Elections in Nigeria.* Kaduna: Klamidas Books.

US Agency for International Development, with Management Systems International. 2009. *Guide to the Drivers of Violent Extremism.* Washington, DC.

Varshney, Ashutosh. 2007. "Ethnicity and Ethnic Conflict." In *The Oxford Handbook of Comparative Politics*, edited by Carles Boix and Susan Stokes, 274–94. Oxford and New York: Oxford University Press.

Vinson, Laura. 2017. *Religion, Violence, and Local Power-Sharing in Nigeria.* New York: Cambridge University Press.

Wahman, Michael. 2014. "Democratization and Electoral Turnovers in Sub-Saharan Africa and Beyond." *Democratization* no. 21 (2):220–43.

Walsh, James I. and James A. Piazza. 2010. "Why Respecting Physical Integrity Reduces Terrorism." *Comparative Political Studies* no. 43 (5):551–77.

Warner, Jason and Hilary Matfess. 2017. *Exploding Stereotypes: The Unexpected Operational and Demographic Characteristics of Boko Haram's Suicide Bombers*. United States Military Academy, West Point, NY: Combating Terrorism Center at West Point.

Weghorst, Keith R. and Staffan I. Lindberg. 2011. "Effective Opposition Strategies: Collective Goods or Clientelism?" *Democratization* no. 18 (5):1193–214.

Widner, Jennifer A. 1994. *Economic Change and Political Liberalization in Sub-Saharan Africa*. Baltimore: Johns Hopkins University Press.

Williams, Paul D. 2016. *War and Conflict in Africa*. 2nd edition. Malden, MA: Polity Press.

Wing, S.D. 2016. "French Intervention in Mali: Strategic Alliances, Long-term Regional Presence?" *Small Wars and Insurgencies* no. 27 (1):59–80.

Wood, Elisabeth Jean. 2000. *Forging Democracy from Below: Insurgent Transitions in South Africa and El Salvador, Cambridge Studies in Comparative Politics*. Cambridge and New York: Cambridge University Press.

Yinka Fashagba, Joseph. 2014. "Party Switching in the Senate under Nigeria's Fourth Republic." *The Journal of Legislative Studies* no. 20 (4):516–41.

Zenn, Jacob. 2014. "Leadership Analysis of Boko Haram and Ansaru in Nigeria." *CTC Sentinel* no. 7 (2):23–9.

Index